T0131790

On the Lower Frequencies:

A SECRET HISTORY OF THE CITY

Erick Lyle

SOFT SKULL PRESS • NEW YORK

Library of Congress Cataloging-in-Publication Data has been
applied for.
ISBN (10) 1-933368985
ISBN (13) 978-1-933368-98-6

Printed in the United States of America

Soft Skull Press
New York, NY

www.softskull.com

AUTHOR'S NOTE

Stories that were once dispatches from an ongoing political struggle or that were, literally, given away free on the streets, have now become this book. Virtually all of the material in this book originally appeared in the following publications: my magazine, *Scam*, issues #4 (2000), #5 (2005), and #5.5 (2006); my street newspaper the *Turd-Filled Donut*, issues #1–8 (1997-2001), *Nosedive* (2002), *Rice Harvester* (2006), *Full Gallop* (2001), *949 Market* (2001), *Long Ago and Far Away* (2004); Chris Carlsson's book *The Political Edge* (2004), or NPR's radio show *This American Life*. This is the first time they have been assembled all in one place. Big thanks to Luke Gerwe, Ammi Emergency, Icky Apparatus, John Hocevar, Jeff Miller, and Richard Nash for help in putting it all together! This one is dedicated to Ivy, my lifelong partner in crime.

A RISING TIDE THAT SINKS ALL BOATS

When I first moved to the city, TV news had run a story about the donut shop on the corner, the one with the huge sign that proudly proclaimed it was "Open 25 Hours." The story called the corner, "The Epicenter of Crime," and they meant for all of San Francisco. It was a staggering idea. I would sit in the donut shop and try to imagine crime, disturbance, discontent radiating outward across the entire city from that very spot TWENTY FIVE HOURS A DAY. Years later, I moved into my friend Jimmy's house on the alley behind the donut shop, and got to sit back and watch it all.

On San Carlos Street there was a daily sweet and sad procession, a never ending back and forth, that we could watch from our steps. There was the sound of men pushing fruit bar carts up the alley, clanging their bells, calling out; and there was that tense, menacing no-sound sound of cops cruising slowly the wrong way down the alley. The girl down the street that I had a crush on would walk by, short sleeves in the Mission sun, smiling sleepily on her way to morning coffee at 1:00 PM, and Eddie the drug dealer would walk the other way, looking exhausted, sagging against a palm tree with gang tags carved into its weathered trunk. My favorite time on San Carlos was 6:00 AM, just before the street woke up. Staring down the alley past the tired old Victorians and shoes dangling from telephone wires, I could imagine 10, 20, 100 years of 6:00 AM, each day exactly like this one, yawning and stretching into the past. It was a working class street, a ghetto alley, a place with problems that money wouldn't solve—but, for now, asleep and dreaming.

The aspiration of a city, of a neighborhood, or a street, is not that everyone in it would be best friends, but that everyone would, at least, tolerate and respect each other. This idea held our block together. The landlord of the house on the other side of us probably didn't LOVE it that Jimmy would climb up the telephone pole across the street to hang flea market paintings on it with a screw gun, but he still brought us free loaves of bread that he got from his friend who worked at a bakery. Eddie knew we wouldn't call the cops on him and when our friend's bike got stolen from in front of the house, it was Eddie who helped get it back. The antique bookbinder guy down the block could have called the cops on the homeless guy who slept in his doorway; instead, he actually offered him a job, teaching him the art of bookbinding, paying him, and letting him stay in the doorway.

The last I heard, the homeless guy was turning out to be a lousy bookbinder, though. He had to smoke crack every morning when he got up and it ruined his concentration. I heard that the bookbinder and homeless guy were even starting to hate each other a little. But I think that's why I always liked that story. It didn't have a feel-good, happy ending, but they were still trying to work it out. This back and forth, this trying to work it out seemed like it would go on, 25 hours a day, forever.

But the Mission was changing. Streets that had been called "down and out" were now called "gritty," and the Mission's turd-and-graffiti motif was now fashionable. Termite-ridden, drafty old Victorians were bought at exorbitant prices, not to live in, but to immediately resell, like Internet stocks. Everyone in San Francisco had a dream that somehow hinged on real estate. The stock market was pumping so much easy cash into the neighborhood—the good times were so GOOD—that the dream even had a name: "Cleaning up the Mission." Developers and slumming hipsters congratulated themselves, believing that ordinary greed was actually a moral force, a rising tide to lift all boats.

Our landlord up on the hill had bought into this dream, too.

Our landlord, who I'll call Jacque, was a dour-looking, henpecked little French guy—a self-employed electrician who happened to own a couple houses. When I think of Jacque, I always think of him standing in the driveway with his plumbing tools and his sad, black mustache, as Jimmy came from the flea market, driving his huge, green, graffiti-covered cargo van. At those times, Jacque always seemed to be thinking, "How did this happen to ME?" He had bought our house eight years before and inherited Jimmy as his tenant. San Francisco's rent control laws are a stronger "'til death do us part" legal bind than marriage, and, by law, Jimmy and Jacque would go to their graves with Jim still paying a sweet 1988 rent.

In the twelve years Jimmy had lived on San Carlos, he'd become as much a part of the street as the street sign. Everybody knew Jimmy. Even the gang kids dressed in blue shook their heads and laughed when the green van drove by. Jim was a self-employed scavenger who sold trash at flea markets and gave away more of it to anyone who asked. Homeless guys came by for clothes and blankets. Jim's friends came by looking for baseball gloves or super-eight projectors

or a PA for a protest at Civic Center, and he usually hooked everyone up. He was also a long-time neighborhood bartender and had a
band. Just about everyone in the Mission had either bought a beer
from Jimmy or played drums in his band.

Even though the Mission District Real Estate Gold Mine was becoming national news, Jacque never seemed ambitious enough to
try to evict Jimmy and cash in. But he was married to Claire, a
sour, sneering woman with upwardly mobile aspirations of her own.
Claire hated Jimmy. It was easy to imagine her up there on the hill,
working on Jacque, telling him that if he were any kind of a man,
he'd get rid of that wingnut flea market trash salesman tenant of his
so they could sell the house and be rich. Or maybe she wanted to
evict us and move into our house in the trendy, up and coming Mission—a neighborhood that now even had valet parking. We knew
that Jacque's first wife had left him several years ago for another
woman. Maybe Jacque thought if he got left behind in the Get Rich
Quick housing market, Claire would leave him too.

Whatever he thought, our house was now something else to him,
a symbol of some brighter, well-heeled future. It was a chance for a
henpecked plumber to finally hit it big, to be where the action was,
to not be a small time landlord anymore. And all they would have
to do would be get rid of US.

We always paid our rent on time and had no problems with Jacque.
It would be nearly impossible for him to legally evict us. So Jacque
hired a notoriously ruthless and shark-like eviction lawyer, a man so
stereotypically vile that when tenants' rights protestors staged demonstrations on his lawn, he would come out and greet them, waving
and yelling, "Smile!" as he videotaped them in action.

Jacque's hotshot lawyer had never lost a case. He had a secret
weapon, a little-known California state law called the Ellis Act that
allows landlords to evict their tenants if they're taking the property
off the rental market forever. After they evict the tenants, they can
sell the property, move into it, or turn it into a condo, but there is
one catch: if the property is re-rented anytime in the next ten years,
it has to be offered first, at the old rent, to the evicted tenants. This
was not a big deal for Jacque's lawyer. The joke around the Mission was that he mostly used the Ellis Act on tenants who spoke no
English and didn't know their rights, or elderly tenants who were
so shocked by the sudden eviction that they would often die before
there was even a settlement.

The lawyer served eviction notices to our downstairs neighbors and us. Within a month, the neighbors took a settlement and left the city. But Jimmy decided to hire a lawyer and fight in court. As long as the lawsuit went on, we would continue to live there and Jacque could not collect rent. Jacque and Claire were confident. They sold their house on the hill and moved to the Mission. In fact, they moved right into the unit downstairs.

The first month was awful. Jim said he could hear them through his walls, giggling and having sex in the bathtub—something I did NOT want to imagine. They were clearly enjoying their new life-style in the resurgent Mission, playing the part of wealthy real estate movers and shakers. Claire had taken to smoking cigars and she would stand on the porch and sneer with great satisfaction at us, with her arms folded, saying things like, "Have any luck finding a new place yet, Jim? Better start looking!" They would have their one friend over and talk with him loudly in front of the house about how they would soon be rid of us.

But I actually felt sorry for Jacque. The Mission was no place for this kind of hubris, and I think he knew it. The electrician was in over his head. And he was about to meet Jorge.

Jorge was the homeless guy who slept under our stairs, but to say Jorge was just some homeless guy would be to say Shakespeare was just some writer. Jorge re-invented the role. With his trench coat, his thick, greasy beard, and his wild mass of jet-black hair, Jorge was more of an ominous presence, a force—not so much a harbinger of doom, but a reminder that you WERE doomed; a feeling, like a hangover, that had always been part of San Carlos Street and always would be.

While everyone else in town was worried about eviction, Jorge wandered the streets, unconcerned, because he was, in fact, in charge. He slept anywhere he wanted at any time of the day. He would go to the pizza place on the corner, put his feet up on the sidewalk table, and throw his head back, surveying his domain through always squinting eyes. He would not buy a thing. Instead, he had the power to assess taxes on passersby. If you had a six-pack, Jorge would always get a cold one off you. If you gave him a cigarette, Jorge would stroke his beard and command, "Give me TWO!" Jorge also left massive turds in front of our garage door every morning. There was nothing you could really do about it, but he was pretty good about going in a bucket if you put one out for him. Since Jacque was new downstairs, we decided to see if he could figure this out.

Jacque had lived on Bernal Hill, a NICE neighborhood full of kindly, older dykes, where everyone always seemed to be walking their dog. It was a pretty part of town with trees and views. Nothing there could have prepared him for Jorge.

We would sit and drink beer on the steps and watch Jacque clean up after Jorge.

After a week or so of this, he installed one of those annoying security floodlights that turn on if anyone walks within, say, a hundred yards of it. We were blinded anytime we walked up our steps at night. Historians will note that this was the first device of its kind installed on our block EVER and we were, understandably, embarrassed. We had to explain to Eddie and the gang kids that we hadn't suddenly become narcs.

I found out that if you just unscrewed the light bulb a little bit it wouldn't work. But, one day, Jorge came by and Jimmy asked him what he thought of the new light.

Jorge said, "Oh, I LOVE those things. I can make sure I have all my things together before the light goes out and I go to sleep."

After that, we quit unscrewing it.

The case dragged on, and weeks with Jorge stretched into months. Jacque and Claire's lone friend came over less and less and then not at all. The bill from the hotshot attorney was mounting and the flood of money into the neighborhood wasn't exactly cleaning up the Mission.

If a rising tide was going to lift all boats, in the Mission that tide would not be money, but urine. The most visible example of the "economic revitalization" was that the people pissing in our garden at night were now wearing more expensive clothes. I'd come home to find giggling drunk girls in those huge shoes with their pants down, peeing away in the driveway while their boyfriends drunkenly tried to pick all of Jim's flowers to give to them. I saw people mastering the art of pissing with one hand and talking on a cell phone with the other. The Latino working class bars of the Mission had all been systematically closed by the police, ostensibly because the patrons sold crack and got into fights with each other. They'd now all been replaced by hipster bars where the patrons all did coke and then fought each other. I'd see leather-coated, side-burn-wearing yuppie guys scoring heroin on the Sixteenth and I would think, "Damn! It's like these people couldn't wait to move to the ghetto and lose their minds!"

Jacque, apparently frustrated, next turned against the very thing that might make him rich: the property itself. He ordered Jimmy to remove the garden, where Jorge was now living. You would think a well-maintained garden would be a SELLING point in a house, but I guess Jorge is a pretty loud snorer. Jacque claimed that since he was a tenant of half of the house, he was entitled to half the space where the garden was. Jimmy had no choice but to comply. He cleared out half the space in the corner by the garage door, a barren cement area that soon filled up with "Lake Jorge"—a foul, yellow pool refreshed daily by a natural spring.

Then, probably inspired by the high-ceilinged, white-walled lofts that all the kids were into these days, Jacque started gutting the downstairs interior, ripping out the solid redwood cabinets and the countertops that had been constructed over a hundred years ago out of trees brought over on ships from New Zealand. The craftsmanship had stood up through three major earthquakes, but it would not survive a Mission real estate craze.

The legal case had by this time dragged on so long that it was no longer clear what "winning" might mean. Jacque and Claire were always locked inside now—their security alarms feebly protecting them from the Epicenter of Crime a mere TWENTY FOUR hours a day. The downstairs unit had sunk into a bunker-like paranoia. One day, our phone wasn't working so we had a guy from the phone company come look at it. "Well, HERE'S your problem!" he yelled in disbelief as he looked at our grey box. Jacque and Claire were TAPPING our phone!

Later, a small dispute over parking in the driveway ended with Claire punching Jimmy's girlfriend in the head. Soon after that, Claire apparently moved away, curiously being escorted by a younger man who carried her bags and opened the car door for her while she leered up at him. No more sex in the bathtub for Jacque. After that, we almost never saw Jacque except when he came home from work and slammed his door.

And as for Jimmy, the block he had lived on for twelve years had changed considerably in a short time. Three Latino families down the block had been evicted under the Ellis Act. Now their former houses stood empty because they were more valuable that way. One was surrounded by rubble where the owner had tried to turn the Victorian into a loft but had run out of money. Most of our friends had had no choice but to just move away. There were no weekend garage sales at Jim's and no one really came to hang out on the step. No one had anything good to talk about anyway—just more eviction news.

After nearly a year, the judge ruled against Jimmy and we had to move out. Jacque's winning deposition was a monumental four-page list of over seventy complaints against us—a staggering paranoid epic, detailing Jacque's almost Kurtz-like collapse since he'd moved to the Mission. He accused us of having our house open at all hours, day and night, so homeless people could come in and wash their clothes. One innocent time when Claire found Jim and two male friends working on the car in the garage was described as "an orgy." In another complaint, Jacque accused us of "dragging heavy items across the floor all night in order to tape record the sounds." Well, it was easy to see why the judge had ruled against us! Jacque was just trying to do what he wished with his OWN property that he had bought legally, when he had found himself at the center of a sordid and vast avant-garde homosexual underground, a Mission netherworld where the unclean and un-housed traded sex for laundry at twisted 4:00 AM art shows! I said, "Man, I only WISH we were that cool!"

The day we moved out was the only time I every actually SAW Jacque's famous hotshot attorney. Everyone was there waiting for the sheriff to come serve the final papers. Jacque came out to the top of his steps to wait. Claire finally pulled up, chauffeured by the younger man. The lawyer pulled up in his SUV. He was the only one smiling. He strode confidently to the top of the stairs, looking out into the alley, grinning, as if about to address a crowded plaza full of supporters. After all, he'd never lost a case and he'd built a personal fortune on the one tried and true San Francisco idea that went all the way back to the first gold rush, the principle the town was founded on: you don't get rich panning for gold; you get rich selling Levis to all the fools who show up here every day to pan for gold.

The sheriff finally came, papers in hand, and the lawyer led him up into our old place. A moment later, they came out confused. They couldn't find Jim to serve him the papers. Suddenly the shark was worried; he turned to us, irritated, and said, "Where the hell did he go?"

Just then, Jimmy came out of the house next door and casually said, "Oh, I'll take those. Thanks." See, a couple of days before, Jimmy had worked out a deal with the landlord next door—the one who always gave us the free bread—and now Jimmy was moving into a room in the very next house! Jim said, "Hey, Ig, can you give me a hand with these plants?" and Jacque and Claire watched in disbelief as we dragged the planter boxes across the driveway to their new home, a mere ten feet away! They wouldn't be able to rent the house to anyone but Jimmy for ten years, and he would be right next door, watching.

Jacque stood at the top of the steps looking out across San Carlos Street, a street with problems money couldn't fix. How could he have known what would happen next, that within a year the real estate boom would bust, the stock market would flounder and lofts would stand vacant all over town? How could he have known that in only a few months he would move out of the house that was his dream, his dream to be where the action was, to not be small time? And that, after that, the house would soon be covered in graffiti and trash, that the driveway would be full of homeless guys sleeping on couches and that Jorge would move to the top of the stairs. How could Jacque know that the get rich quick scheme would fail and that he would be unable to even sell the house because no one wanted to rent it to Jimmy at a 1988 rent?

I don't know, but from the look on his face, I could tell Jacque had figured it out, all at once. His high-paid lawyer got in his SUV and sped away. The younger man opened the car door for Claire, and they drove away, too. The house was finally all his. And, somewhere, Jorge was stirring for his morning rounds.

THIS ISSUE: PROTEST, RIOTS, BEER...

CIVIC CENTER POETRY!

WHEN CITY WORKERS RECENTLY STARTED TAKING ALL THE TREES OUT OF CIVIC CENTER, I THOUGHT IT WAS JUST ANOTHER CYNICAL PLOY TO TAKE AWAY PLACES FOR HOMELESS FOLKS AND DRUG DEALERS TO HIDE OUT. BUT WAS I WRONG! IT TURNS OUT THAT THEY'RE FINALLY _____ THAT SPACE OPEN FOR POETRY READINGS! THIS GOT THE TURD-FILLED DONUT STAFF SO EXCITED THAT WE WENT TO WORK ON OUR POEMS TO READ AT CIVIC CENTER RIGHT AWAY! HERE'S 6 HAIKUS BY AESOP

THIS CIVIC CENTER
This Civic Center
Not quite civic nor centered
Let's get some hard drugs

Karl's
This Karl Jr. sucks
Bathroom. Customer's only.
Pee on salad bar

Malt
Malt liquour is sweet
an elixir I drink up
this world ain't so bad

Farmer's Market
Bought a live chicken
three bucks in fuckin' food stamps
not allowed on bus

My Bike
Some ass stole my bike
smoking crack by the fountain
fuck you, its my bike

Kools
Kools, Newports, Salem
Do you got a menthol, man?
No, go fuck yourself!

6th STREET MAN SUES SENECA HOTEL--- AND WINS!!!
59 MORE TENANTS AWAIT COURT DATE IN BACK RENT SUIT

Anybody who lives in a hotel downtown knows the feeling of hopelessness you can get from creaking, day after day, with the average hotel's poor living conditions and unresponsive management. Most of us who take all your money; treat you like a criminal, and still refuse to paint the walls, or fix the elevator. But Jerome Reid, and 59 other tenants at the notoriously troubled Seneca Hotel (6th/Stevenson) are proving that you can fight back in court—and win!

It's been a long summer over at The Seneca. Since June, there has been a fire, putting 30 rooms out of service for various lengths of time, and causing the evacuation and relocation of many residents. Even worse, many residents complained of burglaries that occur DURING the evacuations! The elevator has been broken for much of the year and, according to Seneca tenant representative, Johnny Durden, drug dealers are still used to bribe their way into the building, deal in the halls, and prey on elderly residents. "You can still get a room at the Seneca for crack," says Durden.

Jerome Reid, a Seneca resident for 9 months, had finally had enough after the room he shares with his girlfriend was burglarized on May 22nd. Stuff was stolen from his room with NO FORCED ENTRY! As it turned out, 20 OTHER TENANTS that month complained to the Tenderloin Housing Clinic of similar burglaries with no forced entry. You might think the night doorman, a known heroin addict who has access to all the hotel's room keys, would be a prime suspect, but, when Reid called the cops, he says, "They acted like me and my girlfriend were just crackheads, and that one of us must have sold the missing stuff when the other was out of the room. They didn't do anything."

So Jerome sued the Seneca in small claims court for $2,000 in damages. The Seneca's owner, infamous 6th Street slumlord, Raymond Patel, who also owns The Sharon, The Hart, The Raymond, and The Mintu-Lee, didn't even show up in court to refute the charges. So Jerome won the case! "It's important for people to know that they don't have to just sit back and take it," says Reid. "People should try to get every penny they got coming to them."

Meanwhile, tenant rep Durden has helped organize 59 other Seneca tenants in a lawsuit against the Seneca to win payments of back rent. "If the elevator's broke for a month, if there's no heat, no hot water, there's garbage in the halls, then people should get money back for the time that that's not fixed," says Durden. Their case goes up before an arbitrator for the Rent Board on September 29. "It was hard to get people to sue, at first," Durden said, "but once they saw that if they work together, they might really get something, then they wanted to try."

In the meantime, Durden says the legal pressure has brought about positive change at the hotel. "I can't change overnight, but they are starting to fix things." The elevator is working again, and the doorman has been fired. And, what do you know? There hasn't been a burglary since.

weekend garage sales at Jim's and no one really came to hang out on the step. No one had anything good to talk about anyway—just more eviction news.

After nearly a year, the judge ruled against Jimmy and we had to move out. Jacque's winning deposition was a monumental four-page list of over seventy complaints against us—a staggering paranoid epic, detailing Jacque's almost Kurtz-like collapse since he'd moved to the Mission. He accused us of having our house open at all hours, day and night, so homeless people could come in and wash their clothes. One innocent time when Claire found Jim and two male friends working on the car in the garage was described as "an orgy." In another complaint, Jacque accused us of "dragging heavy items across the floor all night in order to tape record the sounds." Well, it was easy to see why the judge had ruled against us! Jacque was just trying to do what he wished with his OWN property that he had bought legally, when he had found himself at the center of a sordid and vast avant-garde homosexual underground, a Mission netherworld where the unclean and un-housed traded sex for laundry at twisted 4:00 AM art shows! I said, "Man, I only WISH we were that cool!"

The day we moved out was the only time I every actually SAW Jacque's famous hotshot attorney. Everyone was there waiting for the sheriff to come serve the final papers. Jacque came out to the top of his steps to wait. Claire finally pulled up, chauffeured by the younger man. The lawyer pulled up in his SUV. He was the only one smiling. He strode confidently to the top of the stairs, looking out into the alley, grinning, as if about to address a crowded plaza full of supporters. After all, he'd never lost a case and he'd built a personal fortune on the one tried and true San Francisco idea that went all the way back to the first gold rush, the principle the town was founded on: you don't get rich panning for gold; you get rich selling Levis to all the fools who show up here every day to pan for gold.

The sheriff finally came, papers in hand, and the lawyer led him up into our old place. A moment later, they came out confused. They couldn't find Jim to serve him the papers. Suddenly the shark was worried; he turned to us, irritated, and said, "Where the hell did he go?"

Just then, Jimmy came out of the house next door and casually said, "Oh, I'll take those. Thanks." See, a couple of days before, Jimmy had worked out a deal with the landlord next door—the one who always gave us the free bread—and now Jimmy was moving into a room in the very next house! Jim said, "Hey, Ig, can you give me a hand with these plants?" and Jacque and Claire watched in disbelief as we dragged the planter boxes across the driveway to their new home, a mere ten feet away! They wouldn't be able to rent the house to anyone but Jimmy for ten years, and he would be right next door, watching.

Jacque stood at the top of the steps looking out across San Carlos Street, a street with problems money couldn't fix. How could he have known what would happen next, that within a year the real estate boom would bust, the stock market would flounder and lofts would stand vacant all over town? How could he have known that in only a few months he would move out of the house that was his dream, his dream to be where the action was, to not be small time? And that, after that, the house would soon be covered in graffiti and trash, that the driveway would be full of homeless guys sleeping on couches and that Jorge would move to the top of the stairs. How could Jacque know that the get rich quick scheme would fail and that he would be unable to even sell the house because no one wanted to rent it to Jimmy at a 1988 rent?

I don't know, but from the look on his face, I could tell Jacque had figured it out, all at once. His high-paid lawyer got in his SUV and sped away. The younger man opened the car door for Claire, and they drove away, too. The house was finally all his. And, somewhere, Jorge was stirring for his morning rounds.

DECEMBER 98
ISSUE NO. 4

THE TURD-FILLED DONUT

THIS ISSUE:
CHRISTMAS
TOILETS
NEEDLES

pt. 1 : TURDS, DONUTS, AND PUNK SHOWS IN THE STREETS!

WORKFARE DIARY
CHAPTER ONE - STEALING MUNI RIDES

THE FIRST ANNUAL 6th Street TREASURE HUNT for BEER!

QUESTIONS, COMMENTS, CONTRIBUTIONS?

keep track of your clues to find the prize!

1.
2.
3.
4.
5.
6.

FIRE AT THE THOR HOTEL

A SURVIVOR'S STORY

BY THUMPER

THE ZEROS

The big Y2K New Year's plan was to go to Hunt's Donuts, since the sign says it's "OPEN 25 HOURS," and just sit in there, at 20th and Mission, champagne at midnight, watching the streets go crazy through the window. It really would be the 25th hour! The rest of the world would be in 2000, but we'd be somewhere no one had ever been before.

But the streets weren't going to go crazy. As The Zeros dawned, the cops were shutting the city down. We rode downtown in the afternoon to watch the Financial District workers throw all their calendars out of the skyscraper windows, like they do every year, and all the windows on Market Street were boarded up. It looked like after a riot, but it was before. Before what, I wondered. As we watched the little pieces of calendar paper flutter down from Transamerica into the almost deserted streets, it seemed so weird to actually be going into the year 2000. It seems like my whole life, people have been telling me the world is about to end, for some reason or another, but here it was, another year's days fluttering into the past.

By nighttime, the cops were everywhere and they all had huge ropes of those plastic handcuffs hanging off their belts. Mission Street was dead. You know how when you're in a protest it feels weird to be in the middle of the street looking out at familiar buildings, that feeling of disruption of the usual order? Standing on Mission Street it felt like that except for what was actively happening was NOTHING. The non-event was so actively planned.

We had no choice but to go undercover. We, the punks, had obtained some police radios just for this night—not scanners, but actual cops' radios that you could talk on—and now we were going to see Jimmy's band play at some bar on Mission Street. I felt like a narc going into the punk show with the radio well concealed under my clothes. What if it fell out, or someone grabbed me to dance and felt it? And what about that annoying squawking between songs?

It was fine, though. I kept the volume down and played half the show for the cops over the dispatch—especially the between song dedications Jimmy made to the cops. Soon it was midnight, so I headed to Hunt's with Anandi to meet Greta and Bill, who had the champagne.

We popped the cork and walked around. It really was dead. Bill said, "It's the complete fusion of police control and the media. The cops and the media say nothing's happening, so nothing happens."

But I wasn't so sure. The night ended with me and Anandi on a roof, listening to the cop radio and watching Mission Street. The radio announced that the power was out at the Sunnydale Projects. There were fist fights. A man was standing in the road, screaming on Geneva Avenue. There was discontent, chaos as '99 rolled into '00. Scattered incidents.

And there was us saying on the radio, "We need backup at 24th and Balmy. Three cops are pepper spraying an unarmed Latino man to death."

This is a look back at the decade that dawned, the chatter on the police radio. It started with an enormous pile of flyers, train maps, old letters, hitchhiking signs, wheat-pasted scraps, and ended up here: a look at what worked and didn't work, a look at the things punks invented. I'm not sure what it all added up to. But I know when the cops say that nothing is happening, they're wrong!

THE TURD-FILLED DONUT STORY

When I moved back to SF in late 1997, IIvy was already living here in a welfare hotel on 6th Street—SF's Skid Row. She already had a workfare job, passing out condoms and clothes and doing needle exchange with teen runaways on Haight Street. By my third day back, I'm proud to say, I was back on welfare myself and had my own hotel room, a block up 6th from hers. At the end of a week, I'd started doing my "alternative workfare," a requirement of work to receive my welfare, at the Tenderloin AIDS Resource Center. I passed out condoms, bags of snacks, and clean water to HIV-positive clients, two days a week.

As far as I was concerned, this was the *SCAM* lifestyle. I had a place to live, food stamps, and spending money left over, and all I had to do was a couple hours of social service work, which I'd gladly do anyways. I had plenty of time to ride my bike all over town, hop swimming pools, and hang out at donut shops, drinking too much coffee. My hotel was clean and friendly, and old timers drank beer and listened to ball games on AM radio on the steps. I had a window facing the streets and a girlfriend who came over to yell up at it. Life was good.

But you wouldn't know it was possible for life to be good in the Tenderloin from reading any papers in town. The mainstream newspapers only came to 6th Street when the police talked about "cleaning it up." In the liberal, free weekly *San Francisco Bay Guardian*, hotels were never clean and friendly; they were always rat-infested, disease-filled fire traps full of impoverished victims. Even the graphics of *The Street Sheet*, the homeless newspaper, only depicted the poor cowering in the shadows from the impending attack of a policemen. To read the *Street Sheet*, you'd think nothing ever happens to homeless people except getting hassled by cops and lit on fire by frat boys.

This completely denied the reality I saw every day in the neighborhood: the sweetness among the day-in/day-out regulars at the donut shop, the humor of the dive-bar bartenders and Tenderloin junk store owners, the bravery of the drag queens who came in to my work for the bag lunch. I wanted to do a paper that wrote about this sweet stuff all mixed in with the evictions and the struggling—something to laugh about that also showed poor people fighting back for a change. So, at a time when the supposedly-liberal mayor, Willie Brown, was trying to launch the biggest anti-homeless police sweeps in the city's history, Ivy and I launched our street newspaper, the *Turd-Filled Donut*. Issue #1 was a 6-page "XMas Issue. Our masthead read, "This is Issue #1 of the *Turd-Filled Donut*. We cover the Tenderloin, 6th Street, the Mission, and any other part of SF that the city wishes would just disappear!"

The first issue, featuring the debut of "Turd Caen," the 6th Street gossip column based on legendary *San Francisco Chronicle* columnist Herb Caen, did fairly well. We printed around 400, and, of course, stole all the copies from Kinko's. We passed the papers out on the street, at the welfare office, and at a couple social service agencies. We also snuck some into copies of the *Guardian* and the *SF Weekly* on newsracks, and wheat-pasted the issue, in its entirety, around the alleys off 6th, and down in China Basin, where people live in their cars. It seemed to be a big hit among the somewhat jaded Tenderloin outreach workers, and I started seeing faxed copies of our back cover—a shopping cart with a sign reading, "Fuck you, Willie Brown!" taped to it—appearing tacked up in cubicles at various social service agencies and non-profits. Rumor was that some crusty punks even thought our joke announcement of "The Critical Piss" ("We're not blocking traffic! We're pissing!"), a protest of the lack of public restrooms in SF to be held in filthy Stevenson Alley, was real and showed up!

But I was still sort of bummed that no one wrote or called us about the first issue, and that no one answered our ad at the end seeking writers for the paper. Our distribution sucked. I figured our only hope was to get our own *Turd-Filled Donut* newspaper box and put it on 6th Street.

Ivy suggested a spot she'd scoped out, around 4th and Market, where there were about 10 newspaper boxes in a long line. Who would miss just one? We pushed a shopping cart over there and selected the box of the mysterious publication, *Downtown S.F.* The box was empty, and neither of us had either seen or heard of *Downtown S.F.* When the sidewalk seemed relatively free of traffic, we got it up and into the cart, and headed up Market. It was a pretty sketchy scene—us just pushing this big old news box down the street—but I knew if we could just get it the couple blocks to 6th, the box would, like all stolen property, magically disappear there forever. We stopped to repaint the box in Natoma Alley off 6th, while some crusties we knew hung out with us and drank. At one point a cop rolled by us, but, sure enough, the box was already invisible. Seeing six dirty punks with a dog, spray painting a newspaper box, the cop simply smiled, waved, and said, "Nice dog!"

I decided to store the box in my hotel room until issue #2 was done. When I struggled to carry it up the stairs into the hotel, the night doorman, a middle aged black guy who always wore mirrored sunglasses at night, greeted me with the same inscrutable expression he always wore, whether I came home with two 12-packs of beer, or covered in spray paint, or with a girl with blue hair. He'd seen it all.

Issue #2 finally came out. with a cover by Greta Mudflap, more Turd Caen, a celebration of legal drinking in parks of SF, and Ivy's article on cheap or free spots to go on dates in the Tenderloin. In the alley at 6th and Jessie, we chained our box to an official city sign that ordered—or you might say begged—people not to piss in public. However, we were so excited to get the paper out, that when we were collating the copies and drinking beer in the alley, we weren't paying attention, and didn't see the cops rolling up. We got drinking in public tickets. How ironic! Luckily, our article on drinking in parks also had legal advice on what to do if you got caught. We took our tickets to The Coalition on Homelessness like the article said, and their legal representatives got the tickets thrown out of court!

With issue #2, we finally got some response. The weird, crack-smoking mechanics at the bike shop around the corner from my place called to tell us they loved us and wanted us to do a story on them. Yeah, right! Then a middle-aged drag queen named Queen Antoinetta, who was the tenant rep at Baldwin House, called us every day for weeks to see if we'd interview her. One day, I woke up to her banging on my door. She gave me her card, which read "Antoinetta—The Queen of 6ᵗʰ Street." She never ended up writing for us. But, for a while, the guys in my hotel would joke with me, "Hey Iggy! There was some dude here lookin' for ya... a dude in a dress! Is that your new old lady? Or your old MAN?"

Soon, however, we did get a couple of new columnists and even a second newspaper box. Twist gave us the box and we put it over by St. Anthony's Soup Kitchen at Jones and Golden Gate, the *Turd-Filled Donut*'s first march north of Market Street. RG (pronounced "URG") Goudy, an organizer at the workfare rights union, P.O.W.E.R., started writing a "workfare diary" about his experiences cleaning city buses for his welfare check. His first column was about the fine art of making fake bus transfers for free rides. Jimmy started writing "The Wandering Scavenger" column, directing people to where big trash nights would be in different neighborhoods across town, so they could go dig through rich folks' trash for free stuff!

The problem with the newspaper boxes turned out to be that the cops kept taking them. The girls from Tom's Grocery said they saw a cop actually borrow bolt cutters from a pawn shop to cut our lock and take our box! However, we found a newsbox supply place in China Basin that always had five or ten boxes outside their fence. Whenever the cops would take one, we would go get another one and repaint it until, finally, the cops seemed to give up. Once, we had the same box for a record 5 months! The issues flew fast out of the box and, on many sunny days, the box also served as a bench for street drinkers.

Our biggest breakthrough, though, toward becoming a credible paper happened when Ivy actually scored a *Turd-Filled Donut* interview with Willie Brown, the hated mayor of San Francisco! Once a month, Brown had an event at City Hall where he would meet individually with twenty-five SF citizens, one at a time, for fifteen minutes each. The press loved it and always showed up to get pictures of Willie listening attentively to his poor citizens' grievances. In order to see Da Mayor, you'd have to line up on a certain day at City

Hall at 5:00 AM and be one of the first twenty-five people in line. Ivy went down there bright and early and managed to get a ticket. Then we asked people on 6th Street what questions they wished they could ask the mayor if they had a chance to talk to him.

Apparently, Brown didn't take his talk with the lowly *Turd-Filled Donut* very seriously. Despite a very visible tape recorder that Ivy had told him was recording the interview, he made slip-up after slip-up. Many of the questions from 6th Street residents concerned the safety, upkeep, and cleanliness of the 6th Street single-room occupancy hotels in which many of our readers and us lived. Brown was surprised to learn that there are no kitchens in SRO hotel rooms and that you can't buy hot meals with food stamps. He was just so out of touch. He told his aide, "No kitchens? Let's get right on this! First thing, Monday morning!" As if they could start building kitchens in 70-year old hotel rooms, just like that!

But Brown's biggest fuck-up came when talking about the controversies raging in the city over gentrification. Illegal evictions, welfare cuts, and the influx of rich dot-commers were working to completely remove the poor from San Francisco—a city that already had one of the highest median rents in the country. Brown actually came out and said, "I say to people who are poverty stricken, you are better off going where the cost of living is not so great..." He had come right out and said it: if you're poor, get lost!

This interview ended being reprinted in the *Guardian* under the telling headline "Brown to Poor: Leave Town!" KUSF borrowed the tape so they could play it on the air repeatedly. A year later, during Brown's run for re-election, this offhand remark to the *T.F.D.* was still being used against him in the *Chronicle, Examiner,* and *The Guardian*, as well as being cited in the campaign literature of his progressive opponent, Tom Ammiano. During the campaign, Brown's quote from the *T.F.D.* appeared on countless anti-Brown stickers and wheat-pastings all over town. The most exciting thing for me was hearing that our "election issue" from November '99, in which we endorsed Ammiano, was spotted tacked to a wall at Ammiano's election headquarters!

The *T.F.D.* printed a wide variety of articles over three years. We wrote about people winning lawsuits against their slumlord hotel owners, we covered Coalition on Homelessness demonstrations demanding civil rights for the homeless, and we interviewed the UN Plaza Homeless Project, a group of homeless people who were doing sit-ins in City Hall and demanding that the city give them an abandoned building to fix up for housing. We wrote about transgender history in the Tenderloin and the Biotic Baking Brigade, a group of activists who famously attacked Mayor Brown with a pie at a press conference.

But I think our most well known story, besides the Brown interview, was one with no morally or politically upgrading benefits, "The 6th Street Treasure Hunt for Beer." Greta and I hid a 6-pack of beer and the centerfold to Issue #5 featured a big map and clues to find it. It was actually pretty hard, but if you solved it—and all the clues were right on 6th Street—then you would've found the beer in a suitcase, floating in the bay, at the end of a rope tied to a ladder on Pier 7! That's how the beer was guaranteed to be cold; it was in the icy bay! It turned out my bike messenger friends, Ravi and Sean, found the beer within a week, so we put more out there. One day, I went to check on the second 6-pack and I found the rope up on the dock next to a bunch of crushed Tecate cans. Someone had found that one, too!

The *T.F.D.* broke a major story in an election year, and publicized resistance against gentrification and redevelopment on 6th Street and in the Mission. It was read widely—at both the welfare office and in City Hall. Yet, mostly, when people stop me on the streets to talk about it, they just ask me when I'm going to hide some more beer.

TENDERLOIN SECRET HISTORY

1

In an old hotel, downtown, off a small alley. It was a neighborhood where, if the cops came, no one ever saw anything. There were surveillance cameras everywhere. Some days, men on every corner would be talking to themselves, as if humming along to a radio station that only they got. Rainy mornings, lost under umbrellas, collecting cans. I walked in crowds between tall buildings. Everyday streets, walked deeper and deeper into a maze. There were dead ends, secret places. Hotel hallways and darkened bars. From my window I could see the hidden spot behind a dumpster where a different man shot up every morning.

I did street outreach, passing out flyers about our services to men in doorways. There were black guys with trash bags on their feet, men selling trash they'd found. Often, I'd see our clients in line at a corner store, or waiting to be buzzed in at a hotel. If they were with a non-client, I'd avoid eye contact. I knew their biggest secret.

Secrets. Past lives. Hiding places. When she and I had sex, I'd hear the hum of old elevators coming to life. All I remembered was the murmur of pigeons in the airshaft between buildings, where the sun would never shine.

A man with a white mask over his mouth would empty trash into the dumpster across the alley every morning. Cops walked the streets with white latex gloves on. I passed out condoms and lube to HIV-positive men only.

On the fifth floor of the new main library, I found a book that said my hotel was 62 years old. There were crowded days and old newspapers. Steaming coffee, waiting. She would stand in the alley and yell my name, like a neon sign in a bar.

When I moved out, I still had her umbrella. Stuff was sad, the things you had owned. They lasted too long. Joseph Loya, for instance, apparently died on Jones Street, but his stuff made it to a sidewalk sale, two blocks further up Turk. All of the letters for sale were addressed to him. He had been to the Russian Orthodox Church in the Avenues in 1981. Someone named Buddy had sent him a postcard of the St. Louis arch in 1980 addressed to his room at the YMCA in Houston. Now, someone was trying to sell it on Turk Street. I took it home and put it on my wall.

That night I lay in bed, listening to the sounds in the alley. Sixty-two years. I would catch myself, sometimes, falling asleep, and sit bolt upright in bed.

2

There was a mysterious smokestack that I could see from my window, maybe two blocks from my place, that sometimes gave off a steamy emission. I had always felt oddly drawn to it, and one day, I set out to once and for all find its exact location. When I found it, down an alley, in the center of the block, the fence in front of it was lined with men, smoking crack.

In my room, there was an ornamental strip of wood that ran around the perimeter of the room, about a foot and a half from the ceiling. After I'd lived there for about six months, I noticed a small orange dot out of the corner of my eye, just at the edge of this wood. I climbed up on a chair to see what it was. It was a clean, unused syringe with an orange safety tip. The last occupant, or maybe the occupant before, had hidden it up there. Holding it, I felt time seemed to blur. This could be any of the hotel's 62 years. Dead ends and hiding places. Secrets and past lives. I put it back up there for the next guy to find when I moved out.

Our office was a converted storefront. The place was old, from before the world had ever heard of AIDS, or even the CIA. We had everyone's name on a list. I knew most of our clients by sight, but if I didn't know them, I'd have to look them up on the list. Everyone on the list had an incurable disease. But, day in and day out, they were surprisingly upbeat people. They only got upset if I had to get out the list. The very sight of it would enrage them. A 6-foot tall guy with a red wig on and a very ill-fitting skirt would come in, who I had never seen before, and I'd say, "Name, please..." He'd say, "Ginger." I'd say, no, I need your full name. "But I come here every day!" he'd yell. Finally, though, if he wanted his food bag, he would settle down and whisper, "Michael Ellis." The disease didn't seem to bother them, in a way, as much as their real names.

It seems we never get to control our real names in the library, either. We never get to see the list. The secret history might be in the old library, across the street from the new one, which spent much of the last few years surrounded by huge weeds and unmowed grass. I imagined the old history in places where time stood still. Sometimes, blackout drunk, she and I would have sex and she would try to put it in without a condom. I'd think of elevator shafts and alleys and hidden needles, and feel myself falling. And not wanting to catch myself.

In our office in the old storefront, a tranny sighed, "I wonder what this place used to BE...."

3

January turned into February. It was still raining. A girl at work told me about people who lived in tunnels under the Tenderloin and downtown. She said she'd found tunnels in the basement of her old squat, and that she and her friends had gone in them and explored a little.

I became sort of obsessed with finding the tunnels. I started by looking for entrances in the crater lots downtown where buildings had been knocked down. There was one behind my hotel, full of weeds and broken TV's. With most of the lots, from the sidewalk you just saw a fence. But if you snuck in there'd be a huge field, walls covered with graffiti, and, sometimes, whole communities of people living just under the sidewalk. But I found no tunnels.

An old-timer in Chinatown told me, "Of course I know about the tunnels. People go in 'em down on Commerce Street, around the corner." Commerce turned out to be a one-block dead end on the other side of North Beach. Did he maybe mean "Commercial," which WAS right around the corner?

I checked every manhole cover on Commercial, but there was nothing. I searched for some kind of old tunnel map in the new library. But the new library, with its huge unassailable-looking walls, looked like it was built just to keep the information from the streets out of it. I couldn't find anything. It seemed like they only had computers now, and no books.

Later, I read an article about the library that said they HAD thrown away tons of books. They had first put them in storage... in a tunnel under Civic Center.

<h1 style="text-align:center">4</h1>

Lately, I've had my own secret. I've been hiding stuff in the library. I started by putting stuff in the clipping files. I'd write stuff and just put it in. I put all my magazines in them, in the corresponding files. Then, I started making my own files. I took pictures of old bar signs in the Tenderloin and made a "Signs" file of my own and put it in. I started working on a punk flyer file. I go back and check and it is all still there.

I've also made name tags for shelves so I could put my magazines up in the periodical section and make it look like the library ordered them. I mean, sure, they're already in the Special Collections, but whoever can find out when that room is even open? Now, I prefer just to get it right up on the shelf. Piece by piece, I'm building a secret history collection.

TURDS IN THE SUN

For the first time in weeks, the rain has stopped, Bell's Donuts is empty, and the shopping carts roll, once more, down 6th Street in the sun. The gutter punks are out front of the teen drop-in center on Turk Street, mapping out freight train routes, the guy from Tenderloin Petals on Hyde is out, talking to his plants on the sidewalk, and the *Turd-Filled Donut* staff is busy, sneaking into downtown hotels' swimming pools! In the 'Loin, love is in the air. A couple skips, arm in arm, down Golden Gate, past the Self-Help Center, and someone in the crowd asks, loudly, "What are THEY on?!?" The couple turns around, and cheerfully yells, "PILLS!"

Meanwhile, revolution is in the air up at the Ha Ra bar on Geary. New graffiti in the toilet reads, "It is the duty of all men to ignor (sic) any law that turns citizen against citizen!" What are they pissed about? Proposed welfare check cuts? Cops fucking with the homeless? NO! They're pissed about the new NO-SMOKING-IN-BARS-LAW!!! Of course, you can still smoke in the Ha Ra, or any self-respecting Tenderloin bar, AND you can still get a strong whiskey sour, for two bucks and a quarter...

Down at the Hall of Injustice, 850 Bryant, the *Turd-Filled Donut* staff was on hand for the Vehicularly Housed Residents' Association's protest and press conference. For those who don't know, the VHRA is a real, live neighborhood organization for folks who live in their cars in China Basin. The SFPD was having their annual Police Commission Hearing, where they basically pat themselves on the mustache for what a great job they've been doing all year. The VHRA packed the hearing room with supporters, including the Mayor of China Basin himself, and all held signs that read, "SAVE OUR HOMES!" One after another, they spoke at the podium, telling the cops to stop towing the cars that they live in. It all went real well, except one whiny old guy from the "Polk/Sutter Neighborhood Committee" or something came up to speak, and, ignoring the massive car dweller demonstration, launched into a pathetic speech about how the cops won't arrest prostitutes in front of his store on Sutter. Ah, poor BABY! Where does he think he LIVES, anyways? I wanted to change my sign in solidarity: "SAVE OUR HO'S!"

MORE PROTESTS out in the Av-a-Snooze: The owners of the BEACH HOTEL at 42nd Avenue and Judah, want to illegally convert their residential hotel into a tourist hotel, and kick out the poor folks who can afford to stay there now. At a hearing about it, the place was packed with whiny rich folks, but they had nowhere to sit because the TENDERLOIN HOUSING CLINIC had lured a huge crowd of protesters with the promise of FREE PIZZA! The terrified Avenues residents were snide and condescending, saying things like, "We're not saying we're better than YOU PEOPLE, but we DO pay more taxes…" and "We don't want our neighborhoods ruined by the junkies and prostitutes who stay in THESE hotels…" which prompted Prince Bush, the Tenant's Organization leader at the Jefferson Hotel in the 'Loin, to get outraged and yell back, "So how come you all drive your Mercedes down to MY neighborhood to buy your drugs and pick up prostitutes?!?" Fuck yeah!

BACK HOME on 6th: TOM'S GROCERY at 6th and Mish has long been known for their pre-cooked meals that you can buy with food stamps and reheat at home, but the Health Department has told them that the meat has to go! From now on, there are no ribs, beef sandwiches, or chicken. But you can still get salads, beans and rice, and potato salad, and it's still 6th Street's only 24-hour store… OVERHEARD: In front of the ALDER HOTEL, a guy takes a mighty hit off his crackpipe, passes it to his partner, exhales, and yells, "LORD, I THINK I CAN FLY!" And, at Bell's Donuts, a customer tosses an SF FREE TOILET TOKEN on the counter, and yells to the surrounding crowd, "Wow! Check it out! Now, I can shit for free, forever!" Sorry, buddy. You actually only get 20 minutes inside the toilet…

SHOPPING CARTS ON THE RUNWAY: Here's the latest in TENDERLOIN RAIN FASHION: A lot of folks are sporting the PLASTIC-BAGS-TIED-AROUND-YOUR-SHOES-LOOK these days, and still more are going for the PLASTIC-BAG-TIED-AROUND-YOUR-HUGE-BLASTING-RADIO-LOOK!!! But the best new style yet was spotted by a *Turd-Filled Donut* staffer at the temporary emergency shelter at 6th and Folsom: A guy in the food line was wearing a BIG ORANGE LIFE PRESERVER!!! Take that, El Nino! Another guy in line pointed and whispered, "Now HE sure ready for a flood!!!"

THERE GOES THE NEIGHBORHOOD: A *Turd-Filled Donut* staffer claims to have spotted a lone rollerblader, apparently on crack, weaving around 6th Street at 3:00 AM last Friday night... And at 9th and Market, a *Turd-Filled Donut* subscriber spotted Da Mayor himself, WILLIE BROWN, walking down the street. Our man yelled at the mayor, "Why do you hate poor people?" three times. There was no response, until the mayor reached his car, and getting in, yelled back, "I don't hate poor people. I just hate YOU!"

ALL WE ARE IS TURDS IN THE WIND: at EL CAN-CUN (6th/ Market) a TFD staffer was eating, when a drug dealer approached, offering, "Good weed." The staffer said, "No thanks." The guy got this real hurt look in his eye, and said, "NO. it's GOOD weed!" We said no. The drug dealer looked deeply sad. "But it's really good weed!" he repeated mournfully. We said, "Look, man, we don't smoke!" and the drug dealer walked slowly to the door, hanging his head and muttering to himself, "But it's really GOOD!" Poor guy. Who says 6th Street doesn't have a sensitive side? Later, at Bell's, on one of those long, rain-soaked, coffee-swilling, newspaper-reading afternoons, the regulars ask the counter guy, "What kind of music do you like, man?" Without pause, he replies, "I like SCOTT MCKENZIE!" and puts on a tape of the 60s SF folk star! The crowd gets wistful as Scott drones through, "If you're going to San Francisco, wear a flower in your hair" and then slowly starts to remember the words and sing along to "Come on, people, now!" Soon, the whole shop is muttering, "Come on, people, now! Blah blah blah, Everybody get together and try to love one another, right now..." It was a touching moment. One guy smiled ear to ear, and said, "I LOVE music!" I said, "I love DONUTS!" and got another buttermilk bar (glazed).

HOW I GOT RICH BEFORE I TURNED 30 IN THE NEW DOT-COM ECONOMY!

When I lived downtown, I used to go for lunch many days to Martin de Porres, the venerable Mission District soup kitchen. My theme song was that old MDC song from the 80s, "Soup Kitchen Celebrity." The hours were still the same as in the song, open every day from 12 to 3! I even saw Zara there sometimes, though if I saw the drummer of the Dead Kennedys, as promised by the song, I didn't recognize him.

Around the corner from Marty's, one day I noticed a gathering of twenty-something white hipster kids. They stood, smoking and talking, in a configuration that resembled a younger version of the group of homeless men milling around outside the soup kitchen down the block. But they were standing in front of a dot-com company that was housed in an old red brick building. When one guy, probably about five years younger than me, stubbed out his smoke and opened the front door, I impulsively nodded a greeting and followed him inside.

A guard at the front desk didn't look up. As I passed the lobby, some employees headed outside didn't give me a second look either. For about ten full minutes, I strode confidently around the work area, poking my head into conference rooms and greeting people in the halls. I found the main work area, a vast, high-ceilinged room filled with young white kids, each wearing headphones and stationed in long rows in front of computers. A couple of kids looked up at me as I approached, nodded, and went back to typing. I realized I could probably sit down at a computer and pretend I worked there for days and no one would ever know I didn't belong there. It seemed likely that no one knew just who worked there.

I later read an article in The Baffler where a guy wrote about doing exactly that: showing up at a dot-com company in New York City and pretending to work. But that sounded boring to me. I went for the beer! The Silicon Valley start-ups that were now overrunning our neighborhood were famous, of course, for their informal workplaces, and I soon found the Internet era's fabled beer-stocked fridges and overflowing cabinets of food in the employee kitchen. I took my time, making a sandwich and enjoying some fresh, organic juices. Then I got some coffee for the road, noting that there were not one but TWO good beers on tap.

After that I went back a few times, avoiding Martin de Porres's gas-producing split pea soup in favor of dot-com sandwiches, trail mix, and the occasional fancy beer raised in toast to my new co-workers, milling awkwardly around the kitchen with me, their headphones still in their ears. Ironically, it was because I never got kicked out that I finally quit going. After a while, being somewhere that could be anywhere with people who could be anybody was just too damn creepy. I couldn't handle the sterile atmosphere that was also creeping out into our entire neighborhood. At least Martin de Porres was like a family.

SCAM PUNKS VS. STARBUCKS

Could this shitty homemade coupon (below) get you and 12,000 of your friends free coffee at Starbucks? Xerox it at home and try for yourself! *Scam* recommends colored Paper.

COME GET TO KNOW US!!!
STARBUCK'S is probably coming to a corner near you.
Come try one *Venti* **"COFFEE OF THE DAY"**, or a
Solo **Espresso** drink, **ABSOLUTELY FREE!**
No purchase necessary. Offer valid at any Starbuck's
(Expiration 01/01/01)

www.starbucks.com

The "fake coupon" scam has, of course, been around for a long time now. You know—people using fairly primitive computer graphics programs to make fake coupons that you can trade in for coffee grounds and free ice cream and stuff. Sometimes it even works if you just photocopy real ones. It's not hard to convince your average underpaid, teenage employee at a chain store that your shitty homemade coupon is real and to give you free shit.

But what about convincing EVERYONE IN DOWNTOWN SAN FRANCISCO that your coupon is real? Anandi and I decided to see what would happen if we used a computer and a scanner to make coupons for Starbucks and then copied, oh, say, *twelve thousand* of them and passed them out in the Financial District.

Our coupons, despite being printed on colored paper, turned out pretty ghetto looking. Somehow that seemed even better. It was almost funnier to see how ridiculously bad could you make them and still have them actually *work*. After endless days of half-assedly cutting out the tiny crooked strips, we went downtown to see.

Antonio took a pile to Powell and Market and Sarah went to Union Square, leaving Anandi and me at Montgomery Street Muni Station. We were just two blocks from a Starbucks. Actually, EVERY corner downtown is just two blocks from Starbucks. That was the best part.

When we showed up at Montgomery, luckily there were already some women passing out sample packets of Excedrin, which added legitimacy to our actions. When the first oddly cut, irregular-looking coupon was passed from my hand to the hands of a passing suit, I was excited. It was starting!

Montgomery Street is the capital of the whole fake economy. The stock trading, Internet stocks, real estate speculation—this is where it all goes down. If everyone in the Bay Area could be convinced that the economic boom would never end, or that our creaky, cockroach-filled ghetto houses were worth millions, then our coupons would be an easy sell. Sure enough, after a couple minutes of handing them out, people in suits were running back, begging for more. People were quite literally walking one way with the coupon, and then walking back by moments later, holding big, free cups of coffee!

Anandi herself decided she needed coffee, so she went to the one near Powell. She said there was a big pile of our coupons by the register and a line out the door; EVERYONE was getting free coffee! Which raises the question, "If I say it's a coupon for free coffee, and the store gives them free coffee, is it still a FAKE coupon?"

Apparently, yes. After we'd been there close to two hours and had probably, at all three spots, put over 2,000 coupons on the street, a man came up to me and said, "I'm a Starbucks representative. You have no authorization to pass these out! Give them all to me!" He was mad. I shrugged and handed him the four or five left in my hand. I said, "Look, man, this guy gave me twenty bucks to pass these out for four hours, and it looks like I'm done in two!" and I started walking away. The guy tried to intercept Anandi as she quickly split the other way. He yelled, "Stop! You're under citizen's arrest!" But she just said, "Yeah right!" and kept going. Now that we can't pass the coupons out in the street, I think we'll just have to leave the other ten thousand or so of them in stacks at laundromats and thrift stores, and mail them to punks in other cities.

On the way home, for the hell of it, I tried to get coffee at the Starbucks at Powell and Market. When I showed my coupon, the girl behind the counter flipped out and yelled, "We don't take those! I don't know who made them but we're flooded with them! Our real coupons all have UPC codes on them to scan!" Well, thanks for the info. Readers of *Scam # 1* will remember that U.P.C codes still work when you photocopy them!

A REAL RAIN?

THE OLD NEIGHBORHOOD'S NOT THE SAME. At least, that's what everyone's always saying. Even the gruff, but lovable, British guy who did the Sunday afternoon Tenderloin walking tours out of the Edinburgh Castle (POLK/GEARY) has called it quits and given up on the Tenderloin. "Look at this place!" he snarls bitterly, nursing a hangover and a pint of Guinness. "Dis place used to be all junkies and 'ores, mate! Now da bloody fockin' yuppies are coming up 'ere! Its bloody disgustin' is what it is!" And sure enough, the cops are out in full force, too. Up on Polk Street, Officer "Scarface" Robles has been writing tickets for "Sitting on a MUNI bench without intent to board a bus" again, and believe it or not, beat cops have started to walk up and down 6th Street! Is it the end of an era? Early indications are that "cleaning up" our neighborhood's going to be harder than they think. Just ask the cops who came out to find people laughing and their windshield lovingly covered in fresh, runny pigeon shit... Or you could ask the company who put up the ad for "Real Mexican Tequila" on the billboard by King's Diner (10th and Mish). It featured a real, plugged-in TV set and read "Real Mexican TV Show" with an arrow pointing at it. It took about two days for someone to figure out how to climb up there and rip off the TV! Doesn't it make you proud to live downtown?

PEOPLE'S PUKE: The tiny grass patches at UN Plaza are, once again, public domain. The city tried to barricade them off, and even had an army of police on hand to arrest Food Not Bombs protesters who demanded the return of the public grass. But finally The City gave in, and the two patches have returned to their rightful state: covered in trash and home to an army of shirtless men, swilling 40's in the sun! How did they think they could stop us? Someone better tell the British guy things aren't so bad after all...

SUMMER OF LOVE ON 6th? Cops, or not, it's summer on 6th Street. Love is in the air, there's singing in the halls of the Hotel Auburn, and, down the block at 5th and Minna, an enthusiastic couple was observed the other day at noon, having loud, passionate anal sex behind a dumpster. Talk about looking for love in all the wrong doorways... And there's protest brewing, too. The city's workfare workers have started a union to demand the city hire them for real jobs with real pay. Check for more info later in this issue... Less promising sounding, however, is the "Drug User's Union" that they're attempting to start over at Tenderloin Self-Help (193 Golden Gate). Flyers posted across the Tenderloin read, "Drug Users Unite! Stop being treated like 2nd-class citizens!" An admirable idea, to be sure, but still, one that sounds like it was conceived, by, well, DRUG USERS. A self-help staffer said that 6 people came to the 1st meeting, and 4 were there "by accident." Only in Ess Eff?

OVERHEARD: On heroin row, on 16th between Mission and Valencia, a jaywalker stumbles in front of an oncoming car, but turns to face it, halts it with an upright palm, and sings, like The Supremes, "Stop! In the name of drugs!"

DYING TO KNOW, TOO AFRAID TO ASK DEPT.: The *Turd-Filled Donut* has learned that, yes, you CAN, buy a live chicken at the UN Plaza Farmers' Market with food stamps. They cost 6 bucks. Too bad hotels won't let you have pets...

SOCIETY NEWS: Bell's Donuts (6th/Market) regular, Slim, announced to a crowded Bell's that he landed a guest role on a TV show called "Party of Five." Since no one there has a TV set anyway, we all believed him...

The 7th and Minna alley dwellers have started a band. Someone got an acoustic guitar, and they can now be heard many afternoons, singing loudly and playing "Hotel California" over and over again. Minna resident, Miami, a Philadelphia native, known for his red beret, has been spotted wearing a new, gray, felt hat...

BIG BROTHER IS WATCHING YOU PEE: The new surveillance camera and sign saying, "Warning! This area is being filmed 24 hours a day!" at 6th and Stevenson was put up—believe it or not—by new 6th Street tenants, the SF AIDS FOUNDATION! This is the same so-called public health organization that withdrew funding for needle-exchange in the Haight because it was too controversial for the Haight's yuppies. I'm glad I'm not the guy who has to watch that 24-hour footage of folks in the alley, though. There is a surveillance camera you CAN watch at the bar MR. LEE-ONA'S (Turk/Leavenworth). It points at the street in front of the bar, so you can drink and watch the entertainment outside. Broke drunks take note—they also give away a free shot to anyone in the bar when the 49ers score a touchdown! I love to think of a clean Mormon jerk like Steve Young laboring away to help get us folks back in the Tenderloin a drink...

CRIME, PUNISHMENT, AND DONUTS: Hunt's Donuts, at 20th and Mission, long known as THE place in el Mission to buy excellent buttermilk donuts, AND stolen merchandise off the street, has now put up not one, not two, not three, but FOUR signs saying, "No buying or selling of merchandise in the store!" One even says "By order of the District Attorney." Could it be—Terrence Hallinan, the DA, at Hunt's? Like, Terry came for a cruller, and somebody tried to sell him a bag of socks and an electric toothbrush so he got pissed and threatened to shut 'em down? Meanwhile, at Bell's the other day, one of the regulars stepped out for a smoke, and came back to find his cinnamon roll stolen off his plate! He looked so sad, that the nice counter lady came over, gave him another one, and in a stern, but motherly voice, said, "You keep eye on it this time!" It was so sweet. But really I couldn't help wondering, where's a cop in this neighborhood when you really NEED one?

SAN FRANCISCO MAYOR, WILLIE BROWN: THE TURD-FILLED DONUT INTERVIEW

TURD-FILLED DONUT: A lot of people on 6th Street have concerns about their residential hotels and their upkeep. Since The City subcontracts with the hotels, namely through the GA program, don't you feel responsible, partially, to make sure the hotel owners stay up to code? I lived in a hotel, so I have firsthand experiences...

WILLIE BROWN: And they were horrible...

TFD: Yeah, and I received food stamps, but none of these rooms are made for people to get off welfare. You can't save if you live off of $345 a month, and the hotels don't have kitchens. So you get food stamps but you can't cook at home. You're forced to eat "snacks as a mini-meal" like that pamphlet they put out in the welfare office recommends. So, in light of that, can't you do more to force the owners to do the upkeep on their hotels?

WB: Well, absolutely. We can always do more. I did not know that the hotels had no kitchens. Thank you for calling that to my attention. I just had no idea that there were no kitchens for someone receiving food stamps... I mean, why would you receive food stamps if you could not cook the food? [turning to his staff at the table] Did you guys know about this? That there are no requirements for cooking facilities in these places?

STAFF: [nodding sheepishly, they murmur assent that they, in fact, had known this]

WB: What?!? Then shouldn't we try to figure out how to transfer these foodstamps into money, so people can actually buy MEALS?!? We ought to explore that. She's right! No kitchens? That's like having NO BATHROOMS!

TFD: Well, there are no bathrooms really, either...

WB: I think that, frankly, we ought to be able to REQUIRE a COMMUNITY kitchen in every hotel...

TFD: Yeah. Another concern, though, is that the hotel owners are not held accountable for the living conditions. I was on GA and lived in a hotel, but I had to leave because there was a fire twice in one week.

WB: Well, people start them by smoking. Humans start those fires.

TFD: Well, sometimes the humans could be the owners themselves, because their wiring is so ancient. The Sharon Hotel (6th/ Howard), where I lived, was so badly wired that if anyone was using any kind of extra electricity plugged into the outlets, the power would go out (on the entire floor). It discouraged me from even wanting to go home in the evenings, because the power went out every five minutes! It seems that with stuff like that, you wouldn't have to evict everyone. You could just renovate and work around them...

WB: Well, theoretically, our inspection programs are supposed to catch the kind of things you're talking about. That's our fault, if the inspectors aren't catching that. Now that you have called this to our attention, our inspectors are obviously going to be at the Sharon Hotel, first thing Monday!

TFD: Yeah, but that's just one hotel out of so many like that.
WB: Of course! But we do it one at a time, right?

TFD: So, do you feel responsible for their upkeep?
WB: Totally. If we are causing the funding that goes into the owner's pockets, we have a responsibility to ensure that we are getting legitimately what the owner represented to us.

TFD: Another concern is that the $345 monthly GA grant just is not a living wage in this city.
WB: No, it is not.

TFD: And, actually, now it has been cut to $279 for people not involved in the additional hassle of the PAES program. If the hotels take your whole check, you won't ever be able to save up and get off welfare.
WB: Well, we do pay the highest welfare grant in the state.

TFD: Right, but it's also the most expensive place to live—possibly on the whole planet!
WB: And that's why I say to people who are poverty stricken, I know how much you love San Francisco, but, because of the nature of the cost of living here, you are better off being poverty stricken where the cost of living is not so great.

TFD: But that would mean displacing people who have lived here their whole lives!
[Editor's note: soon after this, the "interview" degenerated into an argument, and then the allotted time was up...]

INTERVIEW WITH THE BIOTIC BAKING BRIGADE

Later that day, we also interviewed members of the Biotic Baking Brigade, the folks who made nationwide news that year by hitting Willie Brown in the face with a pie at a press conference.

TURD-FILLED DONUT: Could you just start by telling us a little about the Biotic Baking Brigade's history?

BIOTIC BAKING BRIGADE: The first time we pied anyone was Charles Hurwitz, the CEO of Maxxam. They bought out Pacific Lumber and are the ones cutting down the Headwaters. He's just totally evil. Then we got Milton Friedman, the economist. He was speaking at a conference on privatizing education, so he got a pie. Then there was Robert Shapiro, the head of Monsanto Corporation. They produce Round Up, the herbicide, and they have made other fucked up stuff like Agent Orange. Their new thing is Agricultural Biotechnology. Basically, they're altering the genetic makeup of plants. Farmers in India are burning Monsanto fields in protest now, because Monsanto is creating plants that will not grow without chemicals, and of course you have to buy the chemicals from Monsanto! Then, we got Gavin Newsom from the Board of Supervisors. We did that one at the party he had at his restaurant on election night. All the people there were wasted, well-dressed people just totally sloshed. There were girls with 3-inch heels puking in the toilet. Newsom's always been pretty anti-tenant, so we hit him up with TWO pies.

TFD: Did you get arrested?
BBB: No, he didn't want to press charges. He just laughed it off.

TFD: Was he loaded?
BBB: I'm not sure. He said, "Are you guys from the tenants' union?" And we said, "Why? Do you have a guilty conscience or something?"

TFD: So next up was Willie Brown...
BBB: Yeah. We got the Mayor with 3 pies when he was having a press conference at City Hall to announce his Great Sweep program, where he gets a bunch of volunteers to go out and pick up trash in different neighborhoods. We did it because at the same time that he was announcing that he was also coming out with these other programs against the homeless that don't really do anything but sweep people out of different areas like The Castro, or Union Square, or The Haight. A couple weeks before he had been quoted in the paper as saying he was to the point where he just wanted to see people "swept off the streets" and that was really offensive to me. I mean, no matter how down and out people get, they're still people, you know? They're not just trash or a hamburger wrapper, or something you can sweep up.

So, we figured we could just go out with signs and picket, or something, and no one would notice; but pies are sexier and make better news stories. He was about to announce a surprise deal for the 49ers stadium at the Great Sweep press conference. He said, "I have something dramatic to announce..." and that's when we got him!

TFD: What happened after you threw the pies?
BBB: Brown tried to tackle one of us. He got one of us in a headlock. Some bodyguard tackled me and broke my collarbone. I was screaming in pain! We all got arrested. An ambulance took me to the hospital first and all the doctors and nurses were all so cool to me. They were all like, "Good job! Way to go!" Then, everyone in jail was totally glad we did it, too.

TFD: Of course! Everyone in town thinks its cool except like 5 people who write for the *Chronicle*.
BBB: Right. Well, the people who don't like what we have to say are never going to like the way we say it. People have said that it was violent, but, I mean, it's a pie. It's not non-violent in the same way that a sit-in is, but the whole point is that no one gets hurt. I do feel a little bad, because, it turns out that Brown has glaucoma and he can't see too well, so he didn't actually know what hit him.

TFD: Yeah, when I interviewed him, I noticed he has these wandering eyes. I tried to look him in the eye but it was impossible. I thought he was a robot, or something.
BBB: Yeah, I don't think any jury in SF will convict us.

TFD: What's next for the Biotic Baking Brigade?
BBB: Well, personally, with my broken shoulder, I will only be BAKING pies for a while. But, I believe the pastry uprising will continue. There's a lot of people out there who deserve a pie, and a lot of people who are capable of delivering them. To be in the Biotic Baking Brigade, all you need is a pie and a vision of a better world.

TFD: Do you have anything else you want to say to our readers?
BBB: Well, we really hope that people enjoyed this. Things get bleak sometimes, but we choose to get our politics across this way, because it's funny. People—especially the people most affected by Brown's lack of action and lack of compassion—need a good laugh sometimes.

JOEY RAMONE DAY

It seems like punk rock has been around long enough now to have its own holidays. With that in mind, a couple of us here in San Francisco got together to celebrate Joey Ramone Day to honor Joey on April 15th, the anniversary of his death. Anandi, Kat, Paul, Sara, Arwen, and I spent the afternoon and night walking and riding the bus all over the city, drinking beer and blasting the Ramones on a little radio. We also spray painted "RAMONES" everywhere, covering SF with mysterious Ramones tags—some of which, I was glad to see, stayed up for months. Unfortunately, the photo of the one on the cop car didn't come out good enough to be on the cover of *Maximum Rock and Roll*. Maybe next time!

But you don't have to get wasted to celebrate Joey Ramone Day. This year, Kat found an actual town on the map named Rockaway Beach, just 8 miles south of SF near Pacifica. She wanted us all to go there and have some sort of picnic with a Secret Santa thing, where we exchanged mix tapes. It was a cool idea. I liked the idea of the spirit of Joey being a cause for a day of gift giving. But, at the last minute, Kat couldn't go or drive us down there. So Sweet Tooth, Ben Ditch, Joey Alone, and I met up at Hunt's Donuts to see if we could, in fact, hitch a ride to Rockaway Beach.

"What if it IS far?" Joey grouched as we got on Muni, blasting our tape of the Ramones' first record. "What if it IS hard to reach?" But the music got us into the spirit. Those songs sound so fucking great when you're playing them loud on the street! After a couple of Muni rides, we got to the Daly City line where all four of us scummy punks would now stand together with our thumbs out on the side of the road in the suburbs. It was probably the first time in history anyone had ever attempted to hitch a ride at that spot, but hopes were high. After all, it was only eight miles away and Ben was even wearing a leather jacket! Our cardboard sign read, "Rock...Rock...Rockaway Beach!" Sadly, motorists looked right through it for hours.

Of course, it actually IS possible to take a bus to Rockaway Beach, just like the Ramones conceivably could have skipped all the hassle and hopped the turnstile of the damn A train for a more certain ride out to Far Rockaway. It's pretty funny, today, to go to Rockaway

Beach in Queens, a fairly suburban-looking part of New York, and try to imagine the four Ramones lurking around on the boardwalk or sitting on the sand in their leather jackets. They must have had an aunt or a granny that lived down there or something.

But we COULDN'T take the bus; it was Joey Ramone Day and we HAD to hitch a ride, just like in the song. It just didn't work, though. We stood there for hours and probably would have just WALKED the rest of the way to Rockaway Beach if I didn't have to get back to The City to play a show in a couple of hours.

But there was one magic Joey moment on the side of the road. I had sort of zoned out for a minute, as the cars whizzed past, but once I came to, I realized that we were all standing there with our thumbs out, quietly singing along with the tape.

Whoah-oh-oh. We got nowhere to go oh-oh.
It may sound funny, but it's true. Woo-ooo.

Finally, we spray painted RAMONES really big on the ground to mark our spot and went to SF State to table dive at the food court before the show...

PUNK SHOWS ON MISSION STREET!
MIAMI AND SHOTWELL LIVE AT LEEDS 5/21/98

Underground scenes had to adapt quickly to the city's shifting land-scape. As we struggled to survive the rapid changes and imperma-nence of the dot-com era, our events and protests started to embody it. Without the anchor of genuine community space, illegal street takeovers and shows in squats became common.

The cops shut down all the places to play, except a couple awful dive bars so we, the punks, decided to just get a generator and have free shows in the streets! A couple folks around town, like John Geek and Marcus Da Anarchist, were already having free, illegal shows out in abandoned industrial areas like the Toxic Golf Course (a.k.a. "Tire Beach"), but we thought shows should be right there on Mission Street in the heart of our neighborhood. After seeing how huge the crowd was at the May Day march, I figured we had a big enough crowd to do whatever the fuck we wanted.

We decided to have our first show in the spacious doorway of the abandoned Leed's shoe store at 22nd and Mission. After we got the flyers out, people were asking me all week if the show was really going to happen. I was starting to wonder myself. We couldn't find John Geek to borrow his generator until hours before the show and when me and Jimmy finally pulled up to Leed's, on time, with the P.A., amps, and generator, there was almost no one there. Would anyone show? What if we played, got busted, and no one even CAME?!? Fuck!

But then I spotted the unmistakable profile of a lone punk rocker, bottle in hand, striding triumphantly toward us past the fruit stands and taquerias on Mission, and I knew the shit was on!

Within minutes, there were 50 or 60 punks jamming the sidewalk, bus stop, and doorway in front of Leed's. Everyone was there— the punks who lived in the laundromat in Oakland, the girls who worked at Tom's Grocery on 6th, even the Mohawk-sporting kids who panhandle at Fishermen's Wharf. Floyd showed up with a huge carton of nachos. Tommy Strange even came with his dog, Flipper. Yes, everyone was there except Shotwell's current bassist and drummer who were AFRAID to play, because they didn't want to get arrested! Luckily, everyone in the Mission has played drums in Shotwell, and Pete, the most recent ex-drummer, happened to walk by to check out the show. He was quickly enlisted to play drums and save the rock!

Anticipation filled the air. Would the cops show up? Would we get arrested? And, most importantly, where was Ivy?!? The street was filled with drinking punks, the cops were already circling, and she was late. What if we got busted before we even played a chord?

Then we realized the bass amp was missing! I was about to run down to Hunt's Donuts at 20th to see if someone had stolen it and was trying to sell it, but then Ravi, Jeff, and Sean-The-Dead-Guy from the laundromat in Oakland came up and presented me a ransom note. It read, "Give us beer and we'll give you your amp." They were trashed and could barely speak. Gradually I came to realize they had wheeled the amp around the corner to San Carlos Street. Barely containing my rage and exasperation, I grabbed Sean and growled that he really would be dead if he didn't run back with the amp.

They split, and, a moment later, Jeff wheeled the amp up. "We've decided to return the amp," he burped, gravely.

Finally, Jim struck the opening notes of "Libertyville on The Rocks" and the dancing started right there on Mission Street! Ivy ran up just as Shotwell started, someone handed me an ice-cold 40, and the girl I had a crush on flashed me the kind of look from across the crowd that only a girl who has a crush on you can flash. We played tag-team style, each band playing a couple songs and then switching off, so that everyone would get a chance to play in case the show was stopped. Every time Jimmy would intro a song, all bitter and convincing, like, "This is for the people who work all their lives for shit and get sent off to die in wars," the cops would drive by at that moment and everyone would turn and look at them like, "Yeah! Fuck you!" and the Mission Street Latino guys, who'd stopped to check out the show would nod, solemnly, in agreement. It was a great show.

Somewhere in all this, ex-Shotwell bassist Greg showed up. He was walking by and saw Shotwell playing without a bassist, so someone handed him a bass and he finished out the set. Ivy dedicated Miami's last song, "The City That Never Sleeps," to the all night #14 Mission Bus and then, as the song ended, it actually pulled up to the stop and everyone cheered. The bus driver looked sort of startled, but he took it in stride and waved to the crowd.

Finally, Jim announced the last song, the hit "Ghacked," his ode to summertime drinking in the streets. Just then, a cop pulled up, but everyone kept dancing and drinking. In a couple minutes, the show was over, and there was nothing the cop could do. And that was it—a huge crowd of punks, two bands, beer, an hour of rock, and no cop hassle! I went home and I could not sleep!

CLEANING UP THE MISSION

Mission Street today looks surprisingly similar to photos of Mission Street thirty years ago. The theater signs are all still there, as is the Leed's sign. The front door at Hunt's has been "Open 25 Hours" the whole time. I have squatted in one abandoned theater, played punk shows in every abandoned building's doorway on Mission, and marched countless times down the middle of the street with hundreds of angry protesters. But it is in just walking down the old main drag every day past these same old signs and produce stands that I've felt smaller memories of my own life—making out on the roof of El Capitan, walking home in the rain drunk, spending the night in a cell at Mission station—blur into something larger, the memory of the street, something sweet and sad that won't go away. A history flowing continuously, but buried deep beneath the street, like Mission Creek.

Against this backdrop, history has come back to the Mission to repeat itself again and again. The Thor Hotel, a dive at 17th and Mission, burned down in the 70s and was remodeled in the 80s. The new tenants organized a tenants' union to demand that the new owner make the hotel cleaner and safer. The owners responded by calling the cops to break up their union meetings and hiring thugs to beat the organizers in their rooms. The union was effectively destroyed.

In 1999 the Thor Hotel once again suffered a mysterious fire, and this time burned down for good. The hotel and storefront it was built over still loom, creepy and burnt out, over the nightly crowds of hipsters who now come to the Mission, and the cops who cruise alongside to safely escort their wallets into the Beauty Bar.

In late 1998, in a still unsolved case, an old abandoned warehouse on Hoff Street, just off 16th and Mission, burned spectacularly to the ground as the tenants from the nearby Thor and King hotels watched anxiously in the blocked off streets. The police believed it to be arson and immediately searched for "an unidentified homeless man" they claimed may have started it. The investigation, however, didn't in any way stop the owner from building a brand new live/work space on the property in one short year.

And by the time the Hoff Street live/work space was completed, the King Hotel, too, had burned to the ground.

One of the most often repeated and least questioned statements about gentrification is that we, the punks, can't do anything because it is our fault. This line of reasoning, widely believed by even the punks themselves, goes that gentrification, like other economic forces, is somehow a "natural" process, like the weather, and that it "naturally" occurs when punks and artists move into a ghetto for the cheap rents. After we arrive, the rents "naturally" rise, the poor are "naturally" kicked out, etc. While I am sure that such traditional punk contributions to Mission District life as providing warehouse space for teenagers to get wasted in at punk shows, buying pills at Evergreen, doing graffiti, and dealing speed have caused the Mission real estate values to skyrocket, as we see with the fires at the

Thor and King hotels, sometimes these "natural" economic forces need a more sinister kick-start to help get the process going. Long before the punks and artists arrived, the "cleaning up" of the Mission campaign, as we now know it, probably started in earnest on the night of December 12, 1975, when a still unknown person or persons entered the cheap and rundown Gartland Apartments at 16th and Valencia, soaked the stairwell with gasoline, and dropped a lit match.

At least 12 people died in the confirmed arson. A temporary morgue was established on 16th Street in front of the Wells Fargo bank. The hotel was not rebuilt. The people who lived there had to go somewhere else, while the "Gartland Pit" remained empty until the early 90s. No one was ever arrested for starting the fire.

By the mid-80s, punks, artists, and activists had shown up in the Mission, and the Gartland Pit was often used as a site for protests, film showings, even punk shows. This may be gentrification, but it is gentrification that was started not by "the yuppies taking over," but by violence against poor people's homes.

The Mission cleanup was devised by city planners, though, long before the Gartland burned. In the 60s, after urban renewal had successfully removed most of the housing where black people lived in the Fillmore, and was clearing out the SRO hotels South of Market, The City planned to use the BART to drive the Latino concentration out of the Mission. Following the lead of Manhattan, SF planned to de-industrialize and base its economy on stock trading, insurance, and real estate. The idea was to bulldoze the Mission and build new apartment towers on the main thoroughfares to house the young office workers that would work in the Financial District. The new BART trains would provide easy access to Montgomery Street. Despite massive opposition, the BART was built under Mission Street, but the gleaming offices and apartments planned for the 16th and Mission BART plaza obviously never materialized.

So much for urban planning. Today, 16th and Mission is the sight of a foul-smelling market that sells boar and ostrich meat, a donut/pornography store called "The Fun Spot," and the largest open-air heroin market between LA and Vancouver.

But from the late 60s on, the Mission was under attack when landlords realized how much their property would be worth if they could just get rid of the people who lived in it. As in today's homeless sweeps, the message was often beaten home by the SFPD. Officers

Brodnik and McGoran, a duo code-named "Mission 11," walked the beat on Mission Street, a couple of old time, racist Irish cops from the Mission with a special hatred for Mexicans. Brodnik's infamous 2-foot rubber hose that he carried to work over uncooperative kids is the stuff of subconscious Mission Street history; you can feel it in the street. But it didn't do him any good on May 1, 1969, when Mission 11 stopped some kids in Noe Valley and a scuffle broke out, during which McGoran's gun was discharged and Brodnik was shot down dead—the incident that led to the landmark Los Siete De La Raza trial.

The massive organization in the Mission for legal defense of Los Siete proved that the neighborhood was going to be harder to put down than the cops thought. In the year before the acquittal of Los Siete, the community created a Mission newspaper, *Basta Ya*, and free legal defense programs. There was a free breakfast program at St. Peter's church on Alabama Street, and a worker-run restaurant next to the Levi-Strauss factory on Valencia, that provided cheap food and attempted to organize the Latina women who worked at Levi's.

A couple years later, in 1973, activist attorney Oscar Acosta came back to SF to write *Revolt of the Cockroach People*, the classic of the Chicano movement, at the Royan Hotel—"The Mission's Finest"—on Valencia, just down the block from the still- unburned Gartland. I have an old *Chronicle* clipping that shows a big, heavy-set, long-haired Latino guy—identified in the caption as "Walter Acosta," but obviously the Brown Buffalo himself—walking on 24th at South Van Ness. Behind him is an old mural that shows cartoon pigs in SFPD uniforms herding cartoon rats with Latino features and work clothes into a paddy wagon.

The mural is gone today. Those were different times. But it still says, "Free Los Siete," written in the sidewalk cement on Clinton Park next to the Levi factory.

And the burned out Thor Hotel still looms over Mission Street. I walk by it and get a bitter taste in my mouth every time.

Summer officially came to the Mission on July 4th this year. Jorge, the San Carlos street drinker, usually seen slumbering heavily and uncomfortably in a weighty black coat, emerged from his doorway that morning, looked right, looked left, and... took off his shirt! It's like Groundhog Day; when the shirt comes off, Jorge predicts three more months of sun.

The news spreads fast. The 4th of July explosions started at 10:00 AM. The Cisco rack at Lakeside Liquors was cleared out by 11:00 and all the guys in front of El Can Cun were drunk at noon. And Jorge staggered through it all, with his eyes half shut, rubbing his chest and smiling in the sun, maybe dreaming of a cold lake in El Salvador.

It's summer, but the poor guys selling weed in Dolores Park can't give it away. The park's been full of cops all year. For a while, there were huge "Stop the NATO Bombing" protests in the park every week, and the police would always be there, too, in full force on the foot bridge where the dealers usually hang out.

No, this ain't the summer of love. The fruit bar pushcart guys sold a few cold bars to sweaty anti-war marchers, but the pushcart guys weren't doing that good, either. Most of their business is selling drugs, too.

Then the NATO bombing finally ended, but there were more protests. The new Mission yuppies held a protest to complain about the Mission Yuppie Eradication Project's anti-yuppie flyers, and the cops were there, too.

But then the "yuppies" protesting turned out to be fake. They were actually "artists" who were pretending to be "yuppies." Either way, they weren't buying any drugs and REALLY helping out the neighborhood economy. Meanwhile, this reporter spotted Nestor Mahkno, the man behind the Yuppie Eradication Project, several times at the possibly yuppie Atlas Cafe on 20th and Alabama. Is it time to eradicate the eradicator?

Yeah, it's summer, but it's cold and foggy and everything seems a little backwards, except that it's an election year, and as usual everyone's talking about "Cleaning up The City." What else is new? A bitter and largely unspoken war is on in the streets over every inch of space in this town. The cops kick the homeless out of Civic Center and they move across the street to UN Plaza. The cops start to sweep UN Plaza and the punk rockers across town start throwing rocks through the windows of Harrison Street live/work lofts. A landlord in Noe Valley is even making news for trying to kick a 90-year-old woman out of a house she's lived in for over 40 years. You'd think a landlord would be a little self-conscious about doing such a stereotypical "Evil Landlord" thing, but I guess not. The Eviction Defense Network organized a good protest, with thirty or so folks picketing the landlord's office. It went well, with passersby honking and yelling in support, but don't you think next time we should get the same thirty people and just evict the LANDLORD? We could get all the stuff out of his office and into the streets in five minutes!

Summer's here but the time just ain't right for dancing in the streets. Supervisor Amos Brown doesn't just want to clean up the streets; he wants to clean up the MEDIANS in the middle of the streets. He's proposing legislation—believe it or not—to make it illegal to stand in the medians. Why? Because panhandlers stand in medians. A couple weeks back, a crowd of activists and panhandlers and day laborers staged a demonstration in front of City Hall and marched into the building to present oversized "Standing on the Median" tickets to each of the twelve supervisors. They haven't voted on it yet, but as of this writing, it is still legal to stand on a traffic median in The City of San Francisco.

Clint Reilly's set up his campaign offices for his run for mayor in the old abandoned Leed's shoe store on Mission Street. He just put out a 48-page booklet, outlining HIS plan to "solve the homeless problem." Meanwhile, the homeless themselves are patiently waiting for him to go ahead and lose the election, so they can go back to sleeping in the spacious Leed's doorway.

And Jim Reid, another candidate for mayor has weighed in, too, with his own rather bold and astonishing "homeless plan." Reid, best known for driving a red pickup with a patch of green lawn laid in the back, to symbolize his "grassroots candidacy," calls for all homeless who have not lived in SF for one full year to be given bus tickets to anywhere else in the country. Then, the remaining home-less will be interred at nine shelters across the city.

"The police will patrol the areas around the shelters, protecting the homeless from predators, and directing the homeless to appro-priate facilities," instructs his campaign literature. "The H bus line could drive through neighborhoods frequented by homeless and de-liver them to shelters," it goes on to speculate. And when Reid's program is fully operational (read: NEVER), "the police would be mandated to move the homeless to the shelters, because there will be no excuse to live or sleep on the street." Well, obviously a home-less person would be advised to think twice before stepping into any shower installed by der führer Reid. That's the one good thing about this town: if they ever get the concentration camps for the homeless up and running, we'd never actually die in them, because all the trains going there would be run by MUNI.

Meanwhile, Reid has alerted the media that the lawn was stolen out of the back of his truck when it was parked at 15th and Mission the other night. If you want to call Reid and tell him you have the lawn, and make some demands, his number is 826-6106.

Yeah, it's summer, but it still seems like there's less to go around. Overheard at the Tom Waddell clinic: "I got stabbed up at Bush and Webster on the 4th. I just wish people would start trying to rob RICH people for a change. I gave 'em everything in my cart!" You're not alone, brother. A guy across the waiting room spoke up, "You got stabbed on Bush Street on the 4th? Me, too!" A move-ment is born?

Yes, something's missing this summer. In the GA line, a security guard says to the guy in front of me, "Hey, I know you, man! But you was younger." Weren't we all? The guard shakes his head and repeats, "Yep, you was younger then," and a shadow passes across the guy in line's face, like a southbound shopping cart slowly drag-ging across the Francis "Lefty" O'Doul bridge.

And, just like that, summer's gone. And I saw Jorge passed out in front of Hunt's and he had his old coat back on.

And there is no cold lake by Lakeside Liquors.

But, as usual, a regular at Bell's Donuts has it all figured out. "Do you know what this city needs?" he asks. "This City needs the Boy Scouts. The kids need to learn manners and honor, stuff the Boy Scouts teach. We need Boy Scouts helping old ladies across the street!" And the guy at the next table nods enthusiastically, "Yeah, we need THAT! But you know what else is wrong?" he implores, confidentially. "The Chinese are TAKING OVER!"

Someone took over. The old City ain't the same. Where have all the shopping carts of summer gone? Can you still buy crack at the Crack Burrito? I know something's wrong when a young mota sales-man in Dolores Park offers me a one for one trade, one joint for one regular cigarette! Or when a homeless guy on Market Street tells me, "Sure the cops are always waking my ass up, but, hey, you got to give them a break. They got a hard job!" He must be a heavy sleeper... Now the Coalition on Homelessness is buying shopping carts for people. They already put five out on the streets, with plans for thirty more. The five carts, painted all black and dubbed "stealth carts," carry signs declaring them to be the property of the homeless person they are assigned to, so that cops and shopping cart poachers can't steal them. I think it's great for people to have their own carts, but wouldn't it be better to give homeless people CROWBARS?

And now the Poor People's Eradication Project has come to the Tenderloin. Right after the Yuppie Eradication Poster guy got arrest-ed in the Mission, these somewhat hysterical flyers started appearing at Civic Center BART and UN Plaza, saying "SF officials refuse to do anything about the junkies, drunks, and drug dealers who hang our around Civic Center Station. We are most heartily sick of the urine fumes and the feces all around." So what's next? Keying nice, new black shopping carts? Replacing all the ENSURE with lattes? I mean, this is our QUALITY OF LIFE they're threatening!

But, the flyer went on to eerily warn, "Either get rid of the creeps or we will buy guns and do it ourselves! The creeps must be gone by precisely 6 AM, July 1st, or our extermination begins!!!"

The cops finally found out who put them up and it wasn't a Nazi businessman who went off the deep end or some Taxi Driver-style psycho. It was a middle-aged, divorced black lady from the Tender-loin whose son had been killed by a stray bullet. She didn't really have any guns and she didn't really intend to shoot everyone who pushed a shopping cart. She was just mad as hell and didn't want to take it any-more, and wanted someone to pay attention to what she was saying.

A week later, she had new, less virulent flyers out for a rally in front of City Hall for people who "want to clean up the Tender-loin," presumably without guns. On a gray and cold summer morn-ing, I went to check out her rally. It turned out to be only her, a lone, fed-up woman, pacing back and forth in front of City Hall with a picket sign reading "Mayor Brown and Chief Lau have abandoned the Tenderloin." *Turd-Filled Donut* and Liberation Radio reporter, RG, showed up to interview her. He told me, "She's really on our side, deep down. She's saying what we're saying, that the government needs to be more responsive to the people."

Watching her, I wasn't so sure. Her rally made me want to push a shopping cart into City Hall, talking to myself. It made me want to ask every dot-com jerk in town for a dollar. It made me want to sit in the summer sun and drink beer after beer.

But there's no summer sun. Something's just wrong. I saw Jorge at Hunt's Donuts, looking wise and important with his half-closed eyes, imposing black beard, and bare feet. I wanted to ask him what happened to summer, but, first, Zen-like, he answered my question with a question of his own. "Do you want to buy a wrench?"

So I got a beer and drank it in Dolores Park. One more protest, against "Cleaning up The City," and, this time, no cops!

But there's just one last thing: what was Turd Caen doing at the Atlas anyway?

(Answer: I was stealing the toilet paper, of course!)

AN INTERVIEW WITH MATTY LUV AND RO GIULIANO OF SAN FRANCISCO NEEDLE EXCHANGE

I'm always interested in what kind of punk skills, attitudes, and ideas punks bring with them when they get involved in activism. How does being a punk affect their goals or tactics? What will we create in the world besides music? The San Francisco Needle Exchange is a public health activist group that got started the punk way—by fighting the cops! When the San Francisco Department of Health decided needle exchange was too controversial for the Haight, SFNE got independent funding to start their own exchange. And when the cops shut 'em down, they kept going back!

Not only is this country's right wing drug war filling prisons with non-violent offenders, and filling the pockets of police departments and prison builders with taxpayer money, but it also keeps sensible harm reduction drug policies from being implemented. The spread of HIV and Hepatitis is a public health emergency that could be slowed by needle exchange, but even comparatively liberal cities like San Francisco let anti-drug hysteria dictate public health policy. In the early part of this century, it was illegal to publicly advocate birth control. If you read Emma Goldman's books, she and Ben Reitman and their contemporaries were always getting arrested or having cops raid their halls and shut down their speeches about CONDOMS. Today, SFNE and the clean needle are fighting the same uphill battle. I talked with SFNE's Ro Giuliano and Matty Luv (who many SCAM readers know from his old band, Hickey...).

SCAM: OK, you might just want to start off with a brief rundown of the idea behind needle exchange, and just what the basic idea of harm reduction is, for some of our readers who may not know much about it.

MATTY LUV: Harm reduction is non-judgmental medical treatment around issues of drug use. Rather than saying abstinence from drugs is best, we take the position that people use drugs and always have used drugs, no matter what the law is. Instead of treating drug use as immoral, the idea is that any positive change in drug use is good, is a step towards greater health. By using clean needles, you can stop the spread of HIV and Hepatitis. By teaching people what to do if someone OD's, you can save lives. Abstinence is not the issue, but, if people stay alive and healthy, maybe, one day down the road, they might be interested in that.

RO GIULIANO: In San Francisco, there are four overdoses a day, and soft tissue abscesses are the #1 cause of visits to the emergency room at SF General. The City spends $18 million on abscess care, when it is easily preventable, because they're more interested in trying to ARREST users.

SCAM: OK, so what events led to the formation of the SF Needle Exchange?

ML: OK, well, some background on the Haight... The Haight is pretty much a police state. If you're on the streets and you don't look like you own property, or shop there, you're liable to get stopped by the cops and shaken down for no reason.

RG: Teenage runaways from all over the country still come to the Haight. Mayor Brown shut down the east end of Golden Gate Park in the Haight in November 1997, basically because he didn't want the kids there. Brown had this whole ruse about building a children's playground and a skating rink...

ML: But now it's over two years later, and there's still just a fence there...

SCAM: Right, I remember that was when I moved back to SF. I was shocked. Here was Brown talking about using helicopters with NIGHT VISION to root out homeless people sleeping in the park... I went to these real crazy Haight Ashbury Neighborhood Council (HANC) public forums about it. People were at each other's throats...

ML: Yeah, it was a very politically charged environment we started in...

RG: I had a job as an outreach worker in the Haight at that time, working with street kids.

ML: And I had just got back from the Hickey tour, with Ivy, who we brought back to SF with us. We got on GA (SF welfare) and got our GA workfare jobs at the AIDS Foundation. We were supposed to be helping street kids in the Haight make a fanzine and a leather workshop. We weren't supposed to be doing needle exchange at all...

RG: But, when Golden Gate Park closed, the Department of Health stopped all their needle exchange in the Haight, because it was just too politically hot. This left a huge gap in services. They expected the kids to go all the way past the Castro to the Department of Health site behind the Safeway on DuBoce, but these kids never even go past Masonic, or even Ashbury! So the outreach worker who was doing needle exchange before supplied me with needles and I started doing the exchange myself, VERY covertly. Then Matty and Ivy started helping me.

ML: For a long time, we did a roving exchange, handing needles out of our Zo Bags... But then, one time, we told, like, 4 people to meet us on the side of the Cala Supermarket at Haight and Stanyan and, like, 50 kids came. So we started doing two-hour shifts, three days a week at the corner of Oak and Shrader in Panhandle Park.

RG: After that, when the AIDS Foundation found out we'd been doing exchange the whole time, they declared us a secondary site for exchange. So, we got the right to be there, sort of, but they wouldn't give us any legal backing at all...

ML: OR any needles. We still had to turn in all our dirties to get clean ones. I'd always be riding my bike around on Oak Street with, oh, a THOUSAND dirty needles in my bag... But they didn't give us any support, because it was too controversial.

SCAM: This is the AIDS Foundation, too... You'd think they'd have an interest in stopping the spread of HIV...

ML: Well, we were getting harassed by the cops all the time. The AIDS Foundation's brilliant response was "Get out of the Panhandle then! Quit doing it!" Fuck that!

RG: So, then the foundation cut off their funding for the youth program, because they didn't want anything in the Haight. I'd heard through the grapevine that that was going to happen, so I had already started getting funding together so we could become the first independent needle exchange in SF. We had a small start-up grant of 10,000 needles from the North American Syringe Exchange Network. That was enough needles to carry us for awhile until we could write more grants and get more cash.

Now we were independent. We had no legal backing at all, and no organization behind us. Our last day with the AIDS Foundation, officially, was June 30, 1998, and then our first day on our own was July 1. On our first day, Officer McGloughlin came to shut us down.

SCAM: Ah, yes...Good old McGloughlin. He was, I think, according to the *Turd-Filled Donut* story I did, #5 on the list in the whole city of cops who wrote the most "Quality of Life" citations to fuck with homeless people...

RG: One of our HIV-positive participants tried to tell McGloughlin that if there had been a needle exchange for him a couple years ago, he wouldn't have contracted HIV. He asked McGloughlin, "What would you do if I was one of YOUR kids who was addicted to heroin, or got AIDS?" Officer McGloughlin's brilliant response was, "None of my kids would get addicted to heroin or get AIDS!"

SCAM: What is the exact law, anyways? Needle Exchange IS legal, right?

ML: Needle Exchange is legal in a declared Public Health State of Emergency. The State of Emergency is in effect, now, in SF, because of the AIDS epidemic, so exchange is legal, and SFPD policy is to leave exchange sites alone. One time, I was wearing this "Fuck Bush!" button that one of the kids gave me, and Officer McGloughlin rode by. Then he stopped and said, "That button is obscene! There are kids in this park!" I said, "Look, if you're close enough to read my button, by SFPD policy, you're too close to our site..."

RG: So, the first day, he gave us a warning. Of course, we went back, and the next day he came back and arrested us. He took us away in cuffs in front of the whole exchange...

ML: We called the Linda Smith Center, a think-tank on drug policy, and they helped me out with a real good lawyer who got all the charges dropped. Next time I saw McGloughlin, he was pissed. "What happened to that charge?"

I said, "It got dropped, dude. It was harassment." So... he arrested us again!

RG: That time, we both had to go to 850 Bryant because he considered us "Repeat and Dangerous Offenders." We spent 9 hours there, just to get cited out again.

ML: It was cute, though. She was in the girls' cell across from me, and we could wave at each other...

RG: Yeah, but Matty's cell had the phone! After that arrest, the Haight Ashbury Free Clinic and HANC were up in arms, because they'd seen fewer needles on the street because of us. They said, look, we can't have the Haight without needle exchange, because there's tons of young injection users and the Hepatitis C rate is through the roof!

ML: So that arrest led to our meeting with the head of Park Station, Captain Newland. It was supposed to be just a small meeting with Ro, an outreach worker from the Haight Ashbury Youth Outreach Team, a couple cops, and me, but we packed it with our supporters. We brought 13 people. We had to try and legitimize ourselves with the cops. They had just looked at us (before) and thought we were just the kids on the street.

RG: We had representatives from the Harm Reduction Coalition there. ALL the Haight outreach workers. Legal people from the Linda Smith center came all the way from NEW YORK. You came there from the Coalition on Homelessness. The DIRECTOR of the Haight Ashbury Free Clinic was there. The president of HANC...

SCAM: Wasn't that the meeting where Newland had to split to go bowling, and we were saying we should get a crusty bowling team together to settle this once and for all, ON THE LANES!

RG: Well, actually, we found out a lot about the arrests BEFORE they would happen from someone we know who is Newland's bowling partner!

ML: It's true. We're oddly well-connected. They bowl together every Tuesday night at Japantown Bowl on Geary. When there was the threat of impending arrest, the bowling contact would warn us before it happened. Then one of us would stand on Oak and Shrader with no needles or anything and just tell the kids to go to another secret spot where one of us would be waiting with the needles. During the Haight Street Fair, we actually did exchange INSIDE of a Porta-Pottie at Haight and Cole!

RG: You see, Newland wasn't really against us. He just had this one officer, McGloughlin, who has making this his pet peeve issue. Once Newland saw that first hand, we were OK. McGloughlin was at this meeting, yelling at middle-aged homeowners who were saying they WANTED there to be a needle exchange. These are the constituents he's supposed to please. Newland actually told him to shut up a couple of times. At that meeting, Newland said he'd leave us alone if we found an indoor space. Then 409 Clayton let us start doing exchange in their space on a trial basis. We set up strategic planning on how to keep the space. That's why we have a door person. We're responsible for making sure the whole 400 block of Clayton is clean. We have to rake the children's playground in the Panhandle every night for needles—not that we've EVER found a needle in the children's playground. We've been there almost two years without a single complaint.

SCAM: How has punk rock experience helped you start SFNE?

ML: We've been very diligent about the way we run the space. That's the one thing I learned from putting on punk shows over the years, is how to keep things cool on the outside as to not attract the cops.

RG: "No drinking outside the show" became "No smoking and hanging out on the steps"or "No doing drug business on the steps of 409 Clayton."

ML: We culturally identify with the kids we serve, which helped gain their trust, and they're hard kids to reach. We're the only punk-run needle exchange in the country. I mean, Ro, Ivy, and I started it. Our volunteers are mostly punks. Then, there are the organizational skills I learned from booking tours and that problem solving. One of the first things we did to advertise the exchange was make a series of stickers that had the logo of a punk band on it and the exchange days and times and location written real small at the bottom. So, if the kids put it on their skate or their jacket, they'd always have the schedule, and if a cop happened to see it, he'd just think it was a band. There was a Black Flag one, The Misfits...

SCAM: I had The Descendents one!

ML: That was super effective, because they weren't flyers left lying around for cops and angry citizens to find. They got stuck on. We also made these pamphlets, *Alien Meth Fiend*. In any outreach situation, there are all these really dull pamphlets full of HIV or OD prevention info. So we started making punk-style pamphlets with info in an easy-to-understand language and punk-style layouts. The kids actually read them.

RG: Also, after having seen us go to jail for this, the kids had a lot of respect for us and the program. They knew we were there for them. It gave them a real sense of ownership of the program. After the program survived the arrests, they felt like they didn't want to fuck it up...

ML: Basically, we snuck needle exchange into the Haight, based on the fact that we were going to be there and doing it in the Panhandle, three days a week, no matter what. The cops couldn't just keep arresting us.

SCAM: Why did Hickey break up, Matty, and what was the initial appeal for you of doing this kind of work?

ML: I don't really know why Hickey broke up. When we came back from what turned out to be the last tour in 1997, it was just apparent that we weren't going to do it anymore. Hickey was a fairly intense experience: 4 years, 7 US Tours, 2 full records of stuff. I was looking forward to not being in a structured band for a while, but I was looking for a way to stay in touch with the punk community. A lot of the kids from the exchange were the kids who went to our warehouse shows at 17ᵗʰ and Capp. At exchange, I'll see kids with Hickey patches and I'll be like, "Which show did you get that at? Arkansas in '95?" It's cliché—"Doing it for the kids"—but I like the kids. The kids are a lot nicer than a lot of my peers who grew up and turned out to be real fucking drags.

SCAM: Does it bum you out to give a bunch of needles to a kid with a Hickey patch who is all strung out and not doing so great?

ML: Not at all...

RG: Hickey was pretty fucked up, too.

ML: Well, I think it's beneficial for the kids that are really down and out to be involved in the punk scene and to be able to go inside of shows and to have a community.

RG: That shows kids what they can do or what they could become. We're punks who started an exchange. We can help them get involved in SFNE. We can get them into paid positions at some of the user studies in the Haight where they'll hire homeless kids, and then, maybe, they can get a paycheck and a more stable living situation, and still stay true to what they want to do.

At this point, I was going to agree that it's important to use punk as a lifeline for kids who are so under attack from the cops and everybody, but then the phone rang, and Matty had to spend 10 minutes helping the caller find a vein in their ankle to shoot up in, because all their veins were collapsed, and that seemed to make my point nice enough for me...

ON THE BEAT WITH THE TURD-FILLED DONUT

As The City ramped up its homeless sweeps and attacks on the poor, the TFD continued to use OUR punk rock skills to put our DIY paper out on the streets, featuring stories like these:

ALL IN A DAY'S WORK FOR KPIX TV

This may be old news to some, but many people who are trying to get on General Assistance welfare in San Francisco are still wondering why GA no longer accepts the required letters that prove your 15-Day Residency in the city from the Coalition on Homelessness. If you are homeless or on GA, you probably don't have a TV, and you probably don't catch much of KPIX's new coverage. But, last April, KPIX reporter Hank Plante did an "investigative" story where he set about to prove Ye Olde "How Easy It Is For Freeloaders From All Across America To Just Show Up In San Francisco and Get Right On Welfare" Story. The basic idea of this old fable is that droves of people across America move to SF to be homeless just because of the extravagant welfare grants and services The City offers the poor. This always makes me think, "Yeah, right! I heard about SF's whopping $287 a month GA grant, so I immediately quit my job back East and hitchhiked right out here! Now, everyday is a non-stop party from the moment Officer Guerrero kicks my sleeping head awake in the morning. Should I eat the luxurious brunch at Hamilton's, or take my afternoon sun with the one-legged pigeons in line at the Glide Church free lunch? Ah, yes... 52 degrees in July, and rents starting at $800! Nothing but California sun and fun since I got on welfare!"

Anyways, Plante was able to obtain a Letter of Residency from the Coalition for his story, without in any way having to prove he had been here for fifteen days. Of course, this letter alone does not qualify you for welfare. Nonetheless, as a result of Plante's story, The City has decided to no longer accept proof of residency letters from the Coalition! So, basically, this guy with a nice house and job decides to casually fuck up this one tiny helpful thing that is available to an enormously disadvantaged population, all in the name of "a good story."

The *Turd-Filled Donut*, despite an extensive search, was unable to locate Plante's home address, to, uh, register our dissatisfaction with Plante's story. We were able, however, to find his number at the KPIX newsroom and call him up for a few questions.

TURD-FILLED DONUT: I was just calling to tell you I thought that piece was really mean-spirited and terrible.
HANK PLANTE: Well, did you actually SEE it?

TFD: No, man! I'm on GA! I don't have a TV!
HP: Well, I can't talk to you about a story you didn't even SEE.

TFD: Well, I didn't have to see it to know the end result. How could you run this story, knowing the end result would be to take this thing away from poor people, this small edge that can help them? I mean, how do you justify THAT?
HP: It was a good story. It's about taxpayers knowing where their money goes...

TFD: No, it's just the typical, cynical piece that picks on the defenseless homeless!
HP: You didn't even see it. It was a fair piece. They were bending the rules and that affects taxpayers' money.

TFD: So you can just ruin something for these people who have nothing and then go home and sleep and it's all fine because it was "just the facts"?

HP: Look, I'm not going to talk with you about a story you haven't even seen.

Basically, that was how it went. In the interest of Objective Journalism, I should point out that Plante was a nice enough guy who did take time to call me back for my "input" even after he knew I was against the story. I should also point out that Objective Journalism is the lie that these chickenshit, nice guy journalist hacks always try to fall back on. You can call Plante in the KPIX newsroom to give your "input" at 415-765-8610.

TO SERVE, PROTECT, AND CRANK OUT TICKETS: OFFICER CLARK TOP PIG IN TFD CITATION STUDY

Sure, cops are bad, but did you ever notice how much better our "quality of life" would be if it wasn't for just a handful of REALLY terrible asshole cops? There seems to be one or two in every neighborhood. There's Guerrero, roughing up the homeless in the Castro, and old Swiatko, down in China Basin, who is on a one-man crusade to keep people from sleeping in their cars. There's Ludlow in the Mission, who took it upon himself to shut down all the Latino working-class bars for code violations so the hipster bars could buy their liquor licenses. And what about Officer Robles up on Polk Street, rolling up on his bike, and inventing violations like "Sitting at a MUNI stop without intent to board a bus"? Can't these assholes find something else to do?

Apparently not. For the past five years, the Coalition on Homelessness has been helping homeless folks fight their so-called "quality of life" citations in court. In that time, since Willie Brown supposedly called an end to Matrix, they have collected nearly 4200 tickets. Though this data does not represent all tickets written in SF, and only totals those collected by the Coalition's legal workers, it is still an enormous pile of tickets, and it is possible to get an idea just who the biggest anti-homeless assholes on the force are.

For instance, the 4200 tickets collected by the Coalition were written by nearly 600 total officers. However, ONLY 20 COPS WROTE OVER 2100 TICKETS—OR HALF OF THE ENTIRE AMOUNT SINCE 1995!!! Thus, 3% of the cops wrote 49% of the tickets!

Who wrote the most? All of the top five are from Golden Gate Park or the Haight areas. Officer Clark is #1 in this study—a man who cannot, apparently, sleep at night knowing that someone less fortunate than himself may be sleeping in the Park. With little fanfare or public acclaim, he wrote 16% of the entire total, all by himself, demonstrating a fearless and selfless willingness, at any time, to step between a helpless SF citizen and a snoring wino, in the line of duty. It is a thin, blue line.

Next up is the Haight's Officer Wilberg, totaling 14%. Then there's Officer Lam, charting with 10.4% of the total, including 16 citations written to one single individual! Officer Gilbert Gallaread, who was last seen by this reporter forcing a legless man in a wheelchair out of a doorway into the pouring rain, placed only 4th for his enthusiastic efforts with a mere 7.9% percent of the city's tickets since 1995. Rounding up the big five is the Haight's Officer McGlaughlin. Last summer McGlaughlin claimed he would personally "bury" the Haight's needle exchange program. This year, the exchange, cheerfully unburied, has found a new home indoors (409 Clayton) and has received ample grant monies to continue its service. Poor old McGlaughlin can still be found, bitterly scribbling drinking-in-public tickets around the corner by Cala Foods.

And there is no end in sight to the ticketing. In fact, the Mayor's budget was just passed, allocating new funds for two new attorneys who will be hired by the DA's office SPECIFICALLY to prosecute these "quality of life" tickets. This will not provide housing for people on the streets. This will not provide treatment on demand or mental health services for those who need them. But that is not the cops' job. The cops' new job in The City, apparently, is to mercilessly herd the poor from one square to the next on an increasingly militarized downtown chessboard. It is an ugly job. And they've found some ugly men to do it.

INTERVIEW WITH ZARA THUSTRA
Pt. 1

For years, Zara's been consistently doing strong, eye-catching political graffiti in SF but in recent years he has branched out into making more traditional paintings and putting on big events like the Anti-Capitalist Fashion Show. This summer, his art auction to benefit the Coalition on Homelessness raised twenty-five thousand dollars. Zara's always trying to use his art for pretty righteous causes, and has silkscreened countless posters for protests over the years. I did this interview in late 2002 at an interesting time for Zara. The cops' graffiti squad was looking for him hard, while all the graffiti writer crews were looking for him too, to beat his ass over some imagined street beef. At the same time, museums were starting to court him and he was selected to be in the potentially career-making "Bay Area Now" show at the Yerba Buena Museum. We talked about how to use art for social change, about his impressions of the gallery art world, the recent history of SF, and, course, graffiti.

Most people know your art from graffiti. How did you start painting and why did you start with graffiti?

ZARA: I started to do graffiti before I started to paint. My friend, SHUGGS, the writer who brought me up, showed me how to draw and paint. I went out painting with him all the time. I got psyched on painting from there and then it changed my adulthood, my whole outlook.

In what way?

ZARA: I went to rehab for a long time and I was viewing graff as a "red flag" or whatever the rehab terminology for basically abusive behavior is. I was convinced that this was true for a while and I tried to be completely straight and not get arrested. I quit drugs and alcohol, which turned out to be really successful for me, actually. When I started doing graff again, I felt like I needed to have a higher purpose, that I couldn't do the same stuff I was doing. This was right when I moved to SF.

Was this personal inspiration or were you inspired by the city?

ZARA: When I first moved here, I wouldn't tag. I was one of these kids, running around writing "respect" and "revolt," trying to get respect for just that emotion. But respect comes from putting in real work. I came to this conclusion that what I needed to do was to enter the graff scene and get respect for doing hardcore graff. Then I could write my other shit along with it. I wanted to come up in the scene, pay my dues, and when people started to respect me, I would then use that as a platform to speak out.

I started realizing that you can't just step out and write "Revolution" on a wall; you've got to show a proof. You have to be DOING Revolution and then people get the context that it's written in and they respect the word.

Respect from whom?
ZARA: From the community at large, not so much from just graffiti kids. If I was trying to get respect from only graff writers, my technique would be a lot different. A lot of writers do really tight, nice, artistic graff shit that's really technical, but it's only for the graff community. A lot of my stuff is text and bold fonts for more general public folks to read it.

But does a graffiti context help get respect from the larger community? Like, does a harder to reach spot get respect from passersby? Or is it more like, "Well, I want to stop the war, too, but I don't go around writing it on other people's storefronts!"?
ZARA: A little of both. There are people that see property as, like, HUMAN. A large community respects and enjoys graffiti and an even larger faction doesn't want it anywhere and wants it whitewashed.

The whitewashing faction seems, at this point in history, to be so privileged that it's hard for me to take seriously any more. There's a war going on here and you're worried about your paint job?
ZARA: It's severely stupid and ridiculous. Look at New York City. It's really bombed and has a lot of self-expression on the streets. It's really vibrant. In SF, the two most vibrant communities are the two communities that are bombed. When I was thinking about moving away from Delaware, SHUGGS told me never to move anywhere where there's no graffiti. If there's no graffiti, there's no dancing, no art, no subcultures. If there's graff, then all this stuff is alive in different ways. Otherwise, there's a Starbucks on the corner and the property values are high.

TURD SUFFRAGE

Finally, there's only a week until election time—one week until the names Clint Reilly and Frank Jordan are finally shuffled off into the dumpster of history and the homeless can go back to sleeping in the doorway of Reilly's campaign office on Mission. Just one more week, and it'll be another four years until we're treated to the embarrassing sight of a cop leading a line of 4th graders with brooms in a "cleanup" on the 16th and Mission BART Plaza. Yes, it's election time and even the Tenderloin isn't safe from mayoral candidates out shaking hands and looking for votes. In fact, Da Mayor himself, Willie Brown, was spotted getting out the vote at the annual Blessing of The Pets at St. Boniface Church (Jones/Golden Gate). Every year the church offers a service to the city's pets, where they are prayed for and anointed with holy water. While folks lined up with their dogs, cats, and even parakeets, Willie double-parked his limo to get out and pose for pictures with the newly blessed pups, who, like the candidates, had apparently learned at least one new trick: "Shake!" Well, why not? If the dead can vote in this town, why not DOGS? This reporter caught up to Willie as he ducked back into his limo. I yelled, "Hey Willie! How come the PETS in this town got it so good, and all the PEOPLE have to starve on the streets?" He just grinned back and slammed the door, so I turned to the burly cops on horses and asked, "Getting those things BLESSED today?" They just scowled. Lighten up, guys: even pigs can get blessed at St. Boniface.

One *Turd-Filled Donut* reader reports that Brown was also seen working the crowd at the Castro Street Fair last month. Willie was grinning broadly and shaking hands when our correspondent stepped forward to yell point blank into his face, "Willie! Why'd you fuck up my TOWN, man ? Why'd you sell this place OUT ?!?" In true Willie style, Da Mayor was unfazed. He never lost his smile, while grunting under his breath, like a ventriloquist, "Why don't you JUST MOVE AWAY, huh? JUST GO!" Sure, Willie, but can my DOG stay?

SHOPPING CARTS ON THE CAMPAIGN TRAIL: Yeah, it's election time alright. You can't go anywhere without running into some politician. Clint Reilly keeps holding press conferences in front of the bulldozed Mission Rock shelter to call attention to Mayor Brown's failed homeless policies. Judging from Reilly's pamphlets, his policy would be, "Next time, bulldoze the place with the homeless STILL IN IT!" The Wandering Scavenger also reports that he was eating breakfast at the Mission Street dive, JIM'S RESTAURANT, when Reilly and his wife came in to court the 2-dollar-breakfast vote. Our reporter lunged at Reilly and was about to yell, "Get out of our neighborhood, rich creep!" when his girlfriend ordered him to behave at the breakfast table. I'm sure Reilly got what was coming to him, anyway, though, if he got as sick as I do when I eat at Jim's... The *Turd-Filled Donut* had a more successful public encounter with Supervisor Amos Brown. Amos was spotted on Polk, smiling broadly, leisurely taking off his coat and getting into his Mercedes in front of City Hall. This reporter yelled, "Hey Amos..." Brown smiled and nodded and started to wave. I finished, "You fucking suck!!!" He grimaced, quickly got in his car and slammed the door. If you want to tell Amos what YOU think of his anti-homeless legislation, look for his home phone number and address later in this issue...

TAGGERS ENDORSE GONZALEZ? Back in the Mission, graffiti writer Heart 101 tells the *Turd-Filled Donut* that he was motioned over to a car at a stop light on Valencia only to see the driver was candidate for District Attorney Matt Gonzalez. Gonzalez told him, "Tell all the (graffiti) writers to vote for me. If I'm elected I'm going to make graffiti legal!" Wait... so you mean it's ILLEGAL? To write on WALLS ?!?

OVERHEARD: ON PEE-SOAKED SYCAMORE STREET, which should be renamed Sick-A-MOST, a cheerful alley dweller informs, "This is my personal record! I've been smoking crack for 37 days!" See? Everyone sounds like a politician these days...On a rainy night at Hunt's, a man walks in and tries to sell a purple fedora with a feather in it to a Capp Street girl, who has stopped in to buy a hot dog. She yells, "Why the hell do you ask a HOOKER for money?!?" So he puts on the hat and grins, and she warms up a little, "Now that's a nice PIMP hat!" She gets her hot dog and out they go, together in the rain... And, over on Sycamore again, a man tells of getting a urinating in public ticket from an Officer S. Christ. I guess he has a different idea of the Golden Rule...

NO JUSTICE, NO PEE: There's been a lot of marching and protesting in the streets, lately, before the election: three Free Mumia marches, the anti-police brutality march, and the Eviction Defense Network's "March Of The Evicted," which, the name suggests, would likely be attended by half of The City these days. At the Coalition on Homelessness's rally in UN Plaza to kick off a national campaign for homeless folks' civil rights, a speaker condemned The City for leaving sprinklers on all night so people can't sleep in the parks. The Wandering Scavenger yelled out, "If you screw the heads all the way down the sprinklers won't work!" Sound advice... At the 2nd Free Mumia march, the massive crowd surged up Powell past several lonely-looking animal rights activists, dressed in cow suits, handing out vegetarian literature to no one in front of McDonalds. Picked the wrong day, I guess... A hundred homeless folks packed the Local 6 Union Hall to ratify the Homeless People's Congress's Action Plan to End Homelessness, demanding housing and non-police solutions to homelessness. If people keep getting evicted at the current rate, it really WILL be One Big Union.

CHICKEN IN EVERY SHOPPING CART: Now, with Tom Ammiano announced as a write-in candidate, Reilly REALLY looks finished. HUNT'S actually put his sign up in their window, next to Brown's, but he still appears to be failing at trying to win over The City's most sizable voting block, the homeless THEMSELVES! A man at the 19th and Dolores free coffee and donuts drop-in told me that he met Reilly and asked him what his plan was. Reilly responded by saying, "Well, I know what the homeless need because I was homeless myself for one month!" The man was unimpressed. "A month, huh?" he asked the candidate. "Well, did you ever have to sleep in the bushes? Did you ever have to SMOKE CRACK or use drugs like heroin to feel good so you could stand being homeless? Did you ever take speed so you could stay awake all night, so no one would steal your stuff? Did you ever have to sell your body for money so you could eat?!?" Reilly, we're told, turned sort of white, and mumbled, "Uh, no." Just think: if he had said yes, he might have swung the election...

TURD ON ICE: Yes, the election's only a week away and I just can't wait. Finally, an end to the election sweeps! It's become so bad, here in ole Ess Eff that, last week, yours truly became the first person EVER in the HISTORY OF URINE to get ARRESTED for pissing in Sycamore Alley! I mean this is the filthiest alley in all of Ess Eff! I had been drinking beer on Clarion, and went around the corner to pick up another 40, but first stopped off in the shadow of a mini-van to relieve myself. Next thing I knew, a cop had pulled up, and I was being handcuffed! These are dark days, indeed. As the cop car pulled away with me in it, I thought, "Wow, here I am, part of 'The Homeless Problem' that all the candidates are always talking about, one of the 'bums' ruining everyone's 'quality of life.' Just think: my pee is FRONT PAGE NEWS!" What a drag. At 6:00 AM, me and all the other Quality-of-Lifers got out and our crowd made a slow march up 7th, just in time for the stores to start selling again. I thought, "Cheer up guys, in a couple of days, no matter who wins, we can go back to drinking our beers in peace..."

TURD-FILLED ENDORSEMENTS 1999

Voting is an important part of citizenship, maybe important enough to cancel out any of the social stigma people may try to hang on you for getting welfare. Like, how many of those people who call me a bum give enough of a shit to VOTE—or, for that matter, to vote TWICE like I did last year? Remember these two important things about voter fraud. #1: If there is someone registered to vote at your house who has died, moved away, or—most likely—been evicted, then you can vote in their name, too, because no one will check your ID! And #2: If you are approached by campaign workers for Mayor Brown who offer you money to vote, you should take it. Once you're in the booth, you can vote for whomever you want!

Now, on to our endorsements this election:

TOM AMMIANO WRITE-IN FOR MAYOR!

Even though Ammiano never called us back when we left the last issue of TFD in his office with a note offering our endorsement, we still wholeheartedly support his write-in candidacy. After a depressing summer of Frank Jordan flashbacks and ripping down Reilly and Brown campaign signs, there's finally an exciting reason to look forward to the election. At this writing, polls show Ammiano, Reilly, and Jordan deadlocked in 2nd place. Vote Ammiano and force a run-off! It's better than waiting around for an earthquake to save San Francisco from Willie Brown and the dot-commers!

YES ON PROPOSITION J and NO ON PROPOSITION I!

This might be the proposition on this year's ballot that directly affects *Turd-Filled Donut* readers the most. Proposition I, if enacted, would rebuild the measly four blocks of freeway across Market Street to connect with Oak and Fell Streets. Its opponents back Prop. J, that promises to replace the freeway with the new Octavia Boulevard at street level. Backers of Prop J claim this will "beautify" SF and they even cynically say that it's really about new housing that will supposedly be built along the boulevard if J passes. Yeah, right! Do you think any of US are ever going to live in that new, beautified housing? No way! "Beautification" in this town really always means "exclusion." As it stands now, SF barely suffers from the freeway blight of other towns, so let us allow this small chunk to stand so that we can still sleep under it, have sidewalk sales in its shade, and be able to spray paint and put up posters on its supports. Bicyclists take note: Let's keep those cars OFF our streets and up in the air! Octavia Boulevard sounds like a new cyclist death zone like Bayshore!

THE UN PLAZA HOMELESS PROJECT

Last year, after the new Civic Center opened without a single bench or place to sit and even more police presence, UN Plaza across the street became the new capitol of downtown homelessness. This election year has seen relentless police harassment of the UN Plaza homeless to keep them out of sight of tourists and ongoing media pressure to "clean up the UN Plaza," apparently at any cost. The UN Plaza residents even face vigilante attacks from the private shopping cart retrieval company SCOTT'S JR. whose employees have been known to threaten people with fists and knives, all to get their carts back. But, instead of giving up, the UN PLAZA HOMELESS PROJECT *has been started. An organization for the Plaza's homeless, they have been holding weekly meetings and staging actions together since March. Their demand is simple: they want the city to give them an abandoned building, and, in exchange for rent, they will work to bring the building up to code and make it their home. The* Turd-Filled Donut *interviewed project members and Plaza residents Manny and Stanley on the Thursday before the election...*

TURD-FILLED DONUT: Can you give me some background on the Project?

UN PLAZA PROJECT: There are usually 150–175 homeless people in UN Plaza at all times. We started trying to organize in March, because the police harassment was just too much at that time. We had our first real meeting in the basement of the Burger King (9th and Market) in April with 6 people. Now we have meetings every week at the statue in the Plaza, Tuesdays at 1:00. The UN Plaza Homeless Project is about housing, health care, civil rights, and freedom!

TFD: How long have you lived in the Plaza?

STANLEY: I've got 3 years here...

MANNY: I have lived 12 years in San Francisco, 10 years in UN Plaza...

TFD: How many folks come to your meetings?

UNP: well, 6 of us—Manny, Stanley, Tommy, Poppy, John White, Joseph Burns—we are the group that meets with each other and then meets with representatives from The City, a sort-of-committee. But our weekly meetings are open to the whole Plaza and lots of people come over...

TFD: What are your goals?

UNP: We want The City to give us a building that we can rebuild. We don't want a handout. There's a lot of talent out here. A lot more talent than a lot of people who aren't homeless have. And we have, maybe, a small income but not enough for rent. So, we want to be able to work for our roof.

TFD: How have you approached The City?

UNP: We approached Supervisor Leland Yee with our idea, that we be given the abandoned hotel at 144 Eddy. He told us to write a proposal. We did, and he was surprised at how good a job we did. They didn't think the homeless could do it! He said we should talk to the Mayor. So we organized a campout at City Hall to receive tickets to the Mayor's monthly meeting with the public...

TFD: How many people camped out?

UNP: We had 90-100 folks sleeping in front of City Hall, homeless and otherwise...

TFD: What happened then?

UNP: The Mayor acted excited about the idea. He said, "Let's make this happen!" and right there told his homeless coordinator, George Smith, that he would have to meet with us once a week to try and get the building.

TFD: What happened then?

UNP: Well, George Smith disappeared! He met with us a couple times, and then we didn't see him for a whole month! We looked at the building, too, but the price went up. They wanted 3.5 million for it, but when they heard The City was involved, they wanted 4.2. Then when we actually brought a building inspector, it suddenly went up to 6 million!

TFD: Wasn't George Smith homeless himself, before he got this job?

UNP: Yeah, but he even said to us, "I used to be homeless, but I'm still a politician..." He even tried to take certain members of the group aside to offer them shelter for themselves, to try to break up the group. One woman who worked with us got $600 and a room voucher and now we never see her anymore, but the rest of the group is sticking together! We see through that. We want permanent housing, not temporary shelter!

TFD: So, what happened with George Smith?

UNP: We took 30 people and camped out in his office and waited for him to come back! We wouldn't leave! They called him and he came back right away! Now he sees that we're serious, and he's started meeting with us. We're not going to go away...

TFD: Are you having luck with a building?

UNP: Now we're looking at the old Winston Arms at 50 Turk. The City may be able to lease it for us, then we could work for our rent, fix up and run the place ourselves. Cooperative existence... They say, if this works, it could be a model for other buildings...

TFD: What are your plans, though, if The City keeps stalling? What is your deadline?

UNP: Our deadline is the election! If The City doesn't tell us something concrete in the next couple days, we're telling everything to the media, right here in The Plaza! That The City doesn't want people to know about us, that they try to keep people from working for themselves. If we don't hear what we want to hear, we're going to call in the press on Monday!

WHITHER HAULING?

The strange saga of Hyde Street junk store Hauling, and owner, Cheap John, has taken another inscrutable turn. Long known for its unpredictable hours and the angry signs taped to its door, the junk store has now apparently shut down for good.

Earlier this year, signs on the door announced reduced hours because, according to the handwritten notes, John was "going back to school." One day, while seeking to buy either a broken toaster or a bent bicycle wheel—I forget which—I wandered into Hauling, only to find a sign posted that read, "LAST DAY EVER." I asked John what was up, but he would only confirm that the store would close. In answer to my other questions, he would only rock back and forth on his chair, clenching and unclenching his fist, while cryptically muttering, "Oh, they don't know, but they will soon! Knowledge is power, motherfuckers!"

Sure enough, that was the last time I've ever seen the store open and Hauling fans have had to settle for reading John's terse dispatches, newly taped to the window every couple of days. The new Andy's Thrift at 120 Jones has picked up the Tenderloin junk store slack, but, now that Hauling appears to be gone for good, I'd like to at least recount my favorite Hauling moment: One day, I heard piano music coming from the store, so I wandered inside, where I found John sitting at the keys, expertly and gently playing. While I stood there in awe, a Tenderloin oldtimer with a beer in a bag wandered in and leaned against the door, listening with his eyes closed. When the music finished, the oldtimer sighed.

"Pagliacci, huh?"

John nodded. Pagliacci.

TO A BETTER PLACE?

First, Cheap John from Hauling, the Tenderloin junk store, seemingly disappears without a trace, and now the Urine Man's gone. For as long as anyone can remember—at least over 10 years—the famed Urine Man has been living in his parked bus at 24th and Illinois in China Basin, and, as everyone surely knows, he's The Urine Man because he has a huge sign posted on his bus the whole time that reads, "CURE AIDS BY DRINKING YOUR OWN URINE!" Though this controversial and disgusting theory has been widely ignored by the mainstream press, the Urine Man did seem to have built up a small group of adherents, who gathered at this bus to take crystal meth and listen to his terse dispatches about the evils of food and beauty of urine. Now the bus has disappeared. Where could the Urine Man have gone? Coupled with the mysterious disappearance of Hauling it could only signify some sort-of Wingnut Rapture, where they have all disappeared from The City at once. Has the Urine Man, at least, gone to a better place? Early evidence suggests otherwise. A *Turd-Filled Donut* reader spotted his urine-filled bus newly parked up on Iowa Street under the freeway...

The disappearance of Cheap John's store at Hyde and Turk is still a mystery, though. The landlord, an old Asian guy, merely said, "He go! He crazy man!" The lady at the Palace of Fine Junk said, "I never even knew that was his name." A guy selling warm Coronas out of a shopping cart across the street said, "Man, I stayed AWAY from that dude!" Unfortunately, Cheap John himself offered no clues either. I found him standing next to a truck with his piano and mattress loaded in the back, in front of All-Star Donuts. I asked him what happened but he only would clench and unclench his fist and repeat, "They'll pay. Oh, yes, they'll pay..." I asked some shiny 20-somethings who were moving into his old spot what they planned to do in there. "Oh, you know, computer stuff," they said. "Nothing important." I couldn't agree more...

THOUSAND YEAR REICH? Bell's Donuts at 6th and Market has changed their name to the somewhat more expansionist Donut World, and has a map of the globe printed on their new boxes. I looked on the box, but couldn't find 6th Street on the map...

WRITE-IN LOVE: Congratulations go out to TFD workfare diarist, RG, as he is soon to be married! Back in November, RG was so inspired and filled with optimism when Tom Ammiano's surprise write-in candidacy for mayor forced a run-off that he proposed marriage to his long time girlfriend, Roxanne, who works at POWER, the workfare rights union. The couple consulted Ammiano and Tom agreed to perform the marriage if he was elected mayor. Tom didn't win, but RG did; they're getting married later this year... Meanwhile, others in *Turd-Filled Donut* land aren't so lucky in love. One reader reports coming home to his doorway at 6th and Natoma to find a banana with a condom on it...

15 MINUTES OF FAME: Famous panhandler The Bushman was spotted the other day with a small crowd of groupies at 6th and Minna. The Bushman, as often reported in the *Chronicle*, is a 40-something black guy who works the crowd at Fisherman's Wharf. He lurks on the sidewalk, disguised as a bush or shrub, and jumps out of the bush to terrify unwitting tourists, who he then asks for spare change! "I'm going to be in TWO new movies they filmed down there!" Bushman announced, coolly, as he bummed a smoke from a fan. "I'm in the new one with Keanu Reeves." A woman in front of the Hotel Auburn gushed, "I can't believe it's really the Bushman!" I loaned her my pen and he signed autographs all around... The free lunch crowd at St. Anthony's got a break from the Keanu Reeves movie, too. The director rented out St. Anthony's one night when it was closed, to shoot inside the dining hall, and the money went to buy a special steak dinner for everyone...

DOWN IN THE MISSION, on San Carlos Street, this reporter spotted some well-dressed white folks being shown a house by a property manager, while a Latino woman, apparently the current actual RESIDENT, looked on, somewhat stricken. I went up to the smiling, potential buyer, who was oozing wealth and confidence, and said, "So... You thinking of buying the place?" He said yes. I pointed to the blue, spray painted "XIII" graffiti across the street and said, " Well, you DO know what THAT means, right?" A small cloud of worry crept across his face. "No, uh, what does it mean?" "That," I lied gravely, "means that someone was KILLED there on

THAT VERY SPOT." The man now looked alarmed. I followed his widened eyes as he looked slowly around the street and saw that NEARLY EVERY AVAILABLE SURFACE ON THE ENTIRE BLOCK had "XIII" painted on it. As I walked away, I heard the property manager trying to reassure him, "Oh, I don't think it really means that! I'm sure its something else." But the house is still for sale months later, and I never saw THAT guy again...

SEEN AROUND: The Yuppie Eradicator, Nestor Mahkno, was spotted at Hunt's the other night, with a crew of wide-eyed followers who were helping him put up his new Yuppie Eradication Project posters. "Look!" he gushed, holding up a bucket with an Ace hardware bag wrapped around it. "Five gallons of wheat-paste!" Some graffiti writers hanging out there groaned, but I humored Nestor. I lowered my voice, pointed at the "Don't sell it here!" signs, and whispered, "Careful, man. This place is UNDER SURVEILLANCE." Nestor nodded conspiratorially, "Ah... Gotcha..." and split...

I'd like to close this column with some final remembrances of the idiosyncratic junk store, Hauling, a store that was almost never open and had almost nothing for sale, but nevertheless seemed to be at the heart of a very public struggle, a fiercely independent determination to survive. Cheap John's terse dispatches, angrily taped to his bolted door, seemed like a mirror held up to the hard Tenderloin streets. The last one I remember, from last fall, was a Xeroxed photo of John holding a kid, with a note in black marker that read, "This is what they are trying to destroy!"

"He was actually a very sweet and open guy," says Chance Martin, editor of the *Street Sheet*. "Me and Mikey would always go smoke joints with him over by Angelo's garage. When he'd be real pissed, he'd lock himself in the store and you'd hear him playing his piano real loud in there. You should have seen that motorcycle he sold Mikey, though. Mikey took it to the Harley dealer and the guy said, "What is THIS?!? Did you buy this bike from a fuckin' TWEAKER or something?""

Probably no one knew Cheap John better than Mikey. We tried to get some stories from him, but, after eight years living in the Senator Hotel on Ellis Street and working at the Coalition on Homelessness, Mikey and his motorcycle moved to Hawaii last Christmas. Repeated calls, postcards, and e-mails to his island address have gone unanswered.

INTERVIEW WITH ZARA THASTRA
Pt. 2

The boarded-up Mission storefronts were also ever-changing canvases for graffiti. A neighborhood history was written and rewritten nightly in scraps of wheat-pasted flyers and stencil, the neighborhood transition documented on the plywood slats surrounding the deep pits in the earth where buildings had been torn down to make way for condos. While the free art itself would soon appear inside the hipster galleries opening around the neighborhood, a new graffiti police task force out of Mission Station was cracking down, meticulously photographing graffiti to build grand jury cases against graffiti writers. Some artists responded by quitting "graffiti" and instead trying a whole new approach—painting enormous, illegal murals in broad daylight. Evicted artist Aaron Noble came back to town to work with Andrew Schoultz on a huge piece on a crumbling wall in China Basin. They painted the mural for weeks, right out in the open. Zara and I also used paint rollers and extensions to paint a block-long, 20-foot-high text piece that read NO MORE PRISONS on 3rd Street, right where people stuck in traffic from the Giants' games would have to look at it everyday. It took us four or five hours to paint and countless cops rolled by while we were working but what cop has the imagination to think that a project so huge, undertaken in public, could be illegal?

The buildings we painted on, though, were torn down soon to make way for the Mission Bay biotech campus in China Basin, as gentrification spread out from the Mission to other neighborhoods in the Eastern half of The City.

What was some of the response you've had to your graffiti? Are there specific pieces you'd like to talk about?

ZARA: It was fun to do "No More Prisons" stuff in the past couple of years. It impresses me that I can paint a bunch of different stuff and people get it. I think it's because we're all thinking about the same stuff, which is sort of at the core of what's exciting to me about art.

When the dot-com boom was at its worst for the Mission, there was such a conflict of ideas going on here. Graff was the subconscious

of the neighborhood made public in some way. You had everybody thinking about the same thing so hard. There was such a buzz, that any idea put on the street really entered the larger world. It was a time when Nestor Mahkno could show up with those ridiculous anti-yuppie posters and have it make nationwide news.

ZARA: I don't think people who weren't here then can truly relate to what a weird time it was. In '98, when we were out painting, everyone was doing something fresh and different. We'd do buildings with rollers, upside-down throw-ups, even posters. Then, a couple weeks later, five other people would be out there doing the same thing, only slightly different. It was like a spree. Now people are really on top of each other.

Especially with public art. You can see the repression in art. The tags are more furtive and nothing's really big now.

ZARA: Right. People are going to read this and think "Graffiti?!? You're talking about trashy tags and fucked up walls!" But that's based on the art from being repressed. In places where it can thrive more, like Germany, or other countries... or New York, Philly... when you look around at the walls, so many corner stores have graff on their sides and the range is so much deeper. There are more characters, more symbolism, and not just names. In NYC, all kinds of shit is done with spray cans. Store signs, whatever. In SF it is so much more oppressed that it's not accessible to the regular community. For example, in '94, there was that piece that KRUSH and DREAM did at 14th and Folsom that said, "Knowledge is the key to freedom." People used graffiti artists to send a message out to the community. The more oppressed graffiti is, the less that stuff happens.

Speaking of repression, that's is how we met, right? I was working at the Coalition on Homelessness and you came in to do community service. My boss said, "Give this kid some flyers to pass out, or something." How many times have you been arrested now for graff?

ZARA: Nine times now, but under two different names!

THE LIBERATION OF LEEDS

After we got away with the generator show at Leed's, Generator Summer was on. We immediately booked another show at the 16th and Mission BART Plaza with Miami and the Human Beans. This time an even bigger crowd showed up—including a couple folks who showed up in gorilla suits, carrying bananas! The plaza was ours! There were punks standing on the newspaper stands, on the trash cans, even in the trees! Ivy said, "I'll never forget the little old lady who was there taking pictures of the whole thing and dancing right along with us."

The cops didn't stop that one either, so we set up another one in the doorway of the abandoned Cine Latino Theater at Mission and 21st—as Aesop said, "Yet another rock and roll show at the urine-soaked doorway of another piece of wasted SF real estate." This generator show was memorable for many reasons. For one thing, someone forgot to bring the generator! We ended up borrowing an enormous extension cord from the Evergreen Market next door and running it ACROSS MISSION STREET to Mission Records! During a break in traffic, Matty, ever the pro soundguy, duct-taped the cord to the asphalt, just like you'd tape cords down on any stage. Cars ran over it for the whole show, but it worked the whole time. Aesop remembers, "The show proceeded without incident, unless you count the one deranged hippie who was firedancing dangerously close to my head while I played, or the crusty that puked up a hog's head of cheap vodka and then lapped it off the pavement as his scabies-addled dog looked on in disgust, or the crusty punks juggling flaming torches..." This time ONE cop came, but he just sat on the hood of his patrol car, drinking milk and checking out the scene. Not only did he not attempt to shut us down, he even leaned over and plugged the extension cord back in when one of the fire jugglers knocked it out!

After that we did more shows in the Leed's doorway, at the BART, at Tire Beach, and in Dolores Park for the rest of the summer. The shows all brought huge crowds, went off without police hassle, and were even well received by the Mission community. I remember at one show an elderly Latino guy came up to me and put his arm around my shoulder and shouted into my ear, "This is great, what you are doing for the community! This brings people together!" I smiled and nodded, but thought, "No, wait! We are actually punk rockers who hate America, stealing electricity, having an illegal show, and playing loud, awful, anti-government music! Get it right, OK?!?" I guess they saw right through us.

After the show we did on the steps of the Armory at 14th and Mission, we weren't planning on doing any more street shows for a while because the rainy winter season was coming up and the weather would likely be too unpredictable for outdoor rock. It had been a pretty good summer of shows and it would be nice to take a break until spring. But then we were forced into action in early November when a locked metal gate suddenly was installed in the doorway of Leed's to keep people out! What's up with THAT shit?!?

A gate over the Leed's doorway was absolutely intolerable, especially since we'd have to walk past it every day. Now all of the homeless people who slept there nightly would be locked out, just in time for the rainy season. And even if we didn't PLAN on having any more shows for a while, that should be OUR decision to make and not the decision of whoever put up the gate, right?

Then there was the question of why, after all this time that Leed's had been abandoned, would there suddenly be a gate there? Maybe the cops were trying to finally shut us down for good, but it seemed more likely in the context of the boomtown real estate speculation and gentrification in the neighborhood that the appearance of the gate foreshadowed something horrible. Every time a store closes in the Mission these days, everyone thinks Starbucks is moving in. The word on the street this time was that The Gap had bought the Leed's building and was to open the first clothing chain store on Mission Street, but no one knew for sure.

I wanted to have another show at Leed's despite the gate. On closer examination of the gate, it turned out that due to a crucial architectural flaw in the design of the gate, there was still a fairly large hole in the gate between the old shoe display window and the sidewalk on the 22nd Street side of Leed's. Matty went by with a tape measure and determined that we would still be able to still slide our amps UNDER the shoe display, crawl inside, and rock BEHIND BARS! We made flyers right away.

Our first idea was that Miami would play behind the bars just to show that they couldn't stop us from having shows. But Jimmy thought that we actually needed to destroy the gate in some way. So the show we were planning became a Miami/Shotwell show where Miami would play while Shotwell used bolt cutters to cut the lock on the gate. Then, at the end, we would open the gate and leave—a sort-of symbolic "Freeing of The Rock" like when the guy from Iron Maiden swordfights a monster onstage, or something.

There was some debate over how we should go about the show, though. The gate was only held in place with bolts that had been drilled into the ground. Jimmy wanted to just unscrew them right away, weeks before the show, and haul the gate away. We'd play the show as if the gate had never been there. But I thought it would be cooler to play behind the gate. So then Jimmy wanted the crowd to crash down the gate and haul it away DURING the show, starting a riot on Mission Street. I thought that would be pretty rad, except that none of the equipment or the generator belonged to me and I thought that just playing at all was going to be a much bigger risk than we had taken before. I thought we should just play, cut the lock and leave. Then, at a later time, go take apart the gate and haul it away in the middle of the night. All during the week before the show, Jimmy would get drunk and start talking about taking apart the gate early. I'd catch him walking off down the street with a 6-pack and a cordless drill and I'd have to talk him out of it.

In the end we had to change our plans anyway. As if they were reading our minds, a couple days before the show someone drilled a piece of wood over the hole where we were going to slide in our amps. Now we would have to crash down the board, too.

We thought it would be too obvious to go kick out the board in broad daylight, right before the show. It would attract too much attention. The only way to do this, we decided, would be to be even MORE obvious. Matty and I hatched a plan to dress up like construction workers and to take off the board in broad daylight.

On the day of the show, we got together with a cordless drill and a couple pairs of overalls. The idea of Matty and me being construction workers was pretty ridiculous. Matty had enormous dreadlocks and I had long, purple hair. Even in San Francisco, there are no construction workers who look like this. We put on the coveralls, but we still looked sort of pathetic. Matty wasn't worried. He said, "We'll wear hats."

With our hair stuffed into hats, we walked over to Leed's carrying our drill. Yes, just a couple of "construction workers" with no truck and only one tool out for a walk! Anyone who saw us with our drill would have assumed we were on our way to Hunt's Donuts to sell it.

At Leed's, the bolts on the board easily popped out, one at a time. A couple of Latino guys stopped and did a double take, squinting at us a bit, but no one paid too much attention to what we were doing. In minutes, we had the board off. When no one was looking, we hid it behind a dumpster in the Bartlett Alley.

That night, when we showed up with the generator and amps, there was already a pretty good-sized crowd on hand and Pete Shotwell was already halfway through unscrewing the gate's bolts. We slid the gear under where Matty and I had taken out the board and we set everything up. It was pretty funny, looking out at the crowd from behind the bars while we tuned up. Jimmy started working on the bolts, too, and then we started playing.

It was all over pretty fast. Somewhere during the first two songs, Jim had 4/5 of the gate removed. People started hanging on the slumping gate and pulling it apart but there were still a couple of bolts left to take out, so it was just hanging there in this cool, twisted heap while we played. In the middle of the fourth song, the cops screeched up on to the sidewalk. We finished the song, grabbed pieces of equipment and started stuffing them into our waiting van down the block. People in the crowd came up and grabbed stuff to help us clear out of there before we got in trouble. We figured with the gate just hanging there, all wrecked, it would be a good idea to get lost.

But when everything was loaded to go, the cops just took off! What happened? Apparently, the cop had asked Ivy, "Did you guys do this to the gate?" She said, "No! It was just like that when we showed up." The cops then, incredibly, just said, "Well... there's been a noise complaint so you have to stop the music!" and sped off.

After the show, people hung out for a while. More and more people kept showing up. The show had been so short that most folks thought that it still hadn't started! The cops were gone, so I went and got bolt cutters and cut the lock on the gate that was keeping it in the air. Then, a bunch of us started slowly taking apart the gate. It seemed to take forever, but after an hour or so, we got it dismantled.

In the end, I felt a little bad because I realized Jimmy had been right and that the crowd should have been given more of a chance to rip apart the gate themselves, instead of having us do it. I think

I blew that one. But, still, The Rock was freed and the Leed's doorway was open again. But whatever happened to the gate? Rumor has it that the remains of the gate somehow found their way down to Tire Beach in the middle of the night. I sure don't know anything about THAT, but, if it's true, I bet the homeless recyclers down there made a bundle off of it!

THE EPICENTER OF CRIME: THE HUNT'S DONUTS STORY

Like most people, it was the sign that drew me to Hunt's at first. Within minutes of sitting down with my cup of coffee, way past midnight one night back in 1993, I knew that the sign hadn't lied: here was a place that could only be described as being "Open 25 hours." The air was thick with cigarette smoke, the tables were packed with men who were either yelling or sleeping or drinking wine, and the guy behind the counter looked terrified.

An orange-fizz drink the very color of nausea circulated endlessly in a clear, plastic dispenser near the register, and in the corner, the grimy, nicotine-stained wall was inscrutably decorated with a print of the shroud of Turin.

In the swirling drink in Christ's closed eyes, I saw a vision of eternity. "The 25th hour..." I thought. "This is all happening 25 hours a day..." In long nights at Hunt's over the years I would, however, come to see the 25th hour not as a time, but as a PLACE. It was a destination that could only be reached after too much fluorescent light and coffee and donuts.

Or heroin and meth and box wine. I made it to that lost continent that night for the first time, when "New York, New York" by Frank Sinatra came on the old Hunt's jukebox. Suddenly, all the sleeping men in the shop lifted their heads off the table to sing along; they drunkenly shouted, "If you can make it there... you'll make it... anywhere!" The last note of the song was punctuated by one guy pitching forward back on to the table. In the silence that followed, all you could hear was the coffee he knocked over dribbling onto the floor. I felt like I'd been welcomed into a secret society.

There's one other thing about that night that will stick with me forever. At one point, a cop came in and ordered a coffee. The counter guy took advantage of this moment. As the cop took his first sip, the counter guy declared, "I'm going to the bathroom. You watch the place for a minute!" and quickly bounded out the door. The cop's eyes bulged wide and he almost spit out his coffee, but it was too late. He was stuck. He looked warily around him at the huge crowd of wasted men that was already slowly advancing towards the refill pot. One after another, the men refilled their Styrofoam cups without paying, silently, while the cop surveyed the scene like he was watching a horror movie, maybe "Dawn of the Dead."

I was young and new to the Big City. It was the first time I'd seen genuine fear in a policeman's eyes. I went and got my own refill.

While the Mission would change around it over the years, Hunt's remained thoroughly and irreducibly criminal—a fluorescent-lit utopia for lowlifes, a north star guiding the way home for the regulars that answered the pull of the Epicenter of Crime. Hunt's was where prostitutes from Capp Street ate donuts and loudly complained about their pimps into cell phones, while passersby tapped on the floor-to-ceiling windows, trying to sell you crescent wrenches, jackets, or fistfuls of stolen gold necklaces. Hunt's was where you could see gang members and graffiti writers taking donut breaks, side by side. It was where guys just out of prison mingled with men who had fought and killed in the revolutions in El Salvador and Nicaragua.

I have years of memories from there, years of writing all night, sneaking in beers, making out under the tables. For five years in a row, a punk rock "donut night" met every Monday at midnight. And, of course, there were those long years under the court order, when the cops were trying to shut Hunt's down, and the signs on the wall earnestly pleaded, "Don't sell it here," as if the donut shop was not a functioning business but an underground punk venue that could only stay open if we all did our part to keep the cops away.

I did buy stereo speakers once there, but the only thing I consistently bought was new, clean socks that, for some reason, guys always sold there. Bucky told me that when Hunt's closed, he was working on a story about a guy in the Mission who gets his heart stolen. He has to go down to Hunt's, of course, to try and buy it back.

My last time at Hunt's wasn't much different than the first, even if it had long since changed its name to Magic Burgr, just like that without the E. Jimmy and I went to get ice cream cones at 2:00 AM. The counter guy was closing the gate that closed off the back part of the shop for the night. Just then, a kid ran in the front door, yelling, "Wait!" He ducked under the gate, shoved his fist into the soil at the base of a sick-looking plant in the back, and pulled out a bunch of baggies. He grinned sheepishly and said, "I almost forgot my medicine!"

After that I went out of town for the summer and when I came back in August, 2004, Hunt's had closed. Hunt's was such a permanent-seeming fixture of the Mission landscape that I had used to joke that I wanted my ashes sprinkled there. No one had ever imagined it CLOSING. The situation demanded answers. What follows is the results of my search, a sprawling memorial I wrote in November 2004, originally for publication in the *Guardian*. In the end, we couldn't get it in the papers because it in no way really fits the description of "news." It's true. At this late date, nothing about the gentrification of the Mission can really be considered news. The closing of Hunt's could really almost be seen as an afterword, a bookend to that long saga.

But the story of Hunt's is both less than and more than news. It's a rumor, an illicit history, the pull of the gravity of the Epicenter of Crime. At 20th and Mission, battles to control the identity of the Mission have been acted out again and again, between ever-changing sets of police and thieves over the years. In the story that follows we have the Irish cop who shut down the Mission's Latino bars and his cop father who shut down the city's gay bars. We have the young kid who couldn't beat the Hunt's-sponsored team on the baseball diamond who grew up to try to shut down the shop as police captain. We have the Latino teenagers who hung out in front of Hunt's framed for a cop's murder in the famed trail of Los Siete De La Raza. At 20th and Mission, history doubles back and repeats itself in new guises, again and again, like a Borges story about two knives that fight each other for centuries, long after the individual knife fighters die.

When I used to sit at Hunt's, I'd imagine a cop in the basement of Mission Station, ordered to watch and log all the Hunt's Donuts surveillance camera footage, to make a true record of Mission history. It would take a full day to watch each day's footage. The cop would never catch up.

Because the Hunt's day was 25 hours.

1

Hunt's opened in 1952, a year after Bob's Donuts on Polk Street and Silver Crest Donuts on Bayshore opened in their present locations. With their hand-painted signs and egalitarian coffee counters, Bob's and Silver Crest still harken back to a time when the donut shops were a cheap and dependable haven for a working class San Francisco, open 24 hours a day at their current locations ever since.

But Hunt's was open 25 hours.

The donut shop was long a notorious hangout for criminals, but its sign, stretching down the block on 20th Street, announcing "Open 25 Hours" gave Hunt's a certain added mystique. The inscrutable sign that amused or intrigued passersby seemed to taunt police with a hyper-vigilant criminality.

Police brass, like former captain of Mission Station, Greg Suhr, still speak of the donut shop as a respected adversary.

"If you wanted false documents, fake I.D.'s, stolen tools, a radio, or a watch, you would start looking at the donut shop," said Suhr.

Hunt's stories are common to the Mission. They relate a history of Mission criminal ingenuity and straight-up ghetto know-how.

Nosmo King, a legend in bike messenger circles, has been riding for a living for 24 years, and living on Lexington Street and 20th, around the corner from Hunt's, for 15 years, but he is still amazed by a Hunt's experience he had a decade ago.

"Once I went in there (to Hunt's) and told a guy hanging out there I need a pair of green Dickies, size 32 long and size 34 waist," remembers King. "He came back 10 minutes later with the pants, brand new, and only charged me $5 for them!"

Lance Hahn, the guitar player/singer for J Church, too, has seen things at Hunt's that could only have logically taken place in the 25th hour.

"Once I caught some old dude picking my pocket while I was riding 14 in the middle of the day. He saw that I saw and hopped off the bus and I followed him," Hahn says, "He went straight to Hunt's and sat down. I walked right up to him and he handed me my $5. That was the weird, surreal street justice you could expect there."

How you felt about Hunt's Donuts might reveal your position on the changing Mission District.

"Hunt's was a celebration of all that was undomesticated in the Mission," says novelist Peter Plate, who set much of his 2001 novel

Angels of Catastrophe at Hunt's Donuts's scratched Formica tables, and has written three other novels set in the neighborhood. "It was lawless and you liked it that way."

Captain John Goldberg of Mission Station, remembers it much the same way, but prefers to put it differently.

"The donut shop was the focal point for undesirable elements in the Mission," Goldberg said.

Today, Bob's Donuts's storefront window proudly displays a certificate from the Board of Supervisors awarded in 2002 for over 50 years of "service to the community."

But instead of certificates, Hunt's received citations from The City. For the last five years of its life, the Hunt's window displayed an enormous sign, at least 3 feet tall, that announced in bold, red print, "These premises are under court order. Buying and selling of stolen merchandise, panhandling, drug dealing, and loitering are prohibited in this store."

Hunt's Donuts was a thorn in the side of the police at the heart of a neighborhood that has always been a thorn in the side of the police.

The pre-war Mission District was a hardscrabble port of entry for Irish, German, and Jewish immigrants—a sort of Lower East Side for San Francisco. Socialists and anarchists were common in the crowded rooming houses and dining halls of the Mission. There was an IWW hall on Clarion Alley, and Emma Goldman and Alexander Berkman lived on Dolores Street in 1916.

When a bomb went off at a pro-war rally on the Embarcadero that year, police went to the Mission to look for the usual suspects. Police eventually arrested socialists Tom Mooney and Warren K. Billings, who would become the subjects of one of the early 20th century's first huge causes célèbres, when they were both sent to prison for decades for the crime, despite plenty of evidence that they weren't anywhere near the scene of the bombing.

Billings's room was searched and police found several guns. He lived in a boarding house run by a socialist woman at 2410 Mission, the site of today's Ton-Jo room, right next door to the future site of Hunt's.

Plate says he set his novel at 20th and Mission because there is something compelling about the intersection.

"I call it the Bermuda Triangle of Mission real estate," Plate says. "Lives change there and people disappear there. For *Norteños* and *Sureños*, or for police and thieves, it's a heavy place. "

2

Hunt's Quality Donuts opened its doors onto a booming, post-war Mission Street, lined between 16th and 24th streets with furniture storerooms, clothing stores, and diners—the old Miracle Mile, considered the second most important shopping area in The City after Union Square.

Grand art deco neon signs towered over the main drag, vying for the attention of the newly affluent working class families cruising the strip in brand new automobiles. There was Leed's Shoes and El Capitan, and the clock mounted atop the Lochmarquees of the New Mission, the Tower, and the Grand Theaters.

At the center of it all was the donut shop's brand new, fire red sign that featured Frank Hunt's name in one story tall glowing letters. Each letter was encircled by a ring, and, at night, a neon donut would gently fall down the sign, H-U-N-T-S, and splash into a cup of coffee again and again.

Along with the 20th and Mission site, Hunt ran another location in the Marina on Chestnut Street. Hunt donated donuts generously to charities and school rallies and was connected politically, helping campaign for his friend, Mayor Joe Alioto. His shops became a family institution in the old working class Irish Mission and Italian Marina Districts.

Former SF Supervisor and mayoral candidate Angela Alioto still goes with her mother, Angelina, every Sunday to the All-Star Donuts on Chestnut Street, where the Hunt's Donuts of her childhood once stood.

"I grew up at Hunt's Donuts!" Alioto remembers. "My dad and I went to Hunt's every single Sunday right after mass. Dad would buy donuts for his mother and three sisters—four boxes every time."

Suhr, now the Deputy Chief of Field Operations for SFPD, also remembers Hunt's Donuts as a kid. "My dad ran the mortuary on 26th and Valencia," Suhr said. "Every Sunday, he'd bring us home a box of donuts from Hunt's."

By 1970, Hunt ran fourteen successful donut shops throughout the Bay Area and had become head of the Mission Merchants Association. The next year, Mayor Alioto rewarded Hunt for his free donuts at fundraisers with an appointment to the city's Fire Commission. Frank Hunt had come pretty far for a little guy from Shamrock, TX. With glasses perched on a big nose and tiny wisps of cottony hair crowning his bald head, he looked small and slightly comical in photos next to his friend, the robust Alioto. But when the *Chronicle* wrote about Hunt, they called him a "donut tycoon."

Hunt gave his farewell address to the Mission Merchants Association in 1974, celebrating the battles merchants had fought to keep pawn shops and second hand stores out of the Mission. He was a self-made man who believed in the free enterprise system. As he retired he had no way of knowing that his speech was a valedictory tribute to a whole era of chamber of commerce civic boosterism in an almost all-white Mission that had already passed for good.

A few years earlier, a week of explosive events in The City had brought the war between the old and new Mission to the surface. An altercation between white cops and Mission Latino youth in May 1969 left a Mission police officer dead and a group of Latino youths who hung out in front of Hunt's own shop on trial for murder. The resulting trial of Los Siete De La Raza helped change the Mission into a Latino neighborhood in the eyes of The City forever.

3

This November, Oscar Rios, a former four-term mayor of Watsonville, was elected to another term as a city council member in the small agricultural town two hours south of San Francisco where he has served in local government since the late 80s.

In April 1969, Rios was one of the El Salvadoran teenagers that hung out in front of Hunt's Donuts at 20th and Mission.

"That's where everybody met," Rios says. "Either there or the pool hall across the street."

The teenagers who would soon be known as Los Siete De La Raza included Oscar's brother Jose, who hung out there, too.

The teens had attended the College of San Mateo and had become radicalized during a student strike there. Members of the group had also walked the picket line and watched police beat protesters the previous fall at the six-month student and faculty strike at San Francisco State. They had found a social consciousness at school and now urged young Latinos to attend the College Readiness Program, an enrollment program targeting youth of color.

"We would come down (to 20th and Mission) to recruit," remembers Reynaldo Aparicio, a lifelong friend of Rios, who was later active in the Los Siete De La Raza organization that would form to publicize the Los Siete trial. "We would try to politicize the brothers hanging out there to get them so that they could take positive action to change their community."

The kids who hung out in front of Hunt's or the Anchor Billiard Company were just as likely to be politicized by their frequent confrontations with Mission police at the corner, including the infamous plainclothes team out of Mission Station, Brodnik and McGran, that the cops and kids alike called Mission 11.

Joe Brodnik was known on the street for carrying a two-foot rubber hose that he would use to work over uncooperative suspects. Paul McGoran was a huge man, known for his temper and for drinking on duty at Bruno's, across the street from Hunt's, where his girlfriend worked as a waitress.

"We'd see Mission 11 coming in the white truck they drove and we'd split," Rios says. "They were notorious for bullying people."

Brodnick and McGoran, ages 41 and 43 at the time, had both graduated from Mission High School. The Mission District they had been raised in and now patrolled was a changing district in a changing city.

In 1952 when Hunt's Donuts opened, there was not a single taqueria on Mission Street and seven of eleven members of The City's Board of Supervisors were Irish. By 1969, there were no Irish supervisors and The City's Latino population had grown 600% to around 100,000 Latinos. Most of the new immigrants lived in or around the Mission.

In a 1972 book about the Los Siete trial, *Strictly Ghetto Property*, Brodnik's daughter, Colleen, recalls police attitudes towards the new residents of the Mission.

"There was a strong feeling among the police about the brown people of the Mission," Brodnik said. "They said they were going to bring peace to the Mission where the dirty Latinos were."

The police were increasingly being used as the foot soldiers in a city-wide attempt to "clean up" certain neighborhoods. In the Mission, the BART was soon to be built and the Redevelopment Agency was circulating plans for office towers and new condos to be built along 16th and 24th Streets—entirely new redevelopment areas anchored by the new stations. The only Latinos in the agency's proposals were the taco and flower vendors the agency envisioned to be working where a proposed shuttle bus would drop tourists from the BART off at Mission Dolores.

A week before Brodnik's death, a front-page story in the *Chronicle* would ramp up the tension between police and Latinos in the Mission. The story, headlined, "A Gang's Terror in the Mission," was a largely fact-free piece of sensationalistic innuendo describing a reign of terror by the nonexistent "20th Street Gang."

"A loose-knit gang of idlers and hoodlums are slowly closing a fist of fear around the business life of a once bustling Mission District neighborhood," the *Chronicle* wrote.

"The donut shop had a bad image, but we were not in gangs," Rios says. "What they wrote in the paper was a lie."

In a follow up story, members of the Mission Merchants Association—and association president Frank Hunt—dismissed the original story's claims, saying business in the Mission was, in fact, good, and crime in the street was minimal.

"I'm doing better than ever," Hunt told the *Chronicle*. "And I owe it all to the Latinos in the Mission."

But Chief of Police Thomas Cahill, another Mission High graduate with a thick Irish brogue, saw the climate of fear in the article's wake as a chance to push tough, new anti-crime measures in the city. He announced that week that 150 new cops would start patrolling "high crime areas" like 20th and Mission.

Tensions that were already high throughout The City between police and black and brown youths escalated when the Tac Squad raided the Black Panther headquarters on Fillmore Street, just days before Brodnik's death. Police said they had come because a Panther member was speaking into the street through a bullhorn without a permit. The situation escalated into a near riot when police fired tear gas canisters into the Panther storefront and 160 police battled with hundreds of angry black citizens in the streets.

The weeks of tension were about to explode in a gunshot that would change seven lives forever.

May 1st was an unusually hot day. Rios and Aparicio went downtown to check out a "Free Huey" rally at the Federal Building in SF, in honor of the jailed Black Panther leader Huey P. Newton. At the same time, across town in front of Rios's parents' house in Noe Valley at 438 Alvarado Street, Jose Rios and other youths who would soon be known as Los Siete De La Raza—Mario Martinez, Bebe Melendez, Pinky Lescallet, Nelson Rodriguez, and Gio Lopez—were loading furniture out of a van into Rios's house, when a white Dodge pickup truck showed up. It was an unmarked police car driven by Brodnik and McGoran.

Brodnik and McGoran suspected the youths of burglary and started to question them. A scuffle broke out and in the melee McGoran's gun went off twice, killing Brodnik and wounding McGoran.

McGoran would later testify that he was jumped from behind by Lescallet, who took McGoran's gun and shot Brodnik with it. The suspects would testify that McGoran was drunk and aggressive and that he started a fight with Lescallet, in which his gun was accidentally discharged, killing Brodnik and wounding McGoran.

The kids fled the scene. Police filled the neighborhood, raiding Rios's home and shooting 60 rounds of bullets into the walls and furniture.

"We had to leave that day," Rios says, "Our house was totally destroyed."

The youths were all charged with Brodnik's murder. Immediately, Mayor Alioto declared a citywide day of mourning and the *Chronicle* declared the suspects to be "dirty, hippie types." Fearing that the defendants, now know collectively as "Los Siete De La Raza," would be railroaded into the death penalty, the Latino community in the Mission started to organize a campaign on their behalf.

The six defendants—Gio Lopez was never apprehended and soon fled the country—hired Black Panther attorney Charles Garry. Garry, who was also defending Newton, sought to similarly make the case a political trial, highlighting the conditions of poverty and incidents of police brutality in the Mission. The Free Los Siete De La Raza organization, located in a storefront at 21st and Hampshire in the Mission, modeled their defense campaign on Black Panther programs.

To publicize the case, the organization held rallies and protests, but also organized to meet the needs of the Mission Latino community. They started two breakfast programs for elementary school children at St. John's Church on Julian Street and at St. Peter's Church on Alabama Street. They convinced progressive doctors and nurses from San Francisco General Hospital to donate time to the new La Raza Free Medical Clinic that the group opened at 21st and Folsom. They started a newspaper to spread information about the trial, called *Basta Ya*.

"When I got the new issue of *Basta Ya*, I'd always go straight down to the donut shop and sell it," Rios says today. "It was just where everybody was at."

In May 1970, after McGoran's long history of drunkenness and violence had come out on the stand, the jury chose to acquit all six defendants.

Things weren't easy for the former suspects, and over the years they met various fates. The *Chronicle* decried the verdicts and declared that justice had not been served. The youths were under constant surveillance by the police and could not get jobs. Melendez and Lescallet would later get involved in crime and Melendez would be stabbed to death in jail in Tracy in 1977. Lescallet still serves a life sentence in Ione, CA, for the 1979 kidnapping and murder of an elderly school teacher. Lescallet has maintained his innocence to this day.

The Martinez brothers still had to face charges in San Mateo County for stealing a car they used to escape the initial manhunt. Convinced that they would be put away in San Mateo as a penalty for getting off in San Francisco, they fled the country. Today, Tony Martinez is a professor of economics at the University of Mexico City in Mexico, and his brother's whereabouts are unknown.

But the aftereffects of the movement the Los Siete trial birthed in the Mission are still felt today.

"All the things we did then are still happening now," Aparicio says. "The La Raza clinic was eventually taken over by The City and became the Mission clinic on Shotwell. The free breakfast programs became institutionalized by federal government school breakfast and lunch programs."

But, more importantly, the example of immigrants standing up for their rights was instrumental in the Mission becoming recognized as the Latino neighborhood of San Francisco. Throughout the 1970s, contemporaries of Los Siete would form institutions like the Mission Cultural Center and Galeria De La Raza, and work on Latino art programs like the mural project in Balmy Alley that commemorates the struggles in the civil wars of Central America.

"I am friends to this day with people that I met when we went to recruit at the donut shop," says Aparicio, who recently was one of the managers of Renee Saucedo's second place run for Board of Supervisors in the Mission's District Nine. "Most of the people from Free Los Siete are still in the community. They are doctors and lawyers and teachers and they have raised families here in the Mission."

Oscar Rios also has come a long way since police gunfire destroyed his parents' home on Alvarado Street. In 1985, he went to Watsonville to take part in a cannery workers' strike. Soon, he found himself encouraged to run for city council in his new city, when Watsonville had its first district elections in 1988. He went on to become the first Latino mayor in a town long controlled by white agricultural interests, a representative of those who actually worked on Watsonville's farms.

"I was called a dirty illegal immigrant. They said I was just a laborer. But I won," Rios says.

4

By 1993, there were an all-time high of eight donut shops on Mission Street between 16th and 24th Street. After a wave of de-industrialization and real estate speculation, the Mission was out of work and out of luck. The old Miracle Mile drifted into a splendorous disrepair. Dust fell silently in the darkness of abandoned movie theaters, their screens blank after a half century of reels unwound in the dark, working class dreams on the main drag.

Hunt's was often full of old men who lived in the Mission corridor's SRO hotels, men from the long gone port and factories, who wore worn fedoras and argued and laughed. Sometimes it would be almost impossible to see inside because of the amount of cigarette smoke clouding the big windows.

The stasis at Hunt's Donuts echoed the eerie feeling of a Mission Street that seemed to have somehow survived past its prime.

"The donut shop was an anomaly, like the 'Open 25 Hours' sign itself," filmmaker Craig Baldwin, who has lived and worked around the corner for over twenty years, says of the donut shop.

"Time didn't seem to be moving under those fluorescent tubes. It was a place in limbo, like the hour between twenty-four and twenty-five."

The Hunt's art deco falling donut sign, along with the other towering signs from the neighborhood's past, captured the imagination of the punks and artists who were moving into the neighborhood, inheriting the burnt out but still glamorous main drag.

"I always adored the donut shop, like I'd always loved the '17 Reasons Why' sign," Baldwin says, referring to the inscrutable message that stood on top of Thrift Town at 17th Street until 2001. "It was old school, something from Mission history."

Filmmaker Bill Daniel, now splitting time between living in Portland

and traveling the nation interviewing freight train riders for a film, remembers his own fascination with Hunt's.

"I hung out there when I lived on San Carlos in 1988 or '89. I made some audio recordings inside Hunt's; I still have tapes of the jukebox playing some off-brand metal song, mixing with the sounds of the coffee counter, sweeping, and conversations in Spanish."

"I was mesmerized by the sign," says Lance Hahn. After 12 years living in the Mission, Hahn has relocated to Austin and now leads a new lineup of J Church, but Hunt's is still a part of his life.

"When I copyrighted my songs, I named my publishing company 'Open 25 Hours Music,' and to this day, all J Church songs are published under that name."

In 1993, J Church appeared on 17 Reasons Why, a box set of 45's featuring Mission District punk bands singing songs about the Mission. The now legendary sign atop Thrift Town was on the cover.

The songs captured the sweetness and sadness of the downbeat early 90s Mission. Steel Pole Bathtub's song started with a recording of the clacking of an old manual typewriter. Jawbreaker contributed their famous punk rock mix tape essential, "Kiss the Bottle," which evoked lost love and 16th Street hangovers. J Church's own song was "Spilled Corona and the Sound of Mariachi Bands." Hahn remembers the romance in the old world of Hunt's and the Mission.

"Hunt's was a great spot to take a date, because it was in a neighborhood that helped you know immediately how the date was going to go," Hahn said. "Once, I went there with this crazy goth-punk girl named Karrie, and she got a hot dog! That was love."

For their 1994 zine, *You Bet Your Sweet Ass I'm a Turtle*, Matty Luv and Aesop from Hickey wrote of one day's attempt to drink coffee at, hang out in, and write about, every single donut shop in the Mission. Hunt's was their favorite.

Matty had gone to Hunt's for coffee every single morning for the whole year that he dated a girl who lived around the corner on San Carlos Street, because he could not stand the hipster joint, The Club, that was only one block away, at 20th and Valencia, in a now gentrifying parallel Mission universe.

"This is where people go to get the last cup of coffee before they die," Matty wrote. "I love this place!"

"I am convinced this place has a free cup of coffee for anyone with an oozing head wound policy," wrote Aesop.

For punks, the squalor of Hunt's was the principal attraction.

Matty captured an afternoon at Hunt's in 1994 like this:

"Shady dudes out front trying to sell me stolen bicycles, wheel-chair-bound miscreants smoking through tracheotomies, mean counter persons, mismatched tables with 'PUTO' scratched into the formica; and a dazed, old hunchback woman walking from table to table, mumbling, 'Buy me a cup of coffee,' in an evil, nicotine growl."

He summed it up, "Yeah, this place rules."

"Hunt's was a great place for punks to go, drunk and stumbling, and at times I'd go every other night," remembers Hahn. "When I lived with Jawbreaker in the notorious Sycamore Street house, we would try to get to Hunt's at 4:00 AM when the new donuts would come out of the oil."

"Perfect for those 2:00 AM drunken donut quests," Aesop wrote in *Turtle*. "But, buyer beware: you could get shot."

Aesop's warning is echoed to this day for posterity, in a panel of a mural painted by my old roommate, Greta, in 1995 in Clarion Alley, as part of the Clarion Alley Mural Project. Along with people playing soccer in Dolores Park and a couple drinking beers at Original McCarthy's, she painted a scene of someone buying a donut at Hunt's while watching someone getting shot outside, under the neon donut sign.

5

Roger and Lin Chao, immigrants from Cambodia, bought Hunt's Donuts in 1995 and renamed it Magic Donuts. They added some plants and new tables and brought the donut shop into the 90s by introducing different sizes and flavors of coffee and getting rid of the jukebox. But 20th and Mission would change them more than they could change it.

Like the Latino Mission teenagers standing out front of the shop, the Chaos had traveled a long and improbable road to wind up at 20th and Mission in San Francisco. Roger Chao had come to the United States from Cambodia in 1980. Roger and Lin had camped in the Cambodian Jungle for six months to escape from Pol Pot's dictatorship.

Their arrival in the Mission came at a time when many Asian immigrants were now making North Mission their first stop in their new country. It also came at a time when Cambodians had come to dominate the entire California donut industry.

According to *Asian Week* magazine, by the year 2000, there were approximately 5000 independently owned donut shops in California and, incredibly, 90% of them were owned by Cambodians.

Owning a donut shop had become "a way for Cambodian immigrants to become part of the American Dream," Dennis Wong of the Asian Business Association told the magazine in 2000.

Upon his arrival in the US, Roger Chao started working for minimum wage at two Southern California donut shops in the Winchell's chain, working the morning shift at one and then going straight to the night shift at the other, saving up to one day own his own shop.

Magic Donuts was their chance. The falling neon donut sign, still standing tall over the dividing line between red and blue gang turf, was a beacon of hope, a symbol of a chance for a better tomorrow for the Chaos. The family moved to Hayward and worked day and night to make the new shop in The City a success.

While the Chaos were hiding out in the Cambodian jungle, young Greg Suhr was playing high school age baseball in a citywide summer league for the Irving Street Embers, a team sponsored by an Irish bar in the Inner Sunset.

"Hunt's Donuts was the team to beat," Suhr now remembers of the team of Mission and Balboa High School kids that Frank Hunt sponsored. "They were absolutely the New York Yankees of the San Francisco high school summer league baseball."

Suhr could never beat Hunt's Donuts on the baseball diamond, but he would try again later in life. "Who knew one day I'd be the Captain of the Police Department, running sting operations and trying to bust people in there for stolen property?" mused Suhr.

In a series of successful undercover operations, plainclothes police were able to sell stolen jewelry to Magic Donut employees on several occasions over a series of months in 1996. The Chaos fired the employees and spent even more time in the shop themselves.

A sign reading, "Warning: Please do not sale or buy merchandise inside the coffee shop. Thank You." went up in the place where the Shroud of Turin print had once hung. But the Chaos were woefully unprepared to deal with the forty years of criminal history that they had inherited with the shop.

"The family that ran that place was helpless to stop the problems there," Suhr says. "It was in a critical location, on the dividing line between *Norteños* and *Sureños*."

Little did the Chaos know, but when they called the police to complain about drug dealing or fighting in front of the store, the incidents were being compiled in a file that the police were hoping to use to shut the donut shop at the Epicenter of Crime down completely.

And they weren't the only ones complaining about the incidents in front of the shop. The Mission was now full of people who had come there in hopes of turning a slice of Mission real estate into a new life.

A couple of blocks away from the shop, Lexington Street was filling up with young, white dot-commers who were buying old Victorians on the tree-lined street and fixing them up. The new residents of Lexington were also unprepared for their new neighborhood's criminal history, but unlike the Chaos, they were more in a position to do something about it.

Soon a neighborhood watch group called The Lexington Lookouts had formed. Fittingly, the new group met not in person, but online. Their chatrooms overflowed with complains about the donut shop and the group made it a point to call the police every time they saw something they thought might be criminal there.

It is not certain whether it was the heat from the Lexington Lookouts or something else that brought Office Ludlow into the picture. There is much of recent Mission history that can't be traced with empirical facts. It is a history that is at times sensed more than actually verifiably known.

But this much is indisputable: in the late 90s, as the dot-com money flooded the neighborhood, all the cheap, working class Latino bars in the neighborhood gradually closed and became trendy, upscale hotspots that catered to the Silicon Valley newcomers. On many Saturday nights, Officer Jim Ludlow, the permit officer working out of Mission Station, could be found at bars like Docs Clock and Treat Street, bragging to bartenders, door guys, and the newly affluent dot-com clientele about how he personally made it all happen.

While rising rents were driving out Latino and working class renters in the neighborhood, the situation with the bars was more complicated. Because of the moratorium on liquor licenses, you could not simply buy a bar in the Mission, no matter how much money you had. A bar would need to close and sell their license first. This is where Ludlow came in.

Ludlow had announced to the *New Mission News* in 1996 that he was going to shut down all the bars on his "bad bars list" which he gave to the paper to print. One by one, Ludlow fined and ticketed the bars for various code violations until he had, in fact, closed many of them. Then, new buyers came in to the neighborhood and bought up the liquor licenses at a bargain.

Perhaps coincidentally, all the bars on this list were Latino owned and operated, and the new buyers were young and white. Ludlow, whose father and father's father had been Irish SFPD cops, now avenged Brodnik and McGoran in the Mission. Instead of a two-foot rubber hose, he carried a citation book.

Many in the Mission speculated that Ludlow was taking a cut of the profits to help broker these deals. Adam White, the owner of Mission Records, says that when White first met the landlord to rent the Mission Records space at 18th and Mission—the former 7 Coins of Gold Bar—Ludlow himself showed up with another group of prospective tenants. Ludlow assured this group of tenants in front of the landlord and White that he could personally make sure they got their liquor license for a new bar there.

Whether Ludlow was on the take or not has never been proven, but it is known that he hated Hunt's Donuts. In 1996, he took steps to shut it down. Hunt's, Johnny Donuts on 16th and Valencia, and the Western Donut at 16th and Mission did not have permits to remain open 24 hours—let alone 25 hours.

The Western Donut and Johnny Donuts would have to close from 2 to 6 AM as a result of Ludlow's efforts. But the Chaos were able to go to court to get a conditional use permit that would keep them open all night.

Unfortunately for Ludlow, the law he was now enforcing also caused the Happy Donuts at the very low crime corner of 24th and Church in Noe Valley to close from 2 to 6 AM, too.

This time, Ludlow had gone too far. Happy Donuts was the coffee shop of choice for police from Mission and Ingleside stations.

"Everyone's unhappy, including the commander," Ludlow told the *SF Weekly* in 1996. "He was roaming the district one night and couldn't get a cup of coffee and he said, 'What the heck is going on?'"

Ludlow on his own was no match for the shop at the Epicenter of Crime. But soon the piles of complaints added up against Hunt's. Using calls to the police and results of police sting operations as evidence, The City Attorney served the Chaos with a public nuisance complaint in 1999, claiming that it was the shop and not the street corner itself causing all the crime. Eventually, after paying thousands of dollars in legal bills, the Chaos decided to settle out of court in 2000 and pay the city nearly $10,000 in fines.

"I felt so bad for that family that I even offered to get my own coffee there every morning," Suhr remembers. "It seemed like a big gesture for the captain of the police station to come in and personally buy coffee from them. It showed we were paying attention."

The late 90s was an intense time in the Mission. People are still not sure exactly what happened. As the decade ended, there was even a rumor on the street that Ludlow was going to close Hunt's so that a Starbucks could move to 20th and Mission, a move that would be the symbolic death of the old, lawless Mission. By 2000, the falling donut sign, now broken, seemed to sum up the era. The neon donut no longer fell slowly into the cup, but raced frantically through all the stages in seconds, broadcasting a slightly nauseating, hyper-stressed amphetamine twitch to the neighborhood every night.

Whether Suhr's extra attention was a comfort or not to Roger Chao in those times, we'll never know. In early 2001, after years of police harassment and near bankruptcy from legal fees and fines, Roger Chao died of a heart attack. He was only 40.

6

In the Mission, old battles never end. They just change shape and appearance, often on the same site.

For instance, today's era of cutthroat real estate speculation came to the Mission when the Gartland Apartments at 16th and Valencia burned to the ground in a suspected landlord arson in 1975, killing 12 and leaving over a hundred people without homes.

When a new building finally grew out of the pit 15 years later, the ground floor storefront featured a donut shop that was always full of homeless people.

Sometimes the battles just move from generation to generation. My own file on Hunt's Donuts is now overflowing with odd, little irreducible facts that I don't know what to do with—facts somehow peripheral and yet somehow completely related—like this one that I turned up about Officer Jim Ludlow's father.

In 1961, Jose Sarria, the first openly gay man to run for SF Board of Supervisors, was running for office. Jim Ludlow, Sr. reacted to changing times by initiating the police raid on the Tat-Bush Cafe at Taylor and Bush Streets, the largest police raid on a gay bar in the history of the city.

The arrest jailed "101 sexual deviants." Ludlow told the *Chronicle* that he called for the paddy wagons when he saw "25 people dancing and none of them were women."

These layers of history do not sit quite well with each other, especially not in the Mission. There is a feeling sometimes that battles like those that took place at 20th and Mission are still happening, just below the surface.

In 1999, the Mission Branch of the SF Public Library put out a call for old family snapshots from Mission families to be donated to an archive that the library was putting together.

When it opened, I went to look at it. There were eight binders full of family photos. Black and white photos of Irish cops' funeral processions along Guerrero Street were archived in the photo albums next to color photos of Carnival.

In one photo, there is a strong, healthy-looking man, grinning in black and white on the steps of Mission High School. The caption says, "Joe Brodnik in 1948, the year he graduated from Mission High. He was later a police officer and was killed by the Latino Los Siete group."

Another, in color, shows a woman, grinning, holding a child. It says, "Judy Drummond with her daughter. Judy was in the Los Siete organization."

The photo albums don't explain why this gentle-looking woman with the child would join a group that kills cops. There was a disconnect, or at least evidence of an uneasy truce, in the binder's pages.

I went to the librarian at the reference desk and showed her the Brodnik caption. Innocently, I said, "This caption says that Brodnik was killed by the Los Siete. But the members of Los Siete were acquitted of the crime. It shouldn't say they killed him in a book in the library when they were actually found not guilty."

Instead of shrugging and saying she'd look into it, as I'd expected, the woman became livid and started yelling at me, right there in the library. "How am I supposed to know what's on every single thing in there?" she yelled. I had touched a nerve. I studied her more closely. She was in her late 50s or early 60s, most likely. Blonde hair, freckles.

Her name plate said "Colleen."

The two views of Mission history still clash at 20ᵗʰ and Mission.

The last couple of years of Magic Donuts depressingly mirrored many of the increasingly hard times for immigrants and longtime Mission residents. The donut shop had become a place where you could see 19-year-old prostitutes get hit by 17-year-old pimps. It was the place where Chao's nieces, Chan and Ran, worked all night in the shop before taking the early BART back to Hayward to attend high school.

In the last few months of the shop, there was often a 12-year-old boy working all night, alone.

Today, the Sierra Hotel, a 55 unit SRO hotel, remains empty across the street from the boarded up donut shop. The tenants were evicted during the dot-com times from the hotel above the site of the old Anchor Billiard Hall where Rios and Aparicio once recruited.

The donut shop's landlord, Bradley Jones of Novato, refuses to say what kind of business will soon occupy the shop's site. The workers on the site all say it will be a pharmacy.

The closing of the shop after 52 years signals the end of an era for the neighborhood and asks what will come next for the Mission, the longtime thorn in the side of police. A clue to the direction of things to come might be next door where the old neighborhood working class bar, the Ton-Jo Room, is now being threatened with losing its lease.

Ton-Jo Room bartender Richard is a big guy with longish, combed back gray hair and the tough-sounding, old Mission accent that is more Brooklyn than California. He is 68 but looks like he could easily fight and beat men half his age. He was born in the Mission and has lived there his whole life.

"This is the neighborhood, what's left of it," Richard says, looking over a half-full bar of regulars, drinking at noon. "It's not just the same people every day. They sit in the same seats and order the exact same drinks every day."

At the Ton-Jo Room, time seems to stand still, like it once did at Hunt's in the 25ᵗʰ hour. It already seems like something out of the Mission's past, like a black and white photo in the library archive on 24ᵗʰ Street.

The Ton-Jo Room space is currently up for lease on Craigslist. The ad calls 20ᵗʰ and Mission "the most improved part of the Mission," and seeks a tenant to turn the building where Warren K. Billings once hid his guns into a nightclub "within two blocks of the Foreign Cinema and the Andorra Bed and Breakfast."

The real estate agent leasing the Ton-Jo Room is Kevin Strain. I called him to ask him if he knew what might be built in the old Hunt's site. I casually mentioned that I was working on a story about the history of the donut shop.

Strain responded with a completely unprovoked rant, yelling into the phone, uninterrupted for 3 or 4 full minutes.

"You're writing a history of the donut shop? What? A history of pimps, dealers, and whores!?!" he bellowed into the phone. "I can tell from your accent that you're not from around here. Well, let me tell you something. I'm six generations in this city since my family came from Ireland. The Mission is going to be gentrified and there's nothing you socialists who live down there can do about it!"

At 20th and Mission, so one chapter ends as another appears to have begun. But the Epicenter of Crime exerts a curious hold on people. As if on cue, the white hipsters imported to the neighborhoods to "clean it up" have turned to drugs, too. The gang members still come from as far away as El Salvador or Mexico, only to fight each other at an imaginary line dividing the Mission at 20th Street. Is it a new chapter, after all? Or is it the same old film, years of grainy, black and white Hunt's Donuts surveillance camera footage spinning off the reel?

The film that plays again and again in a closed loop. Somewhere in the 25th hour.

THE CITY THAT NEVER WAKES UP

Market Street. A hangover, a blur. I see myself from above, lost in a crowd at Market and 8th, milling around at the heart of The City's Farmer's Market in UN Plaza. There is a murmur, a hum. At the edge of the crowd, a grinning, bearded man sitting on a crate guards a bucket of crabs he's selling. The Black Market. There is something timeless, historical in the looks on the faces of the shoppers examining produce, the homeless men reclining on the lawn. Red bricks and the smell of piss. This is as close to Europe as this self-styled "Paris of the West" ever really gets.

No one knows how it got this way, but this place, UN Plaza, is at the heart of everything happening in The City these days, where everyone comes to get The News. The homeless in the Plaza are the real people that the candidates in the upcoming election are talking about when they talk about "Fixing the Homeless Problem." The mayor wants to use the cops to push them out of sight. His opponents want to put them on the news, a smear on Willie Brown's record. Food Not Bombs wants to feed them. The cops want to arrest them. Activists film the cops trying to harass them, to embarrass the cops. And when Brown ordered the cops to start seizing the homeless' shopping carts, news crews from every TV station in town flooded the plaza to film the shopping carts. Suddenly, shopping carts were front pages news, and UN Plaza was brought to people's living rooms. The former mayor even came out and warned Mayor Brown not to take the carts, not to get involved in a battle at UN Plaza, because that's what cost him the LAST election.

And, sure enough, the Mayor retreated and left the carts alone. There is something going on in UN Plaza that threatens to bring down anyone who gets involved in it.

This year, my own life keeps coming back to UN Plaza, too. Walking through it on my way to work, or on my way to the GA office. Walking past it sometimes on my way to the Free Clinic, my mind preoccupied with various health problems that, without money, remain undiagnosed. It's a place where the very idea of "San Francisco" is stretched too thin. No hills and cable cars here. All the stores sell postcards of someplace else. But I keep coming back.

There should be a mid-Market Street postcard. This is a misunderstood part of town. Deep in the shadows of downtown skyscrapers, you will find the "Instant I.D." store where a man behind the corner makes photo I.D.'s and uses whiteout on the part where the name goes, if you want him to. You can be anyone, or disappear anytime... There is the store that actually sells the designer plastic baggies that drugs come in, the ones with the heart designs or the shamrocks on them. They have boxes and boxes locked away upstairs, possibly handcrafted in a sweatshop in Malaysia. Where they come from no one knows, but they fill the gutters of Market Street... And there's Andy's Sunrise Juice Bar, where each sunrise finds Andy's as boarded-up as the day before. Next door, across the street from UN Plaza, is a long wooden fence covered in a mural. To anyone walking past, it's just a painting, but if you stop and look through the hole in the fence, the other side shows a trash-filled crater, right on Market. Huge rats run there, across broken glass and rubble, just out of sight, 24 hours a day. This is it, the other side of the postcard. The Heart of The City.

There are moments from my walks in UN Plaza this year that are etched in my mind vividly, silent moments with a certain dreamlike poetry. Coming up from the escalator out of MUNI, watching how each step of the escalator has a name graffitied on it, and how they all rise up slowly and disappear into the machine; an old Asian man silently handing a live chicken to another man in the Farmer's Market; newspapers blowing across the plaza, past men in blankets... But I also remember all the protests. I remember playing drums with my band with the statue behind us at a "Stop The Bombing in Yugoslavia!" rally in May, and how the sound guy cut the rally short and the speakers were just old socialists, anyways. I remember the crowd silently dispersing, cheated, as the sun disappeared behind a bank of afternoon fog, and summer suddenly seemed to have disappeared.

I'm back in UN Plaza again when the Free Mumia march gets herded through the plaza, all of us angrily holding torches aloft. It's dark and hard to see. A paint bomb silently flies out of the crowd to splatter the statue with white paint. I wonder why we're marching into the plaza at all and not on to wide-open Market Street. It seems like another trick. And it is. The cops surround us easily in the plaza. As they announce that we're all under arrest, everyone charges the police line.

I'm with a crowd of 15 or 20 who escape by running through the library, back out through the front doors on to Market Street. Back at the line in the plaza, the cops are beating people up.

In the morning, it was like it never happened. It didn't make the papers. It's not even in the books the library took off the shelf and hid away in storage under Civic Center. But it happened, and it happened in the plaza.

Yes, UN Plaza. A place where something is happening that threatens to bring down anyone who gets involved. And I keep going back. It's not abstracted, like the headlines of the papers blowing past on Market, or the language of my friends' eviction papers. It's not something that's happening to someone else, like the booming economy. I have to check my I.D. when I walk past the "Instant I.D." place, and look at the name again. I look at the crater through the hole in the fence, and I can feel a place like that growing somewhere inside of me. Someplace dark, like an Eddy Street bar, pitch-black at noon; hidden away, like a room at the end of a hall on the top floor of the Alder. A place that never changes, the bottom of the broken elevator shaft at the Seneca, where pigeons murmur and rats run in the dark.

A place that's always there. My own bench in UN Plaza.

Back in UN Plaza, newspapers blow past. The names on the escalators rise up and disappear. The man with the bucket of crabs has found a buyer. There's a murmur, a hum. The afternoon fog rolls in. A chill hangs in the air over the men lining the benches. The new decade yawns and stretches ahead. This whole scene is frozen in my mind, a picture of something ABOUT to happen. I pass some guy with carts, drinking beer and camping, and remember a lost TV ad from my childhood. "It doesn't get any better than this." I think it will get better. It HAS to. In an Eddy Street bar at noon, in the basement of Mission Station, backstage at The Strand, all is still. It's the sound of The City, waiting to wake up.

INTERVIEW WITH ZARA THUSTRA Pt. 3

In late 2000, when the gentrification battles of the Mission had reached their highest intensity before everything rolled back, many of the community groups that had been fighting back in the Mission decided to come together under the banner of the Mission Anti-Displacement Coalition (MAC). For a while, it truly seemed like anything would go. Old Latino organizers were working side by side with white punks and tagger kids. There was a feeling of excitement that it was all new, that you couldn't tell where it would end up.

At one point Zara approached MAC and offered to do wheat-pasting for them. They told him to go out and tell people to do wheat-pasting, graffiti, whatever! It was time, they said, to see a unified neighborhood identity in street art and it didn't matter whether it was legal or not.

We ended up making huge posters reading "No Nos Vamos" (We won't go) in bold, black text on white paper and wheat-pasting them all over the neighborhood. The blocks of text looked impressive as I rode past the next day, the whole neighborhood's sentiment, now visible in the streets, united against gentrification.

The community groups' efforts against new live/work lofts and condo development in The Mission would coincide with the return of district elections to San Francisco. After years of being chosen by citywide vote counts, The City's 12 members of the Board of Supervisors would now be chosen neighborhood by neighborhood, making it far easier for grassroots candidates to win election to the board. In the landmark November 2000 elections, progressive, anti-Brown candidates—including Green Party member, Matt Gonzalez, won a majority of the seats on the Board and ushered in what progressives heralded as a new era in city politics.

What about the MAC show at the 16ᵗʰ/Mission BART? That really stands out in my mind as a turning point for a lot of people...

ZARA: We were trying to put all these ideas into action and make it happen. At the BART, we had a cabaret night right on the street. We had an MC. We cooked like 200 burritos and gave them away with Kool-Aid. The MC's talking about good shit, the bands' songs are all about stuff that's happening right now... we had music, bilingual literature. It was tactful and reaching out and not didactic. It was about speaking specifically for yourself, like, "I am a white activist, non-native to SF, who is going to try to step up and take responsibility for my actions," and not trying to speak FOR Latinos. It comes off real when you speak from a true space. There are people with a lot of different experiences watching at a street show, but they can respect you if you're honest.

I liked how MAC let us do whatever we could to spread their message. The pamphlet we made for that show was just bilingual info about MAC and a general call to come to their meetings.

ZARA: Yeah. The show had neighborhood youth come talk and games for the crowd. It was a thin line between corny and innovative.

I think a lot of people started coming together at the end of the dot-com times like, "Fuck! We're the last people still here! We have to fix this!" What were some specific things you remember from that time and how future activism grew out of that time?

ZARA: It was an intense time. I'd been evicted a few times and was pretty stressed out and MAC was a good place to put my energy. MAC was the first structured activist thing I'd ever been involved with. That was like 3, 4 meetings a week. I started to realize what I could bring to the situation. MAC would say, "We're going to show up at this office and call this landlord out and get him to stop this fucked up shit!" and it was clear to me that there needed to be some visuals and someone trying to bring out a vibrant message. There was the SF Print Collective doing a lot of posters at that time. We did billboards, banners. MAC was writing these propositions, pieces of legislation, and we were backing them with our public art. That was fun. I wish that shit was happening now. I wish there were some liberal, crazy folks bashing shit out in this city that we could all support as a community, because right now, as a community, we're still fighting back.

Instead of offering support, how can we turn it around to be about what we're FOR? If you paint something, you're trying to bring something new into the world, to make The City look more like how you want it to look. How does that evolve into strong statements as a group? To be saying, "This is what we want!"

ZARA: I don't know. I think about it all the time. We're all trying to make these cultural events, but I think capitalization and commoditization of expression leads you into making self-serving art and also doing it singularly. As far as painting and making the city look a certain way, well... we all want culture. We don't want whitewashed bullshit. When we go out to paint and we all ask each other what we're going to paint, that's culture. When we think about providing free food for others beside ourselves, we're saying what we want to happen in our community. I struggle with it because it seems really self-important to say, "I'm trying to change the community and I'm trying to change the world." But if we weren't all trying to do that than I think we'd be getting real depressed and taking Paxil.

CHRISTMAS DAY 1999

Lately, my favorite thing has just been hanging out in the train yard. I like to go down there and walk around, spray painting messages on the trains for my friends in other cities. The thing is, they always get them, too. My graffiti somehow gets where it needs to go. I remember Brad and Mike telling me about sitting in the yard in Richmond, on their way down to Miami, watching car after car of my tags go by. Or the time I went on a date in the Alameda Tunnel and later the girl I'd been there with saw the boxcar in another city with "I left my heart in Alameda Tunnel" written on it. One time Anandi was hopping out of Portland, working on a letter to me, and an open boxcar that said "Scam Punks" went by. She should have just put the letter in it! I like going down there to the train yard to miss everybody in the other towns and my friends out there on the road, too. And to hear the ball rattle in the can in the quiet yard, and savor that "End of the World," no-one-else-around feeling.

On Christmas, Ivy and Ian had this cool party. They put out flyers that said "Fuck Christmas! Let's Paint!" and directed everyone to just show up at this wall down in the abandoned, rundown warehouse district by the port to paint murals. They had tons of stolen and donated paint and food and a Bar-B-Q to cook up the veggie dogs. Jimmy brought the generator, of course, and a stereo, and Tracy brought a couple crates of records! Since it was Christmas, the whole city was deserted, and we truly owned the streets. Soon, there were 10 or 15 people painting, records blasting, and food cooking.

As the murals got more elaborate, we started adding to our party. Anandi and I found a couch and dragged it over and put it in the middle of the street. Then, we found some orange cones and put them around us to make it look official. When cars came, they had to go around.

After a while I set out to explore the port. Since it was Christmas, there were all these places you could go where you normally couldn't. I walked all around there, then went into the neighborhood junkyard and climbed to the top of that huge 5-story crane with the graffiti all over it. I'd always wanted to go up there.

Looking down towards the party, I could watch the walls slowly fill up with pictures and look out at the whole city at the same time. In a couple days, supposedly, the computers would all shut down and maybe the world would end and all that. I didn't really think anything would happen, but I was really hoping it would. I could use a couple weeks more like this day.

But what will we do when nothing happens? It seems like, my whole life, people have been waiting for some big event—the end of the world, the revolution. In SF now, people even talk openly of waiting for a huge earthquake to come scare off the yuppies and destroy all the banks. But what if you just lived how you wanted to, instead of waiting? What if we wanted "the beginning" instead of the end?

I left the crane and headed back to the party. It was getting dark. I figured if we started some trash can fires in the street and just had a few more beers we'd really be on our way.

COMMUNITY CONTROL

PART TWO: 949 MARKET

"WE WANTED TO DO SHOWS THAT WEREN'T PROTESTS, BUT WERE MORE ABOUT WHAT WE'RE FOR. SHOWS THAT ASKED WHAT DO WE WANT THE CITY TO LOOK LIKE? HOW CAN WE MAKE IT HAPPEN? SHOWS THAT REMIND PEOPLE OF THE POWER THEY DO HAVE?"

The MAC times were about fighting back. But by the beginning of 2001, the economy was finally failing, there was the new Board of Supervisors, and we felt like we had more breathing room. That's when 949 Market came about...

ZARA: That was more like a celebration. The readers may now know that was an epic show for us here. There were 500 or 600 people there and a lot of people saying, "We're ready to get back to life!" after four years of straight dot-com crush...

You can put on events that really change your life. That night felt like that...

We wanted to do shows or art events that were more about what we are FOR than what we are against. I'm not saying we shouldn't protest; George Bush will certainly keep our hands full with that these next four years. I'm just saying that I'm tired of being expected to self-identify as someone under attack, someone who is powerless and who is being forced out. We wanted to do shows that asked, "What do we WANT the city to look like? How can we make it happen? If we really had all the space everyone says they need to do stuff, what exactly WOULD we do with it?" We wanted to do shows that remind people of the power that they actually DO have.

We had weekly meeting to generate ideas. Could we paint illegal murals in broad daylight that were so big that everyone would just ASSUME they were legal? What about breaking into Mission houses where the tenants had been evicted, and having punk shows with kegs and spray paint? We're trying to come up with ideas of how to take public visual space away from for-profit advertising, how to take housing stock out of for-profit real estate speculation.

You might think it is easier to meet and come up with these ideas than to actually carry them out. However, when I reached my sixth month of having no home and considered my dwindling prospects, I was reminded of how decisive action is so much easier when you don't have any options. When I heard about a vacant two-story Victorian with electricity and running water on sunny Shotwell Street in the Mission that was scheduled to be torn down, I cheerfully dusted off the old crowbar and bolt cutters and, a couple days later, I had a new place to live—a squat!

There is really no such thing as an abandoned building in the Mission these days. Every precious square foot is priced, taxed, owned, rented, coveted, and, ultimately, police-protected. But this turn-of-the-century Victorian with fancy old wood floors was available for the moment. According to the work permit stapled to the front, the house would soon be gutted and turned into an expansive one story loft-like cube with a massive parking garage inside where the first floor currently was. Only the historic façade would remain, leaving a feel-good SF postcard look that is, in fact, mandated by a strict preservation law. My dim hope was not that I could one day own the place through obscure squatter's rights, but that there would be a stock market crash, or an earthquake, something to derail the developer's plans or cause them to run out of money before they could start work—the inevitable shifts in history that market analysts have come to call "corrections."

Everyone has a dream about a space in this town, a dream that hinges on real estate. We do posters and put them up at the bus stop because we have nowhere to do what we want. We put on illegal hit and run shows at the BART station because we have no show spaces, or we do graffiti. We're always doing things that are kind of fleeting. But what if, instead of protesting all the time, you had all the time and space you needed to create something? What would you do with it?

All I really wanted out of my new squat was a quiet room to put a desk in so I could just sit and write. But the young gutterpunks who moved into the upstairs unit were thinking much bigger. They printed out a copy of the so-called "adverse possession law" from the Internet and started making five- and ten-year plans for our new house. Looking out over the empty lot behind the squat, last week's 5th and Market Street drinkers were transformed by the dream. "We could turn this lot into a community garden!" they announced. "We'll build a fence and paint murals on it and turn this squat into a community art center where little kids can come after school and paint!" It was pretty ambitious, but what is a dream about space but a dream about who we might be? What is a city, if not the aspirations of the people who live in it?

This, of course, made it especially poignant when our "community center" was rather unceremoniously evicted by a single cop and a handful of weathered old Irish construction workers a mere two weeks after we moved in. On eviction day, I was invited next door to commiserate by a sympathetic neighbor.

"It's a shame," he said. "Those kids were dumb, but I kind of liked them. And what's going to happen in that space anyway? They're just going to gut the inside and take out all that history. It's just going to leave a FAÇADE? What is that—a fucking Hollywood set or something?"

He talked about his own work in the neighborhood. "I'm a builder. When I go into these old houses around here to work, I see how well made they are, how old the wood is. It's overwhelming. I just think, 'A hundred years!' Like, how much has HAPPENED there, how many people have LIVED in these homes? You ever think about that?"

I said I did, all the time. I thought about the Mission houses, built with trees brought over from New Zealand because Northern California had already been deforested by the turn-of-the-century. I thought about the different layers of time on these streets, all long gone, but also all still there, at the same time, like rings in a tree.

FINDING THE SPACE

ERICK: Didn't you used to play pool at 949 Market when it was still a pool hall in the 80s?

(Jimmy Broustis has been 34 for four years and sings and plays guitar in the band Shotwell, a band known for playing illegal, hit and run shows on the streets of the Mission. Shotwell played the opening of the squat.)

JIM: Yeah! That was Palace Billiards going way back. It was pretty classic. The tables were old. There were a few modern Brunswicks in there, but there were some really nice old snooker tables, like the European crafted jobs. This was like '84, '85... I was 19 or 20... They had a bar in there. There were a lot of pool tables and people were always on them. It seemed like a late-night, after-hours place you could go to after the bars closed.

ERICK: What was it like to go back in there with us, so many years later?

JIM: For the first five minutes I was like, "What is this? What IS this?" Then it clicked. "Whoa!" It was weird with fifteen years of dust and the major pool table removal.

ERICK: What did you feel when you first saw the space?

(Ivy, 25, was involved with the space from the beginning, helping clean the space and painting murals in it.)

IVY: When I walked in for the first time, I felt pretty excited because it was so huge and it didn't have tons of clutter like a lot of abandoned spaces usually have. You could tell that you could do something really great there.

(Zara, 25, has been with the squat since day one. He has been cranking out quality artwork since 1991. Enjoys politics, and walks in the park, no beef—both meat and street grief!)

ZARA: Well, I'm a fan of buildings, you know. I thought it was really nice when we first went in there. It was a nice quiet place really. It was nice to go in there by yourself.

ERICK: It was a big empty space where you could feel free to imagine pretty much anything happening. Zara and I agreed we wanted to put on a big show with a lot of people we know involved, the people we know always need a space to do what they want.

(Anandi, 28, an integral part in the formation of the squat cafe, modeled after The Hangover Cafe, a collective cafe she helped run in Portland, OR.)

ANANDI: That place was a squat because there aren't any places for rent here. If we were somewhere else, that wouldn't have been what people would've been looking for. They probably would've just rented a cheap place.

ERICK: Zara noticed that the sandwich shop and the St. Francis Theater had closed. So now this whole block of buildings was abandoned. So first we went into the theater.

ZARA: I went into the St. Francis Theater specifically thinking that was the place we could do a huge show in, but there had been some exploratory construction in there to look at the foundation and the whole bottom was gutted. The place was just completely destroyed, dirt everywhere. So I went into 949, which was right next door.

IVY: Zara told me he'd originally broken into the space just to paint his name on the huge windows because they faced Market Street, but when he saw the space, he realized this was worth more than just his name on a window. It could be really huge.

PLANNING

Zara and I had been scheming for ages on a way to get a space to do anything. Whatever the size of the space turned out to be would decide what we could do with it. But we had a list of like twenty things: we could have the free food program or the newspaper office or the art space, etc., etc. But 949 Market was a space that was so big it could be whatever you could imagine it to be. It was the kind of space where everyone we know that needed a space could go in there and contribute.

ZARA: First there were three weeks of cleaning. Almost five days a week for the first couple weeks and then we all got tired and took a couple days' break. Then we started to organize days of cleaning because the shit was just not getting cleaned fast enough and it was dirty as fuck. You'd have to mop the floor like five times. We had to vacuum the whole space over and over again and it was still dusty. Fuck, the whole first week we had to wear masks. We also had to put curtains over the holes in the walls and to paint a couple things. And fix some of the fixtures like the counter.

(Melissa, 30, writes fiction zine, Inkling, and performed a spoken-word piece between bands at the first show.)

MELISSA: It seems like there were a lot of people who sort of floated through helping in one way or another. But did you have meetings of the core of people? How many people was that?

ZARA: Altogether it was about 10 to 13 people. We would all sit down and discuss what we wanted to happen and we would discuss how we would do it. One of the interesting things about the core group of people was that anybody could be the core person. All they had to do was show up. If you showed up you had a voice. And if you showed up you were also expected to keep your voice in check as far as showing up and not trying to run the shit right off the bat. And a lot of people didn't go to meetings but helped.

ERICK: What do you feel like your relationship to the space was?

JIMMY: I didn't feel like I really had one, exactly. I just cleaned up some dirt and helped move a lot of weird old stuff around.

MELISSA: It seems like there was something magical, as far as needing something and it just kind of appearing in one way or another.

IVY: There were the three abandoned spaces connected to the show space, like the old theater. Those spaces already had everything in them that we needed to do our event! We found the tables and chairs for the squat cafe in the abandoned sandwich shop. The space provided all... I said, "There's no believing in the Lord, just believe in the space."

ERICK: Yeah, like there were theater seats, so we decided we should build a theater in the squat and show films. When we found the popcorn tubs we were like, "Now we should serve free food, because we have these huge disposable containers to serve food in."

MELISSA: How did you get electricity and water for the space?

ZARA: I was with Erick and we found the electrical fuse box and just started flipping switches. After we flipped one—it was the bathroom switch—the hand dryer just came on in the bathroom. It went "rrRROOOOM!" Pretty random, huh?

ERICK: Someone must've hit the hand dryer button like 13 years ago right before they turned it all off, and it was waiting to go on all this time.

ZARA: Water was pretty hard. We broke into all the abandoned storefronts downstairs in the other part of the building looking for the main water switch, but we couldn't get any on. So we went into the St. Francis looking for water. When we turned it on, the water just went "WOOOOSH!" through the whole building's pipes. The situation was now that the water source was in the theater, 50-75 feet away from the pool hall bathrooms and sinks that we'd need to have working on opening night and to clean beforehand. But we found hoses in the theater. In case construction workers came by for any reason, we had the hose run from the theater sink going up through the ceiling, out an air vent, up on the roof, into the pool hall window, into a sink in the pool hall bathroom. We had this one hose to get water to clean the whole space!

MELISSA: Could you talk about how you guys decided what to paint and what kind of painting ended up there? And did you want to have a theme?

ZARA: We all sat down and we discussed how it would look good. Pretty much everyone that participated, we asked them to do something around "community," but we also asked them to put effort into their work. Then we painted for like three weeks. 20 to 25 people threw up really good murals in there.

ERICK: When Ivy asked me what the basic theme was, I said we wanted it all to be about what we are FOR instead of what we're against.

ZARA: We had a rule, "No tagging in this space," just because we wanted to have it feel respectful. Some of the people that were painting and some of the people that were involved with cleaning the space weren't feeling it in the same way. But there was a lot of talking that was involved in it. A lot of the people that knew each other were able to step up to each other and discuss what was going on the wall, about colors and what they felt the content should be.

IVY: First I thought it was weird that there were guidelines, but as the working on the first show progressed, it seemed to make sense. For example, graffiti writers were asked to not just do a quick throw-up or just write their names real fast. They had to put more thinking and time into it and what came out in the end was amazing: all these different artists made murals that flowed together in a wide range of themes about anything from gentrification to globalization to multinational corporations to empowerment. The rules challenged people to use the space's size and think of the other artists' work to create something together that was bigger than usual. It was a whole mix of folks—some people, too, who maybe didn't know each other so well—all pooling paint, pooling resources, and sharing ideas. It wasn't so much of a competition, like it might be outside the space. Andrew Schoultz painted his famous birds that are so great underneath painting by this really young graffiti writer kid, IRON. They did it at different times, but it came together great.

ERICK: Can you talk specifically about the painting process, about how different people worked together on themes and murals and choosing their space?

IVY: Alicia, Zara, ORFN and I had one side of the room. The images matched and flowed real well. It was mostly about inspiration. My mural was of a girl gardening and it said, "A New Start" in the banner on it. It was about the space bringing in a new era. I did another panel of a boy in a boat and it said, "Looking for a Home" and it was about having a space, being appreciative of this new, big space and being excited. Zara did his thing that said, "Community Control," with shout-outs to other activists that inspired him, so it was this positive thing.

ZARA: On mine I wrote, "Communication Over Capital," because I think it's important for communities to talk and for different kinds of people to talk to each other. Everything steers us away from having conversations. Then I wrote, "Free Food," because I like free food. The other thing I wrote was, "Let's get community control," which is like... well, somebody else should explain that one to me!

IVY: Alicia did a piece about Native American activists. Then on the other end of the room, you had the history-themed film that Erick did, bringing in the movie theater history and the history of the space itself, as well as showing the history footage of SF. That was great because it was not just on the wall—it was a whole corner with a theater and a movie in it. Lucha did this painting about globalization. There was a factory that said, "Bio-warfare," with incarcerated people, a Zapatista figure... Erin Forest painted this big, beautiful lighthouse that shone these rays of light and said, "Keep Watch." It was an amazing thing to see as you walked under into the other room with the posters and photos...

ERICK: The first time that I thought the show was really going to work, after like a month of working on it, was the night we strung up the lights that we had stolen and those worked.

ZARA: One of the last things was the lighting. Erick and I simultaneously and separately had the same idea to get those yellow extension cord things that have a light socket hanging off it like every twelve feet. They have them at construction sites. They're like a hundred feet long sometimes. We went to where they're building this Live/Work loft on the backside of Potrero Hill, but there were TWO security guards working, so we couldn't get it. Erick knew of some lights at the Ferry Building. There was a long 150-foot string of lights running down the dock. So, uh... we went at a very SLOW pace with Erick cutting the zip-ties around the cord while I wound this huge thing of lights around my arm. People and security guards were walking by and we're supposed to be, like, waiting for the fucking ferry or something, at two o'clock in the morning!

ERICK: We threw them in the bike basket and rode like hell.

ZARA: Back at the space, we laid them out and they just exactly covered the whole length of the main room!

ERICK: We didn't really know up until then, of course, if they were going to light the space or not, you know. That was pretty good, though, that it actually worked.

OPENING NIGHT

(Taken from the zine that was passed out for free to everyone as they entered the space at the opening night show of 949 Market)

Market Street: the shadowy heart of SF, the ultimate Hollywood set. Where faded office buildings from Sam Spade's day still lurk and where every luggage or shoe store or every down and out dentist's office seems to be a front for something else. Where the buildings are worth more when they're hollow and empty with postcard shops in the ground floor. Where a buck will get you eight pictures of the Golden Gate Bridge or eight seconds in a room with a grainy porn movie. The land of drug baggies and cheap, second-run movies and fake I.D.'s. Market Street: where everything is for sale, but none of it is something you can really own.

After my squat on Shotwell Street got busted, I found another place to stay that wasn't an abandoned building. But it didn't last and soon I found myself, once again, helping break into an abandoned building to launch a dream. This time it was right here on Market Street, the site of this show.

We had been wondering about this space for years, really, but once inside, we weren't prepared for how great it really was. It was much bigger and better than we would have even hoped for. Practically a block-long room. We could do ANYTHING with it!

It was in a perfect location, too. The guys in the alley out back didn't care if we had bolt cutters, and there were no other neighbors after dark. The block, like all of Market Street, really, had been mysteriously hollowing out for years, until even the sandwich shop and the ancient St. Francis Theater were the last businesses to go, earlier this year.

I spent an afternoon poring over dusty books on the fifth floor of the library, finding a photo from 1925 that may indicate the space was once a piano company's showroom, but it's hard to tell. I was definitely able to chart the history of 949 Market through 65 years of tenants, as far back as 1935 when "SF Billiards" apparently opened on this site. Later, a 1948 ad in the San Francisco phone book announced, "SF Billiards. Largest in the West. We serve sandwiches and beer. Women welcome."

In the 50s the space had a couple year stint as a "Vic Tanny Workout Gym, but health and fitness was never a big priority down in mid-Market, and soon it lapsed into a comfortable seediness as the home of "Palace Billiards."

Palace Billiards used the spot until its doors closed for the last time, apparently, in 1988. A sign taped to a countertop indoors announced, "Check newspapers for a new location." But there wasn't a new location, and the only place the name "Palace Billiards" is known today is where it is laid in the tiles in the doorway—tiles hidden by a roll down door until tonight. For 13 long years, 949 Market has been empty space. Thirteen years of vacancy, probably part of the owner's tax revenue scam, where the big empty room silently fills with dust as somewhere, outside The City, a bank account fills silently with money. Thirteen years of people's dreams about a space.

What would you do with a block-long chunk of open space on Market Street? Is it more important to use it for housing, or entertainment? Would you spend a month working on a space that might only last for one night, and maybe not even that? Should it just be opened and used to do a massive feeding to the guys who live out back in the alley, or should it be used for a punk art show? Can a space that's illegally opened really be open to everyone, safely? What would you do with a block-long space on Market Street?

We asked 10 or 15 people to come down and look at the space to help us imagine what to do with it and then we went to work. The space needed everything, from power and lights to vacuums for all the dust. We found almost everything we needed right next door in the abandoned St. Francis Theater.

With flashlights and dust masks, we went on expeditions into the eerie silence of the old theater, out of the sun and swarm of Market Street into a dark calm at midday. The theater unfolded before our flashlights like a movie, one shot at a time. A movie where we were the only survivors of a nuclear holocaust, or were beings from the future sent to investigate the past.

We searched for fuse boxes and water pipes to turn power and water on. We found ladders, light bulbs, cans of paint. Curtains, old signs. An old theater sound system that we rewired to build a PA for our new space. A hose for water. Popcorn containers to serve free food in. Theater seats to sit in. Every piece of garbage in the old theater could, theoretically, be rigged to build our show space.

Slowly, out of the theater's past, a future developed in our space. We walked—even rode our bikes excitedly around the room—saying, "This is where we'll serve the food! This is where we'll paint! This is where we'll build a new theater!"

But, as the space began to take shape, I found myself spending more time exploring the old theater instead, savoring that feeling of walking out of a downtown day and into the dark, into a place where time stands still—the feeling of going to the movies.

The poor old St. Francis—screens now dark forever after over 75 years of movies, and there wasn't even an article in the paper when it went down. It had started out as a silent movie house with a grand marquee, but its years on the main drag wore it down. In the 60s it still had its name in lights, down and out but proud, like an old man leaving his SRO hotel room in his best suit and hat, only to sit all day at a bus stop bench alone. But Market Street took that, too, and the theater wound out its days with second and third run films. Cheap matinees, and theaters full of men with bottles sleeping it off in a forever darkened afternoon, while the feel-good hits of summers past spun off the reel into the past. Until time at last stood still.

Deeper and deeper into the theater I went, through layers of debris and history. I rummaged methodically through desks in management offices, finding family photos, receipts, licenses. Great piles of unsold tickets and pictures of half-assed graffiti tags on the theater's tired façade before it closed. I found a negative of a woman standing on the deck of a boat, left behind in a folded-up envelope with the questions for the US Citizenship Exam scrawled on it in English and Chinese.

In the projectionist room, I found reels and reels of film and used heroin bags, hidden in a desk. I imagined a down and out Market Street projectionist on the nod in his secret room while the projector fluttered and flickered in a sort of REM sleep. There were film cans and syringes and an old Coca-Cola trailer that I unspooled and watched in the dark with my flashlight. The trailer shows a cornucopia of fruit that slowly turns into a sweating, fizzing Coke as a caption appears, one letter at a time: "It's the real thing."

Down in the basement, in silent rooms and narrow halls, deep under Market Street, I found silent movie projectors in mounds of dust. Marquee letters and old posters. Popcorn machines, broken. Cash registers from the 1920s, rusted shut. And, always, piles of film. Moldy films in rusty cans, never to be seen again.

I look at the piles of film, deep beneath Market Street, and think of a near-century of people sitting in the dark while movies showed. Sitting in the dark, dreaming. Mouths slightly open, waiting. People waiting at crosswalks, watching fog come in. People leaning in doorways and falling asleep on trains, underground. I see the piles of unspooled film on the projectionist room floor and think of a march filing past the theater during the 1934 General Strike. Cop cars burning, cinematically, nearby after the Dan White verdict. Gulf War marches, Rodney King riots. Last century's subconscious ideas surfacing from the dark under the street, ideas fought for and acted out on Market Street.

I think of the ideas that could fill up a free, squatted space on Market Street, one mural at a time—ideas that could fill up the whole city. You are reading this with the benefit of hindsight, knowing how the show turned out. But I still don't know if, in a few hours, our plans will work, or if we'll get shut down and arrested in minutes. I'm on Market Street, where the layers of history are all hidden but still there, like the rings of a tree. I'm in that crowd, leaning in doorways and falling asleep on trains. Underground. Waiting for the inevitable shift in history.

I'm in the front row at the St. Francis, in the dark, mouth open a little. Dreaming.

THE FIRST SHOW 3/30/2001

ZARA: At the grand opening show there were like 600 people. Shotwell played, The Quails played, Inkling spoke, Peter Plate spoke... Feelings on a Grid played which was the super queer presence which was dearly needed.

MELISSA: Not to mention their stellar fashion.

ZARA: And their fucking incredible fashion. They were incredible. Tights. Fluorescent tights. There also was a gallery in the other smaller room in the back where 5 to 8 people hung art in the back for the first show. That all went really well.

ERICK: What kind of meal do you prepare for a show in a squat with 600 people?

(Jet has been running free food programs like CRUMZ for over thirty-five years in SF, starting with his involvement in The Diggers, who fed in Panhandle Park. "I worked for the post office, and was the mailman on Haight Street in the Summer of Love," says Jet, "until LSD intervened.")

JET: Well, that night it wasn't a full-blown meal like I would have done at CRUMZ, a sit-down meal. But there was a seitan goulash sort-of thing that went into the popcorn buckets. There was a vegetable dish—cauliflower, I think. We brought it up in the fire escape in clean white buckets like Food Not Bombs. We planned on a couple hundred who might want this kind of vegan fare.

MELISSA: The concept of free food, I love that. I also appreciate things that are more holistic creatively, like having different kinds of bands, and also including other art forms like the photography stuff in the back and the reading. I thought it was inclusive for a lot of people.

(Kat, the wheels of the operation, delivered furniture, food, etc., for the squat cafe in her truck)

KAT: I had no idea it would be so large. The sheer magnitude of being in a space that was so beyond anything we could imagine actually having access to most of the time and the fact that it was so fixed up and was so gorgeous, that it was covered in murals—that was what probably struck me the most when I was first there.

ANANDI: I've worked on a lot of spaces, and seen the kids have a lot of really great things, but not in a time and place where everyone was so firmly convinced that we couldn't have or do ANYTHING. There has been a lot of pessimism around this city in the past couple years. People lost their houses and are like, "Oh, I can't even find anywhere to live, so I can't even start to think about doing something for the larger community." Everyone gets trapped in that. To see people who were feeling that way see this really was great.

KAT: I was there early watching everyone figure stuff out. Like the lights kept going out, and they were like, "Oh, are we wiring this right?" It felt like something was being built, you know?

ANANDI: I think even at the first show everyone that stepped in there felt we weren't just going to a show somewhere. It was in a very real way our space.

JIM: I thought it was really amazing how there was really so little hostility and so many different groups of people getting together. There wasn't really any freak violence.

ZARA: There were, before the show, a lot of security concerns. We never talked too much about being worried about the police, because we knew if they showed up, we'd have time to evacuate. It'd take 50 officers to clear that space.

ERICK: There was a feeling, too, that with hundreds of people in a space with electricity and food and all those murals on Market Street, it just LOOKED legal. I mean, what cop would have the imagination to think we weren't renting it?

ZARA: We weren't worried about them finding anyone who owned the building to say otherwise on a Friday night. But we were worried about fights breaking out. We were worried about the graffiti kids just bombing the murals and bombing every section of the place. I mean, we were thinking there might be like 400 people. There were a lot of young kids, like fourteen, who were running around, which was cool. A handful of old people, too. We were worried about different communities of people coming together and NOT getting along.

ERICK: Yeah, we didn't want people to think just because it was an abandoned building they could just go totally insane and break stuff or whatever.

ZARA: We discussed all these ways to hopefully disarm people who wanted to come in a big group and clique up in the corner, drinking 40s and getting drunk—people who'd later decide to act up because they weren't having enough fun or whatever. We wanted to find a way to slow them down as they entered the space, and to introduce ourselves so people would feel they were entering a space where they were being asked to show respect. We ended up handing out tickets and 3-D glasses from the theater at the door. There were people there at the door all night, asking people to smoke out back, or pointing the way to the free food—basically saying hello to everyone who was coming in and asking, "What's going on here?" or, "How much is it?"

ERICK: By the time I started working the door, after I played with Shotwell, it was clear things were going good. People just came by to offer me beer.

JET: It was a wonderful mix of types that night—both urban hip and Market Street impoverished. I liked it all, because it was renegade, though for me, at my age, it was too loud, and there were too many cigarettes. I recall what surprised me was hearing some really good political speeches, talking about the Market Street sweeps that were coming up. It was a good reality check. It wasn't entirely frivolous.

MELISSA: I'm glad to have been asked to read something, that it wasn't just rock, and that it included Peter Plate talking about the history of squatting. It was tough at points but I tried to do something that was more interactive, that had a call and response element, about global stuff going on and how it was related to gentrification. There was a refrain, "Take it back!" that I got people to say with me.

PUBLIC ART REVIEW #1: THE VALENCIA STREET FLYER WALL

The famed flyer wall on Valencia near 24th Street has been getting a lot of publicity lately. Now inches thick with tatters of old flyers and wheat-pasted posters, it recently made the cover of one book (Chris Carlsson's *The Political Edge*) and the new literary mag *Instant City*.

But I wonder how many people who wheat-paste stuff there know that this flowering of local democracy is taking place on the front wall of the old Mission Police Station! The old station was sort of a Mission District Guantanamo, a notorious place where old racist

Irish cops like Officers Brodnick and McGoran worked in the 60s and 70s.

In 1970, during the height of Weather Underground bombings across the nation, a time bomb—likely placed by the New World Liberation Front—was discovered on the roof of the station, when an old lady on San Jose Street saw the weird package on the station's roof from her window. It was defused before it could go off.

During the Rodney King riots of 1992, SFPD illegally warehoused arrested protesters in a former Pepsi bottling plant at 17th and Valencia—the very spot that became the site of the NEW Mission Station when the bottling plant was torn down. The old police station was bought by dot-commers in the late 90s, who have allowed the front wall to remain covered in posters and graffiti.

Jimmy Shotwell convinced the new owner to let Jim see the secret room where the cops years ago had beat him up. The owner said, "A lot of people have asked me to show them that room." Jimmy's ribs got broken there, the inspiration for the song "Carbonated Heat," the classic Strawman song in which Jimmy sings of, "Broken ribs, lives, and dumb fuckin' laws."

I only hope he'll get to play it someday in the old Bayview Station on 3rd Street, now abandoned, when IT becomes a squatted punk club!

949 MARKET VS. REDEVELOPMENT

After the big opening night show there was a lot of debate over what to do next. How could we top that show? How could we open the space up to different communities to use? We didn't get busted, so what should we do now? While we were trying to figure out what the next big project to do would be, there were lots of little ones that were almost better.

The week after the opening, Zara put out flyers announcing an "Art show/Bar-b-q"where people could come check out the space's murals in a quiet setting without 600 people there, while veggie burgers were served out back between the theater and the squat. Meanwhile, that same day, Oakie from San Andreas, who played on opening night, filmed scenes of his Super-8 dyke porno movie in the space's bathroom. After the barbeque, a grueling kickball game broke out in the space and, just as THAT was breaking up, those of us who were on the annual 21-Toilet Bike Ride showed up to drink beer and ride our bikes around the space! Art gallery, picnic ground, kickball field, film set, and bicycle race-track all in one day!

Since I needed a place to live I moved into 949 Market and Antonio moved in soon after. Most of my memories of the space now have less to do with the shows than just waking up every morning to the grinding of wharf-bound streetcars out on Market. Drinking coffee and watching crowds out the window, or writing all day and riding my bike around in a circle in the space when I was stuck on something. The pressure to come up with a big show idea was sort of an ongoing frustration. None of us really wanted to start another six weeks of work on a show so soon. Couldn't we use what we already had, somehow? I remember one time Zara came over so we could have a "serious meeting" about the space, but we were sick of thinking about it, so instead we just drank a lot of coffee and played stickball inside.

But while we were trying to figure out what to do next with our little chunk of Mid-Market real estate, everyone else in town was coming forward with their own plans for the neighborhood—AND for 949 Market itself. The redevelopment agency was going to grant a huge chunk of cash to "revitalize" Mid-Market, and everyone wanted a piece of the action. The *Chronicle* was full of daily editorials on different proposals for the money, ranging from reasonable calls for affordable housing and long term leases for artists and non-profit groups, to the rabidly mercenary "Clean up Market Street" factions who called for the closing of all porn theaters, the police sweep of all homeless from the area, and the establishing of a touristy "theatre district" to bring "art" and "culture" to what the *Chronicle* called the "urine-soaked doorways" of the neighborhood. The citywide debate over what to do with our very block reached a fever pitch when the other daily paper, the *Examiner,* launched their own series, "Mess on Market," featuring a daily dose of lurid tales of Mid-Market. In the *Examiner* front-page stories, mentally ill, homeless drug dealers menaced the "decent" people of Market Street with shootings and stabbings, all while a tidal wave of urine stood poised to break loose over The City. There were often full-color photos of bleeding gunshot victims right on the front page. Shootings on 6th and Market had been blacked out of the news for decades, of course, but suddenly Skid Row was news. Perhaps not so coincidentally, the *Examiner* had bought a building for their offices at 5th and Market. Their sensationalist clean-up campaign stood to cynically sell some papers and boost their property value at the same time.

One morning, just what our abandoned space meant to millionaire developers and just what we were getting away with was brought home to me, literally. When I opened up my morning paper inside the squat, I saw the shuttered front door of 949 Market right there on the front page of the *Chronicle's* local section! The article was all about developers' proposals for OUR space. Should it be used for "Art"? For "Culture"? For "Affordable housing"? Or should it just be turned into luxury condos? After all, the space was too big to just be sitting there UNUSED. It was hilarious: everyone in town was talking about our space and no one had a clue about the art, culture and affordable housing inside of it that was already hidden in plain sight behind the shuttered door.

And in our role as editors of the *Turd-Filled Donut*, Ivy and I would soon have a chance to confront the editors of the other Market Street paper, the *Examiner*, in their own offices just across the street from 949 Market.

THE TURD-FILLED DONUT ATTACK
ON THE SF EXAMINER'S OFFICES

In a September 27 meeting, a group of current and former 6th Street residents confronted the editorial board of the *San Francisco Examiner* in their own new 5th and Market offices, and demanded a "full, front page apology to 6th Street" for their "Mess on Market" series. In the meeting, *Turd-Filled Donut* editors and staff forced the *Examiner's* editors to listen to what 6th Street residents had to say about THEM for a change.

Examiner editors Michael Stoll and Jim Mohr opened the meeting by asking for our input on their stories. Input? For nearly an hour our group—*TFD* editors Ivy McClelland and Erick Lyle, and 6th Street residents and TFD writers Allison Lum and Phil Parkman—gave them some input! We repeatedly asked pointed questions like, "Where do you LIVE, anyway?" and, "What gives you the right to just come into a neighborhood and start calling the people who already live there a 'Mess'?" For the record, Stoll admitted to living in turd-free Cole Valley and Mohr, after a pause, admitted to coming into The City every day from gentle Burlingame. But, he added, "At 20, I was homeless on the streets of Japan, so I've BEEN there."

But this was probably the last question they would be able to answer all day. The *Examiner* editors spent much of the meeting scribbling on their notepads, looking at their watches, their faces blank and their responses evasive. For instance, we demanded to see any statistics that show crime is actually rising on 6th Street. In an article last month—headlined in huge, war-time typeface, "Police: Criminals Control 6th Street"—the *Examiner* cited "an internal police memo that says, 'major crime is up 30% in the area,'" but they would not produce the memo.

So we showed them internal police memos that WE had obtained from SFPD through the Freedom of Information Act that suggested that crime in the Mid-Market area is, more or less, the same as ever. They had no response to that, other than to feebly ask, "Can we, uh, make a xerox of YOUR memos?"

When I stated, "You can't just walk into a neighborhood and start calling people names and expect [problems] to go away," Mohr replied that the stories are "crime-related issues and not so much about homelessness." We pointed out that the SFPD statistics we had obtained showed that the focus of stepped-up police presence on Market was, in fact, homelessness-related "crimes" like Drinking in Public and Open Container laws, but they had nothing to say to that.

How about the human side of things? How did the young *Examiner* editors personally feel about the real life consequences that happen to 6th Street residents as a direct result of the things written by the editors who come in to downtown on the train every morning? Phil said, "You all are giving us a stigma. That's what the people of 6th Street are tired of. The only time I hear about crime on 6th Street is when I pass by an *Examiner* box headline. When I see the paper, it ruins my whole day."

Then, referring to police sweeps and Redevelopment Agency plans that are the result of stories like "Mess on Market," Allison asked, "How can you fail to report that homeless people have been swept to 6th Street from all over The City? What's being talked about now is redevelopment, relocation vouchers, and eminent domain of SRO hotels!" If the *Examiner* truly cared about the conditions for residents of 6th, why, she asked, didn't they take on crusades like rehabbing old SRO hotels, or creating more housing for the homeless people they complain about? "Why don't they write that people on 6th are often forced to come up with $45 a night for a single hotel room?"

Ivy was more blunt, stating, "You don't look at the fact that the police commit crimes here, too. They break into people's hotels without warrants, beat people up and arrest them with no charges." They didn't want to know about that.

Phil summed it all up nicely, demanding, "Let's get it down, straight up: Do you walk down 6th Street?"

The editors said, "All the time!" and, "I walk down there every day!"

Phil said, "Then you ain't afraid so why you trippin'?!?"

Finally, in disgust, I yelled, "Is it just lazy reporting or a failure of moral resolve?" which actually caused Stoll to giggle. It was a pretty pathetic performance for the editors of a so-called major big-city newspaper to let the editors of a xeroxed zine come in and videotape them looking dumb as hell for a solid hour in their own office, a performance that we feel clears up any doubts people may have had about whether the *Examiner* is actually being run by publisher Ted Fang to succeed as a paper. It was almost enough to make you feel sorry for them, but not as much as when Mohr asked, "Why do you keep saying we're trying to kill the paper? Why would I work here if I knew I'd be unemployed?" I would have told him to ask Ted Fang about that, but, as you may have noticed, Fang doesn't show up to these meetings.

The *Examiner*'s complete inability to answer our questions leads the *Turd-Filled Donut* to declare, once and for all, that the *Examiner*'s "Mess on Market" campaign is not motivated in any way by actual news or a determined editorial policy, but by a cynical attempt of the *Examiner*'s publisher, Ted Fang, to raise the value of the *Examiner*'s own property in the proposed Mid-Market and 6th Street Redevelopment Areas.

An hour later, we happened to run into Michael Stoll again, out on Market Street, and he had worked up a little indignation since we'd seen him last. "What is your agenda?" he demanded. It was indicative of the position he's writing from that he couldn't believe that none of us were getting paid to do this. Allison is a shelter outreach coordinator for the Coalition On Homelessness, but caring about 6th Street isn't what we do for a living; it's our lives!

Stoll said, "You know, you had a chance to have a reasonable discussion back there, but you blew it." Reasonable? They came in and started running *Weekly World News* stories about our neighborhood, calling it an "open air asylum" and a "mess," and WE are the ones who are supposed to now initiate a reasonable discussion? They dutifully reprint without criticism a police officer's so-called plan to fingerprint and catalogue all residents of 6th Street on the front page in the bold typeface reserved for war and natural disasters and they want US to be REASONABLE? We told him one last time, "If you apologize to 6th Street on the front page, then maybe we can start all over and be 'reasonable,'" and then we walked away.

Before we left, Stoll had one last burning question, though, and I thought it was pretty funny. He wanted to know, "What are you guys going to do with that videotape?" Of course, we showed it publicly several times at the big TFD reading and speaking events we did later on that year to celebrate the release of issue #8!

TOAST AND JAM CAFE

IVY: I think the feeling of the first event was urgent. Maybe the cops would come. We didn't know it would last. After the first show there was a new feeling, like, "NOW what do we do?" and more people wanted to be involved. That's how a long-range plan like the cafe came about.

ERICK: Why a cafe?

ZARA: A cafe was just that basic idea of bringing 50 people into a setting where they can sit down and have conversations. They say you judge the level of repression in a community by their meeting spaces. In the Latino community in the Mission, which is being gentrified, the churches, cultural centers—all these meeting places are being taken away. A lot of the meeting spaces on both sides for the youth of color and the white punk kids are gone. There are no places to have all ages shows. No places to kick it. No time to kick it. You're spending all your money on rent, so you have no money to kick it. And if you don't kick it, nothing happens. If you're sitting around with 10 of your friends, you can come up with an idea and it can naturally happen. I'm also down with service, though. I'm down to put in time and effort to feed folks that need like an hour and a half from shitty-ass street life.

IVY: MSA had a jungle dance party in the space and charged money as a benefit for the first week's food and cafe supplies.

ZARA: At MSA's jungle party we got almost 600 dollars together. And then after that there were three breakfasts in a row. We served coffee, bagels, hard-boiled eggs, peanut butter and jelly, and fruit salad.

MELISSA: How did you get stuff for the breakfasts?

ZARA: Asked a lot of people. Everybody came through. Asked people who'd tell you to go and ask somebody else and then you'd go and ask them and they'd have it... Rainbow Foods donated produce on Saturday night. We'd cut off the bad parts and serve fruit salad. Katz's Bagels was giving us about two hundred and fifty cheap bagels that they'd thrown out the night before. We got food bank food, which is hell-of cheap.

IVY: And someone had to go out and liberate industrial size coffee makers and bagel toasters that were, like, gifts from the Free Gods.

ERICK: You mean stolen.

IVY: Yeah... stolen. It was hard work.

KAT: I have a pick-up truck so I figured I could help out. Then Zara called me, and I helped him to go get some coffee makers and stuff, and Anandi and I started to go dumpster some food. So I guess I kind of just started working on it by default and then I was really excited to be involved.

ANANDI: When was the first time you went to the space?

(Bianca, 26, baker, made homemade muffins for the squat cafe.)

BIANCA: We were walking down the streets and then we see this door, this black door, and we kind of pushed through and there's nothing, just a dark staircase, and we're like, "Whoa. This kind of looks like a place where a deal would be going down," and we're like, "Okay..." and we wander up the stairs and it looks like a gigantic living room, and it's all homey, and it's painted, and there are literally punk rockers everywhere. When you're walking up the staircase, you think it's going to be tiny, it's going to be nothing, and then it's this beautiful room with these enormous windows.

(Kim, Melissa's mother, a 60-something employee for the Washington Post, who visited the space.)

KIM: I expected something like a soup kitchen. But this is a Sunday oasis. People sit at tables and chairs, with enough space between tables for the luxury of not-overheard conversation. Those sitting alone read or write in a private cocoon. A sofa is set out on one side to catch the natural light. There is a row of counters with colorful, fresh protest murals at either end. For me what dominates the room are the elegant floor-to-ceiling windows overlooking Market

Street. These windows frame the soft, natural light filtering through the broad leafy trees and the ornate, wrought-iron street lamps of Market Street. It is like a view of Paris in the spring... the food is nourishing, varied, and lovingly prepared. I, who can afford high-end coffee shops, feel lavished with attention.

(Mike, 43, a homeless resident of Market Street)

MIKE: Nice people, friendly atmosphere... a very nice place for toast, coffee, and some hard-boiled eggs. Very nice.

ANANDI: The cafe wasn't just about giving free food to people. Often, there isn't anything for people in between organizing an event and coming to an event. Whereas with something like this... it's great to have different levels of participation, to have people wipe the tables, serve food, etc...

KAT: One really beautiful thing about the space was seeing all the kids that I see drunk at parties... reading the fucking paper, drinking coffee, doing dishes and stuff. It felt directly connected to my community, and it also felt like I was definitely making an impact. Like, there needs to be food, so we go get fruit. The next morning people are eating fruit. I really like concrete things that I can feel.

(Julianna, drummer of The Quails, who played on opening night.)

JULIANNA: In all, I think I was most charmed by the normalness of 949. Like, "Of course we'd inhabit this room and have this show and eat these bagels."

ERICK: I think the last squat cafe felt really memorable to me. Just looking out across the crowd—I had a lot of out-of-town friends in there. A lot of people from New Orleans were staying over. This guy I know from Philly was showing movies there. People were helping out. The movie started showing and a couple of us started making popcorn. It just felt like this really smooth thing that didn't really have any direct supervision, that everybody just kind of knew what to do and they did it.

(Todd, 30, a visiting straightedge vegan punk from Edmonton, who is a professor at Montreal's McGill University.)

TODD: There was an attempt to launch a squat in a vacant apartment building in Vancouver a few years back and another attempt to squat a vacant downtown Montreal theater earlier this year, but both were shut down within hours. I think the reason for that in both cases

was that the people involved were more interested in making a statement about housing and property than they were in building a viable
squat, so they did things like publicly announce their plans, holding a
press conference as they were breaking in. I think that's kind of noble
in some ways but also pretty bloody futile. If I had a choice between
making a statement like that or running something like the 949 space,
where 150 people got free food and hung out watching movies while
I was there, well, I think statements like that are more noble when
people are fed and have a safe space to chill for a while.

PUBLIC ART REVIEW #2:
RIGO'S TRUTH MURAL, MARKET STREET

The dedication party at UN Plaza for Rigo's new "Truth" mural was
an example of how political public art can actually embody all of the
values it aspires to. The mural is a simple block of text on the side of
the Odd Fellow's Building at 7th and Market, that reads "TRUTH."
At the ceremony, Rigo dedicated the mural to Robert King Wilker-
son, an ex-Black Panther and member of the Angola Three. King had
spent 29 years in solitary confinement in Louisiana's notorious Angola prison for a crime he didn't commit, until being released in 2001.
Mr. King was on hand to address the crowd about his experiences,
adding some extra meaning and poignancy to the terse text of the
mural. Years from now, people will be able to say, "What that mural
is REALLY about is how this Panther got framed on these charges
but truth finally prevailed." In a further tribute to the example of the
Black Panther Party's work in the community, Rigo then passed out a
hundred or so bags of free groceries. Each brown paper grocery bag
was screen-printed with the Black Panther logo, to remind people of
the Panthers' famed food programs for the poor. Then bands and DJs
played for hours, all for free, while people danced in the plaza.

But layers of political meaning aside, the real day-in/day-out
genius of the Truth mural is that UN Plaza offers a clear line of
sight from the mural to City Hall. The enormous letters, partially
obscured at street level, are actually most clearly visible in one
piece from the steps of City Hall. The mayor and others in power
will have to see "TRUTH" every day! Locked in a permanent staring contest with power, the mural seems confident that truth will
eventually win.

TRANNY RIOT ON TURK STREET!
TRANSGENDER ACTIVISM IN THE TENDERLOIN

Did a crowd of drag queens fight the cops on Turk St., three full years before the famous Stonewall Riot in New York? What is the lost history of the Tenderloin? Susan Stryker, a researcher at the SF Gay and Lesbian Historical Society, works full time to uncover Bay Area transgender community history and make it accessible to the public. The Turd-Filled Donut *interviewed her recently at her 5th and Market office about a documentary film she's making called, "Looking for Compton's: The Lost History of Transsexuals in San Francisco."*

TURD-FILLED DONUT: So, can you tell us what you know about the transgender scene in the Tenderloin in the 60s and 70s?

SUSAN STRYKER: You can actually see Compton's from where we're sitting. (points out the window across Market to the intersection of Turk and Taylor.) See that building over there? 111 Taylor? That's where Compton's used to be. So only half a block off Market Street was where a bunch of queers rioted in '66. The first transgender organizations started in early spring '67, so our film looks for what was going on in late '66 and '67 that inspired people to form these TG groups. Why, all of a sudden did people decide, "Hey, we need to have a support group for transsexuals in the Tenderloin"? Well, what we found is that there was some kind of "police altercation" in August of '66 at Compton's Cafeteria.

TFD: Why Compton's?

SS: Compton's was an all-night cafeteria. You could get a bowl of oatmeal there for a quarter or a cup of coffee for a nickel. You could get out of the weather. And if you were too young to get into a bar—

TFD: Or too gender-queer...

SS: Right, because you might get thrown on your butt if you looked like someone the cops might raid the bar over. Or maybe you were too poor; maybe you were some young tranny kid who's run away from home and you're out there selling your ass on Polk Street, looking for some place to get out of the cold night air...

So there were late night places in the Tenderloin—which really don't exist anymore—places where a lot of young, poor gender-queer kids would hang out late at night. But one of the things that made Compton's unique was that it was the meeting place for the first militant queer youth organization, a group called Vanguard, which was organized by ministers at Glide Memorial Church. Young seminary interns were doing outreach right outside the church doors. So who were the people who needed some good old-fashioned Christian charity in the neighborhood? What they found out was that it was a bunch of queers!

Remember, this was the age of Martin Luther King, so although NOW we tend to think of Christians as the Religious Right—Jerry Falwell, Pat Robertson—in the mid-60s, there was a very active African American Civil Rights Movement, which drew a lot of its inspiration from progressive elements of Christianity. A lot of queer organizing in the Tenderloin was coming from people who were coming from the same progressive Christian angle.

So, Vanguard would meet at Compton's to plan their actions and these increasingly militant young queers started getting into it with the security guards. Things began to escalate over the summer of '66. Vanguard had been picketing and flyering Compton's since mid-July 1966, claiming that the cafeteria's twenty-five cent "service charge" on all orders was a discriminatory way to keep poor, queer kids out on the street. According to the descriptions that we have (from the program of SF's first significant gay pride march in 1972), "the SFPD paddy wagon drove up to do its 'usual sweeps' of the street, and cops went into Compton's to harass the drag queens and hustlers sitting at the tables. One of the cops slapped the ass of some drag queen, and she got fed up with it so she threw her coffee in the cop's face!" (laughter) Then, apparently, all hell broke loose. People started throwing their trays, glasses, plates, whatever... they smashed out Compton's windows. They broke out the windows of a cop car and burned a newspaper shack outside the cafe to the ground. Cops were trying to grab the rioters and throw them into the paddy wagon, but the queens started hitting them back, "below the belt" and smashing them in the face "with their extremely heavy purses!" The program claims this riot was the "first ever recorded violence by gays against police anywhere." If it's true, it happened here years before the Stonewall Riot in New York.

TFD: WOW! But are you convinced that version of the story is the real one?

SS: No, not yet. But it's the only description that we have so far. We did an interview with Elliot Blackstone, an SF police officer who actually did tremendous work with the Tenderloin's transgendered community in the late 60s, and he downplayed the scale of the riot.

TFD: Of course! How many cops are going to admit to getting humiliated and getting their asses kicked by a bunch of queers?

SS: Right, he's still a cop. Also, I've found archival footage from a 1967 film called Gay San Francisco, where it shows some queens walking down Turk Street and turning into Compton's Cafeteria. A voiceover says, "Here, at the corner of Turk and Taylor, is a notorious drag queen hangout. Recently, the late-night fights between the queens became so vicious that the police had to close the popular restaurant between midnight and 6:00 AM." (laughter) So, they got it wrong, but there clearly is a reference to something momentous happening at Compton's.

Part of why it is so difficult to pin down exactly what happened is that the transgender population is very transient. People flow in and out of town a lot, they undergo various degrees of gender transition. Some post-ops no longer identify as transgender anymore, and, often when they first start out they live and hang out in the Tenderloin, but then get a job and move to another neighborhood. Plus, a lot of these people live hard lives and many from the late 60s are no longer with us...

TFD: How does this riot at Compton's fit into the bigger picture of the history of Transgender activism?

SS: Prior to 1966, transgender folks were, by and large, forced to exist as undocumented workers, since they weren't allowed to legally change their name or sex on any form of ID, and they had an extremely difficult time finding any work that would hire them at all. As a result, they were forced to make their livings turning tricks, selling drugs, and doing petty crimes. Legal name and sex change on birth certificates, driver's licenses, and passports only became available in the mid-70s after a decade of organizing and agitating from transgender activists of the day.

Starting in 1966, there was more and more agitation for transgender rights in the Tenderloin. After the riots, by 1967, you started to see some groups forming, and by 1968 there was actually a center here called National Transsexual Counseling Unit. Through 1968, transsexuals were able to get access to federal War on Poverty money for job training programs and stuff.

TFD: Was that accessible because they were transgender, or because of their poverty status?
SS: Poverty, basically. It was determined by what neighborhood you lived in. Anyone in the Tenderloin qualified. So, activists were doing organizing specifically with transgender people from the Tenderloin and this group called Conversion Our Goal (COG) got started. A bunch of tranny prostitutes got together and said, "Hey, the only reason we're tricking is because we can't get jobs. If you want to 'abate crime' and 'end poverty' then you have to get us access to hormones, surgery, legal name and gender changes, and civil rights, to keep us from getting busted every time we need to piss in a public restroom! We need you to get the police off our backs and get us trained for jobs because we're severely discriminated against."

Ironically enough, the California Assembly member who helped sponsor and push through a lot of bills decriminalizing homosexuality and allowing transsexuals to change their I.D.'s was Willie Brown!

TFD: Wow, very ironic! How did these new services pan out?
SS: Well, there was the Central City Multi-Service Agency, where transsexuals were trained to do jobs, but the jobs were stereotypical for the gender of their choice. Males-to-Female, for instance, were trained to become beauticians, secretaries, and file clerks because these were the jobs that women were trained for at the time.

A handful of universities, including Stanford here in the Bay Area, knew they needed to open clinics, which they called "gender clinics," to prescribe hormones and sex-change surgery to transsexuals. But, ultimately, the doctors were weirded out by transsexualism, and they ended up making a strict set of rules that must be obeyed if a person wanted hormones or surgery. These were only available if you were straight in the new gender of your choice. If you wanted to become a lesbian or gay man AFTER your transition, you were systematically ruled out.

TFD: Ugh! That must have really sucked to have been a queer tranny back then...
SS: Yeah, but as critical as we are today of these prohibitive rules,

these service providers weren't BAD people. They were just doing the best they could in those days when transsexualism was brand new to Americans. They had a lot of learning and research ahead, and they were, and still are, clueless in a lot of ways.

But, what is never mentioned in historical journals or in medical texts is that the impetus for these laws or access to new medical services did not come from well-intentioned doctors or politicians at all. No one said, "We should be doing something about the problems these unfortunate transsexuals are having." All progress was the result of transgender people wanting, seeking, and ultimately DEMANDING it!

THE DEATH OF A MURAL

Barry McGee's mural in Clarion Alley, which lasted for nine years, was probably one of the best-known murals in the alley. Aaron Noble called me up one day to tell me that Barry's mural was going to be destroyed on purpose and people were being invited to come watch. The mural was painted on the backdoor of Community Thrift. The store was retrofitting their building and the backdoor was to be destroyed in the process. In the time since Barry painted the mural, he has become an international art star and his work sells for thousands of dollars. Aaron thought that the door the mural was on would probably get stolen and sold on e-bay, so, in the spirit of keeping the mural free art for the public, Aaron was going to buff it out with a sander.

I was intrigued. Thinking of the mural being erased made me think of time passing. Barry's graffiti was all over the streets when I moved to SF and I associate it with the excitement of that time, how exciting it was to move to a city where criminal artists were celebrated more than gallery ones.

I thought of Barry. When he'd painted this mural, he was still mostly known for graff, not so much in the galleries yet. So much had happened to him in the ten years of the mural's lifespan. He had become famous, got married, and then his wife, the artist Margaret Kilgallen, had tragically died while giving birth to their child. I wondered what Barry thought of the mural being buffed and called him to ask about it but he was in Italy, doing a show.

Despite all the emails Aaron sent out, in the end, only Megan

Wilson and I showed up that morning to watch Aaron sand away the mural, though passersby would sometimes stop to quietly and respectfully watch. The whole scene was oddly moving in its anticlimax.

After an hour, Aaron made me go to the corner store on Mission to buy the plastic baggies for crack that they sell there. The three of us got on the ground and scooped up pinches of paint flakes, and dust from the famous mural into the crack baggies to keep for souvenirs, a truly fitting Clarion Alley ending.

HOW 949 MARKET CLOSED

The whole basic theory that Zara and I had about the space was that the more out-in-the-open and completely legitimate the whole operation looked, the longer it would last. The murals, the electricity, the huge amount of work, and the big crowds of people attending events made it all look perfectly normal to be there. As long as we all BELIEVED in it, it would be real. That was why we decided to use the front door on Market Street for events, so the big crowds of kids wouldn't be sneaking around a sketchy back door in the alley. We used the back door though, the rest of the time, for bringing in supplies and going in and out.

Ironically, the beginning of the end was when, one night, the huge steel back door simply FELL OFF the hinges!

The next morning, I got up early and called Kal from Survival Research Laboratories. He came and welded it back on for us for the small fee of a pint of carrot juice. It was a pretty "Proud-to-be-in-SF" moment, I thought.

Need a weld? Just call up the guy who makes weird robots that fight each other! A homeless guy in the back alley told me the cops had been there that morning, taking pictures of the door and asking questions about who broke in. The huge door, hanging awkwardly by one hinge, was the first thing about our involvement in the space that looked completely out of place.

Sure enough, on Monday morning, I woke up to the sound of construction workers talking, out in the space between the theater and our squat. They had, apparently, cut our lock on the back alley door and come inside the courtyard area to investigate.

My friends from New Orleans were staying in the squat, because their bands, County Z and Impractical Cockpit had played the day before at the cafe. We all took turns watching, very quietly, out the lone squat window, while the construction workers tried all the doors. They appeared satisfied that no one had broken into the abandoned building at all. They tried the gate to the back door of the squat and we heard them say, "Okay, THAT'S secure. No one touched that." Of course, they didn't realize it was OUR lock! We had passed the test! We weren't caught!

The bad news was, the construction workers then set about newly securing the huge back door to the alley. We watched as they struggled to erect a massive coil of razor wire on top of the door, repeatedly cutting themselves and getting tangled in it, yelling "Ow! Fuck!" It was pretty funny. But then they started welding the back alley door completely shut!

At this point, the front door on Market was locked from the outside and our only way out was the back door. We quickly took stock of the situation. Though we were apparently being sealed into the squat, it was, at least, a squat CAFE.

We had a hundred pounds of coffee, two hundred bagels, a case of peanut butter, boxes of weird protein bars, and several bowls of fruit salad. We had two bands' worth of musical equipment, we had three bikes, and we had an accordion. Ryan from County Z said, "Okay! We'll drink coffee and ride bikes and write songs all day. Then, we'll just have band practice all night!" It didn't sound so bad, except, maybe, the accordion part, and it actually turned out to be a fun day.

While we waited for the construction workers to leave, Dan and Andy practiced songs. I wrote a letter and Stella sewed up her clothes. It was like, "Okay, we'll just keep doing exactly what we're doing, except ... we can never leave!"

Later, we managed to pry the front door open from the inside and sneak out. We went in and out the front door for a couple days, until we came up with a new plan to open the back. It seemed like we had escaped detection and all we had to do was get the back open again. Zara and Todd from Montreal and I went to work on it. When we got it open with a rented angle grinder, I thought that was going to be the watershed moment of the squat history, but it turned out to probably be what got us busted. They came back AGAIN on the next Monday and saw that it was open. And they came back with the cops.

Around ten that morning, I heard people walking in the squat. I've been kicked out of a lot of squats and there's always that moment when you hear the voice of the person that doesn't belong there and you feel that sinking feeling. They walked in and opened the door to my room. I saw a cop. He says, "Good morning! So, like, what the hell are you doing in here?"

I say, "Well, you know, they're going to tear the building down in a while and we're just kind of using the place for art space. We've got a six-month lease. We have a rental agreement, you know."

The cop says, "Oh, well, that's just GREAT! Can I see it?"

I say, "Uh… RIGHT! You want to SEE it? Of course!" I thought I had a fake rental agreement that my friend, Chris, made up one for me, but I was looking for it with the cop standing there, and I couldn't find it. While I looked, about nine other cops came into the room. They stood around, yelling at me. "You're talking out your ass. What's the landlord's NAME, dude? Can you even give us a phone number?" I keep saying stuff like, "Uh…I'm not really the one in charge."

Finally, the biggest and oldest cop gathered us all in a circle and said, "Well, what now?" I said, "How about I'll just go get my stuff and you guys lock it up, and that's that." He says, "Sounds good to me." All the other cops nod. But the construction worker guys get pissed and start whining. "Aw man, our DOOR, man! The grind! You can't just let him go! I mean, look at our door!" So, the cops took me down to the car.

We're going down the stairs and I was just in my underwear and a shirt. The cop says, "You got any ID…?" And I said kind of hopefully, "Yeah, it's in my pants, which are over there. Can I go get it?" And he kind of looks up the stairs, lazily, and shrugs. "Nah, forget it, Let's just go." They took me to 850 Bryant where they just gave me a ticket and let me out in 15 minutes. Then I had to walk really fast, back up to the squat to see if I could get my pants out. I couldn't. I was just another scraggly lone male in his underwear having a little temper tantrum at 6th and Market that day.

THE THING THAT ALWAYS BROKE

It had been a long time since she had yelled up at my window that summer, that summer when I had the room with the window, down in the narrow alleys between the tall buildings. Downtown, behind the *Chronicle* building where the drunks sing and the pigeons swarm and the men load the news onto trucks every morning early. The summer when the sun never came out and the early headline was always about us bombing some new, unexpected country. It always seemed like it had been a long time since she had yelled up at my window.

She stood in the alley smoking.

"How come," she said. "How come when I'd come to see you my bike would always break?"

I looked at her flat tire. "You should leave it here and come with me. We'll play your favorite song."

"Something always broke," she said.

You could hear the march echoing through downtown just a couple blocks away as it came up 5th Street. The flyer had said, "Emergency March to Stop the Bombing." The march was supposed to end at a rally at Civic Center where my band was going to play. Civic Center was one of the few places in town that summer that we'd never gone on a date, or for that matter, had never stayed up all night deciding not to see each other again. We ran to catch up. The sun was out and the streets were filled for blocks, and it looked good.

Everybody was there. There were pissed off hip hop kids from the Western Ad. The Good Vibes girls were there looking tough as fuck, all in black. There were guys I knew from the Coalition On Homelessness—you know, guys who live in the park. Of course that one cop was there, that one who's at every demo. I swear he's even in all of Jim's footage of protests from like 15 years ago.

Presently, Juanita from that Latino storefront drop-in center on Mission Street, all four and a half feet of her, was yelling insults in Spanish up into his face. He didn't like it. I caught myself almost waving to him. After all, we've been marching together for years. We headed up 5th Street to Powell Street, past the cable car turn-around, to Union Square, to yell at all the tourists shopping at Macy's.

The tourists hardly seemed in any way to know what we were protesting about. Bombing? What bombing? Their safe day of shopping while the bombs were dropping hardly seemed threatened by us, either. Instead the tourists were excited. They turned their video cameras away from the Gold Man and the Human Statue and started filming us. You could almost see them back home telling everyone how they went to San Francisco, and how they saw a real live anti-war demonstration.

As we headed down to Market Street again, I found myself stuck behind the Mumia puppet, and I started to have that old sinking feeling. Still, the thing that I had always liked about being in a march was looking back at familiar buildings, from the middle of the blocked off, traffic-free street. The city seemed to come unstuck from its everydayness. And for a short while you could catch a glimpse of a whole different world layered over the top of it. Anything could seem possible.

And, suddenly, everyone was running. The cops didn't want us to go onto Market Street and were trying to push us off onto a side street. But there were too many of us and they were taken by surprise. The crowd surged onto Market Street as cops tried to run ahead, and everything was momentarily silent, except for the crackling of cop radios. In the push of the crowd, she and I were laughing and losing balance like when we used to ride doubles together drunk. She said, "Hey! Remember when we got kicked off that roof in the Mission and we had to run from the cops?"

"Wait... was it the cops? Wasn't it the building super with a machete that time?" I yelled, laughing.

It was suddenly like the old days. She had this look in her eye I hadn't seen for a while, and she was smiling with her mouth slightly open, like someone waiting for a first kiss. I thought of fires in the middle of the street during the Gulf War protest. I thought of burning cop cars and old pictures of Dan White riots. Would this finally be the march where we took over Macy's, when we ran in and said, "No, you CAN'T just shop while these bombs fall on other countries! It has to stop!" Would this be the march that ended up more like we fucking felt?

Well, no. The cops let us have Market Street, and soon we arrived at Civic Center, at the scheduled event. Instantly, an army of old socialists covered in protest buttons fanned out and started trying to sell their shitty newspapers. Everyone started passing out flyers for

NEXT week's emergency protest. The perennial socialist losing candidate for mayor took the stage and started addressing the crowd through a bullhorn, saying, "Send a message to City Hall! Vote for me in November!" while her supporters asked for campaign donations, passing the hat for spare change like the Gold Man or the Human Statue back in Union Square.

We were supposed to play first. I thought that maybe we could keep the energy going. But some horrible hippie speaker ran up and stole our spot. When will this shit end? Finally, we got to play. First song: we broke all the strings and the drums. "NATO bombed my bass pedal!" I yelled, holding up the two halves for the dwindling crowd. We fought off more speakers who wanted to take the stage, while we fixed everything. Then, our singer introduced the second song by telling the Marxists to leave the anarchists alone. The crowd roared and applauded. So, of course, during our third song, the Avengers cover, the power mysteriously got pulled on us. I kept playing the drums and singing as loud as possible all the way to the end of the song, anyway.

But that was it. We had been purged. The sound guy was packing it up. He said, "Look, the cops have been real good about not shutting this down, so, like, we should call it quits before it's too late, don't you think?" It's always the sound guy! He must've been Cointelpro. I said, "With friends like you who needs the cops?" He said, "Hey man, that hurts!" He was a hippie sound guy.

A wave of fog was crossing Twin Peaks in the distance, coming down Market Street. The day had almost imperceptibly darkened. People went their separate ways. The only people left in the plaza were the last of the crowd who were still hoping to get arrested, the people trying to sell them papers, and of course that one cop.

She stood there on the grass, smoking. She said, "I should go. I should get my bike."

I thought of a summer with no sun, and a sound guy with no sound, and a Stop the Bombing march that didn't even try. I thought of a room with a window in a narrow alley, where the drunks sang and the pigeons swarmed and the men loaded the news onto trucks.

I said, " I'll help you fix your flat. So you can go home."

PART THREE:

"WHAT WE'RE FOR

THE RESULTS OF "BILLBOARD SUMMER" 2002:

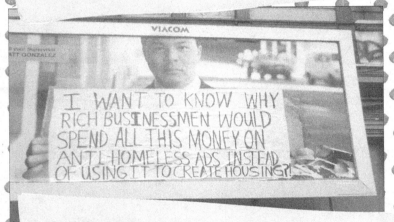

ALTERED BILLBOARDS ALL OVER TOWN FROM THE FIGHT

AGAINST ANTI-HOMELESS, SO-CALLED "CARE NOT CASH" CAMPAIGN

LETTER FROM CHATTANOOGA
DECEMBER 2001

Hey Icky:

It's 3:00 AM and the wind is howling down deserted Houston Street here in downtown Chattanooga tonight. The radio says the US-led Northern Alliance controls Afghanistan, the city of Chattanooga is going to post the Ten Commandments in the county courthouse, and, meanwhile, one of my oldest friends is in the next room, trying to kick heroin. In 24 hours, he will have the fever—great, stinking sweats and an uncontrollable runny nose. In 48 hours he'll be collapsed in gut busting pain, with the shakes and diarrhea. For now, though, out in the hallway, the buckets are filling up with rain where the roof is caving in, and we're not answering the door, because we haven't paid a dime of rent in three months. In just 72 hours, if he can make it, all traces of the drug will have left his system. Until then, there is just the horrible waiting to see How Bad Can It Be, the cowering and the shivering from the expected blow. He nervously downed a last quart of beer hours ago, still in a somewhat hopeful mood, but now he's in there, twisted up in the blankets, wide-eyed and shuddering, saying, almost in wonder, "I feel a chill... like I've never felt before..."

This is not a Real Cool Time to be a dope fiend, Icky. The American people have spoken and they've had enough. Just last week, genuinely concerned for his health, my friend checked himself into the hospital with an abscess in his arm. He's lucky they didn't cuff him to the bed and call the cops. When he asked the doctor how could he get clean, the doctor asked if he'd ever heard the words of Jesus. Jesus? Doc, how can we FORGET?

But maybe a little Jesus IS the answer right about now. I'm seriously thinking of waiting until, say, the morning of the third day, when he's completely lost control of his bowels and is wet with sweat and snot, and then taking him over to a service at the church around the corner. United We Stand, eh, Father?

It'd be an ugly scene. The Good People of the South haven't seen Unity like that since the welcoming party for the Freedom Riders. As for the words of Jesus, he is, apparently, a contributing editor at the *Chattanooga Times-Free Press*, and just today they printed this

150

little bit on the editorial page under the charitable heading of "Bible Wisdom":

The Lord revengeth and is furious; the Lord will take vengeance on his adversaries, and he reserveth his wrath for his enemies. Nahum 1:2

So we're going it alone tonight, without Jesus or even good drugs. We've stocked up on Maalox, Ibuprofen, over the counter sleeping remedies, and the Valerian Root for the days ahead, locked in this house. Normally, in a situation like this, it's good to have something with a little more kick on hand, like a handful of Xanax or Klonapin to stuff down the big bastard's throat when he starts trying to take a swing at me to get out of the house. But, apparently, Jesus himself was riding shotgun with the Chattanooga PD tonight, going, as it were, from cave to cave, because all the North Chattanooga drug dealers have fled the scene and we couldn't find a single pill. *"Come out of the cupboards, you boys and girls!"*

No, this is not the time for downers. Heroin was never really Bush, Jr.'s SCENE. Junkies are too sensitive. It was always cocaine that fuelled W's ambition. Now the cokeheads of the world are grinding their teeth in a thousand-year victory grin, as they line up in formation to stomp the living shit out of the Dope Fiends and Losers of the world, with QB John Ashcroft calling his special night-stick-to-the groin play again and again.

Ashcroft's on the radio again on this long, long night, as the winds howls outside and the big searchlight goes from cave to cave. The voices on the radio seem paranoid and vengeful, booming out across that big American AM radio night. From Louisville, from Philly, WJR from Detroit... There's "The Truckin' Bozo" out of Cincinnati, "Doing it for you all night." There's Paul Harvey, old as the flag, with patriotic reassurances. The Bose Wave Radio and JointRitis... the Big Dark Land that never sleeps. Talk show voices demanding blood and revenge, crisscrossing the land like unseen strands of a huge net, covering all the late night interstates and backroads like roadblocks.

The howling and the groaning in the next room reminds me of the eerie howling in "London Calling," how there was a deadly serious chill in that song that somehow anticipated in 1979 the vicious Reagan/Thatcher gutpunch to come. That chill's blowing in the wind out there tonight, across the sleepless AM radio dial, down Woodward Avenue, down West Madison, down 125th Street. A chill like they've never felt before.

They're feeling it tonight at 20th and Mission, in the fluorescent-lit waiting room of Hunt's Donuts. When the US started bombing Afghanistan, it was the cops that brought the news to the Epicenter of Crime. It was one of those nights when Capp Street was too hot to work and every john was an undercover, so all the girls were in Hunt's waiting it out. An SFPD cruiser pulled up onto the sidewalk. No cop ever actually goes INTO Hunt's. The cop simply motioned for one black girl in an impossibly short skirt to come out and talk to him.

She looked pretty nervous as she stomped out awkwardly in her huge heels to talk to him. But when she came back, she was laughing. She announced to the whole donut shop, "He says that now that the United States is in a war, every cop in SF is on active duty, so there's going to be like, a hundred extra cops on the street with nothing to do but fuck with us. He says he wanted to warn me, and," she paused, laughing, "ask me for a date when he gets off his shift."

But no one else was laughing in the shop. The pimps shifted nervously in their seats and the panhandlers felt a sudden urge to recount their small bits of change and everyone uneasily felt the drugs in their pockets. No, they weren't laughing in the shop. They had been getting away with something for too long, too long on this street in a world they wanted no part of, waiting for the summer to come, but instead finding, almost with wonder, that a new chill had crept up on the wind, sneaking up silently from behind, just like that, like a waiter laying the check, face down.

The check has come due for a lot of people since September 11ᵗʰ. For me, what is interesting is how shocked everyone was. My first thought, when I heard the news, was how much like *déjà vu* it all seemed. As soon as I heard what happened, it all flashed before my eyes, the coming hate and patriotism, the massive bombing of innocent civilians, and the complete crackdown on civil liberties. I could instantly see it all so clearly. And I will admit that, waking up on that morning with someone I'm very much in love with at a time when I'd been so confident of my own plans and future, that my first thoughts were mostly selfish. "Just when I'd finally survived a childhood of Reagan and the fear of nuclear war and we'd finally put Y2K/End of the world obsession to bed for good," I thought. "Just when things were finally going GOOD, here comes ole fascism again."

Yet, we've been saying all along that this was inevitable. The idea that "This world can't last like this" or "One day it's all going to come falling down" is one of the central tenets of activist thought, not to mention the subject of countless punk songs. Now that it was finally happening, watching the towers fall seemed like some secret knowledge that I'd been carrying around for years, a seed of decay I knew was planted in our world from the start.

And now, as my friend groans in the next room, the secret seems so much like the secret of heroin, and how it almost changes your PAST. What about all our hopes and dreams, all the things we planned? Did he know deep down it was all just talk? Can we turn it around? If we just give up, what will we have left then?

As you can see, I've been in edgy, foul humor lately. Every newspaper headline, every radio announcer, every flying flag is just such an insult as I walk down the street. I haven't been so completely surrounded by complete lies, willful ignorance, and casual hate since, well, since the FIRST Bush presidency and the Gulf War. Back then I was just an 18-year-old punk rocker in a small town—possibly the only person against the war in the state of Florida. At the time, I basically wanted to break or spray paint "Fuck You!" on everything. Over the years, happily, I've learned how to get over that feeling, how to get my ideas across to "normal" people and to even like them. I have learned to accept much of the world as it is and even enjoy living in it. How sad that just because a couple of buildings blow up, I suddenly have to feel like I'm 18 again and everyone on the street and TV is my sworn enemy.

In my isolation here in Chattanooga, I've taken to cutting up the free patriotic bumper stickers given out in stores around town that read "God Bless America" and "Proud To Be An American" and rearranging them so that they read "God Fucks America" and "Proud To Be An Asslicker." Then, I put them on cop cars. You have to find fun where you can get it, right? The guy from the convenience store next door has put the word out on the street that he intends to shoot whoever changed the store's sign that read "David's Market" with black spray paint so that it read "Osama's Market." I've been trying to remind myself that not everyone who flies a flag is a bloodthirsty, racist bastard and that is how a lot of well-meaning people—the very people that a legitimate anti-war movement would depend on support from—show their concern.

Nonetheless, when I finished spray painting it, drunk at 5:00 AM, I thought brightly, "THIS will piss those redneck bastards off!"

I keep finding myself daydreaming up crank flyers seeking "Donations to Help Bring Christmas to Afghanistan" and letters to the editor saying things like, "Gentlemen, thus I conclude that if General Braxton Bragg had only had a box of anthrax to use on the retreating Union troops at the Battle of Chickamauga, he would have wiped them out BEFORE the costly battles at Lookout Mountain and Missionary Ridge, thus saving the day and, so it goes, the whole war, for our boys from The South." And why not, Icky? Even rickety old Michael Jordan looks like he could use a baggie of anthrax out on the court these days to clear the way to the basket. As for me, I've started taking anthrax instead of sugar in my coffee, and I recommend it for everybody. You can never be too prepared.

What I've been wondering more than anything is, "Where are the thousands of people who were in the streets protesting globalization a couple of months back?" This whole War on Terrorism will at least give the "It has to get worse before it gets better" crowd something to cheer about while they're looking for their broken teeth under the cops' boots in the streets at the next big demo. But, seriously, things have been pretty quiet. Can things really be "different now" as the media claims?

As someone who has actually put out not one, but TWO zines with covers featuring a city skyline in flames, I have to ask, if we really did know all along that something like this might happen, how CAN things really be any different? Just a couple of months ago, I felt like discontent in this nation had reached an all-time high in my brief lifetime. The huge globalization protests were starting to chart more in the public consciousness and there were a lot of people out there who thought the election was, straight up, stolen. After watching a lot of the things I'd been a part of in the 90s really starting to take off, there's no way I can sit back in silence and let the media try to shove our ideas and our very lives back in the margins again. No fucking way!!

If anything, the now seemingly silent anti-globalization crew has had the perfect issue thrown right into their laps. Now that globalization has been revealed to cause a worldwide hatred of the US government's policies that is violent enough to result in the deaths of innocent American civilians on the US mainland, the media can hardly claim that the protesters aren't protesting anything "tangible." Grimly enough, this is a sort-of version of the Cold War's Mutually Assured Destruction from my childhood years—the idea that US killing of civilians worldwide by bombing OR sanction will likely result in corresponding "collateral damage" in our streets. The issue is simply survival —something that may be able to explain to mainstream folks just why everyone's against globalization.

You have asked me to write a "critique of activist tactics" or something like that for your zine. I'm responding in letter format, because I don't want to seem like I have all the answers or like I'm telling people what they should be doing. I'm more interested in a sort-of list of the questions that nag me at 4:08 AM on nights like this. Anyway, I think that's one of the main problems with activist stuff in general: It's all telling and no asking. Instead of asking folks in your neighborhood what they'd be into organizing to do, activists seem to be more into telling the poor, huddled masses why meat, cars, TV, work, and the stores they shop at are Wrong. (If you're having trouble seeing why this may be annoying and ineffective, try RE-imagining this scenario with you listening as a kid 10 years younger than you tells you why you're not political or punk enough. Happens to me all the time!)

I've recently put out a 10-year-anniversary re-issue package of my zines and records so I've been thinking back a lot lately on the last ten years that brought us from one right-wing Christian Bush administration leading a needless war on an impoverished, trumped-up enemy to, well, ANOTHER one. The media would have us believe that the country has never been this "united," never been so "as one." But, I know that it's simply not true. On these streets, in these zines, there has been a counter-narrative of a secret history, hidden on midnight freight trains, barreling across America, spray painted on walls and booming out of pirate radio stations, left off the dial. On West Madison and West Burnside. In the 25th Hour. A discontent ultimately shouted loud and proud in huge street protests across the world.

I would say now that our scene does seem really strong. (In this text I use "our" and "we" loosely to describe, basically, the people who are likely to read this zine.) Our numbers are big, there's a lot of energy and enthusiasm, nationwide, and when I travel around, I sometimes get all choked up at how many awesome people I'm lucky to know. Nonetheless, only an idiot or someone who only sees what they want to see could look at all this and think that we are, somehow, winning, and the complete shutout of anti-war ideas from recent media debate underscores that. I feel our side is mistaking the loudness and size of street protests for broad support. As it stands, we appear to be in a pretty large intellectual ghetto.

Or maybe it's a suburb. Thinking back on my first zine, which was largely about how to rip off and steal from the then newly emerging chain stores across the land, I remember now that I actually had to take three buses from downtown Ft. Lauderdale where I lived to the vast new suburbs freshly constructed in the former Everglades where the shiny new Office Depot I had written about actually was, so I could steal the copies. Now, a mere 10 years later, there's an Office Depot or Kinko's every mile or so, even in the old urban cores of bigger cities. I've been thinking how ironic it is, then, that in 10 years of being part of this fairly big, traveling scene that survives off scamming these stores, the stores have replicated themselves endlessly, even as we've kept bleeding them for cash. What's worse is, somewhere along the way, as the copycat chain stores have made our cities more rootless and similar and less interesting, our rootlessness and dependence on these stores has seemed to make our individual scenes less interesting and more similar. I remember that I started trying to figure out how to scam stuff from these places as self-defense, but also because crime is a good way to figure out how the world works. Like, I wondered if you really could just Xerox a Greyhound Ameripass and glue the two halves together and travel around the country with it, so I tried it. But after the chain stores became so dominant, I noted while traveling around that everywhere I went, it was like people had the same four scams all involving the same handful of chain stores. It started to seem like everyone wanted to talk about the books they stole, but not the books they had read; everyone talked about the exact spots that the crew change guide said to catch the freights, but no one talked about what it felt like to actually be ON a train. Anyway, now it's 10 years later, and every town has a Kinko's, a Gap, a Starbucks, AND a Food Not Bombs and a Critical Mass. Weird, huh?

I'm not saying these aren't good things to be doing, but I am saying that sometimes it seems like we're missing the point. Today there are far more ready-made political movements that you can join than there were 10 years ago, but maybe, if we question our assumptions about them and try to apply them more locally we can come up with something more interesting. For instance, the last time I cooked Food Not Bombs was last summer in one of those mid-sized fairly cheap cities that fill up with hordes of traveling punks every summer, most of whom quickly descend upon this one scrubby ghetto main drag that is quickly becoming a controversial gentrification hotspot. We would cook the food and then take the food by car a considerable distance to a park downtown where about 5 homeless folks would join 30 mostly out-of-town punks who had ridden bikes from the cookhouse neighborhood to eat it. Now, a free food program successfully run by and for punks is nothing to sneer at, BUT, I had to ask why we didn't just do it back in the gentrifying cookhouse area. Someone said, well, people up there wouldn't be into it. I wondered if that were true. I wondered if maybe their neighbors would be into it if it didn't require eating in a park or an empty lot, or what kind of free food distribution people WOULD be into? Was there a way that punks could use their resources to HELP the neighbors fight gentrification together? How would they know if they didn't ask?

Critical Mass often seems unquestioned to me, too. It makes so much simple, beautiful sense in big cities where there's a reasonable public transportation alternative or really small towns where walking is just as good. But I've seen it imported to the hot, humid, sprawling car-dominated towns of the South with often disastrous results. Once, a few years back, as I watched a kid pulling his mangled mountain bike out from under a car that had deliberately tried to run him over and kill him at a Greensboro, NC Critical Mass, I had to wonder if he really expected that blocking miles of traffic at rush hour on a hot summer day while pounding on hoods and screaming "Ride a fuckin' bike!!!" was going to actually win people over? If so, what KIND of people? I remember that I was, in fact, won over enough to drink beer with those kids until 5 or 6:00 AM, but if I was a guy on his way home from work, I doubt I would have wanted to get out and RIDE BIKES with them. Sometimes it's important to remember that the people in those cars didn't make their shitty world; they just have to sit in gridlock traffic in the hot sun on the way to shitty, non-union jobs at roadside chain stores to survive in it, and, to them, when there's no realistic public transportation option and bike riding is clearly shown to be nearly DEADLY, protesters just look like rich kids with privilege and all the free time in the world to stand around ruining their day and telling them their way of life is Wrong. It might actually not be too hard to convince me that the historical significance of something that wild happening in Greensboro or Little Rock or Chattanooga is worth all of it, but don't you think people should at least ask themselves these questions before they act?

It's this lack of questioning that seems to be holding us back. How can a scene so large be so isolated? How can creative, vibrant activist houses, venues, and collective spaces be located in the heart of existing ghettos around the country and remain so completely insular and often irrelevant to the cities around them? I get frustrated because after a while I just get bored with what we're all doing and wonder what kind of possibilities would break open if we could share the energy and resources of these spaces with the cities around us. It just seems like we're a couple of ideas away from something really big, sometimes.

I've started to think that the problem is that we haven't articulated a clear vision of exactly what kind of world we are supposedly fighting to live in. Much of "Life after the Revolution" as currently imagined in song, zine, and vague sentiment seems to be some hazy "Back to the Land" bullshit or some future "starting over" in the weeds of ruined, fallen cities. But "Back to the Land" fetishization hasn't led to an actual mass movement of activist-run farming or, at least, punks triumphantly throwing off rent forever and owning land. Instead, it seems to manifest itself in a clear mental retreat from the people who don't already agree with us, from the chaos and uncertainty of cities and the very world of possibilities they contain.

As for me, I love cities, the idea of a bunch of people from all walks of life attempting to live and strive together in relative harmony; the democratic ideal that everyone in a city wouldn't have to be best friends but would, at least, be able to tolerate and respect each other. I don't WANT to go Back To The Land. I don't WANT to live on a commune. I certainly don't want to have all the answers. There's no literature in it, no mystery. I want to walk down the street and ponder the layers of history and the lives that came before and the lives to come and the hopes and dreams of all of us who somehow ended up in this place together. And, late at night, I like to think that somewhere out in those streets and alleys, the tunnels and doorways, and sleepless hotel walls, there is an idea that might save us all.

Maybe I don't want the Revolution at all. I certainly don't want to grow my own food. I just have zero interest in it. As Chris Carlson points out in the new *Processed World*, that's the problem: an American people that already work longer hours than any time in their history see The Revolution as a new set of chores. As for me, I've started to fear it as some sort of nightmare where cheerful 20-year-olds lead me on a morning round of Radical Cheerleading before I have to go out and pick the lettuce. Help! Have you ever PICKED lettuce, Icky? On Caty's farm we did it with Exact-o Knives, backs bent in the sun, and it SUCKED! And how cruelly ironic, too, the old instrument of the Revolutionary Stencil, turned against us!

Much to my disappointment, the promise of Seattle has led to the ultimate sort of chain store activism, the huge globalization protests themselves. In all my years of squatting and stuff, I've never been the "Fight the cops" guy, because in general I've found the police are often easily outwitted but so much harder to defeat in armed confrontation. But, now, these huge protests are like the Super Bowl—gritty battles staged once or twice a year in various neutral host cities with all the macho pre-game hype on both opposing sides that goes with it. It is unquestionably a powerful feeling to be in the midst of even a small march, but I've come to see that so much more is needed. It is so much easier to go shout your opinion with a hundred thousand strangers than it is to discuss your opinion and try to create something with just a couple of people. Where does all the energy from those things go when they're over?

Back home, on a much smaller scale, in SF, I've started to notice that most protests require you to self-identify as the helpless victim of something. It always seems like people watching us march tend to agree with us and know that we are right, but can't bring themselves to march with us. Maybe we just look like we're begging too much for help. Or maybe when the flyers are wheat-pasted to the bottoms of telephone poles and backsides of dumpsters, we're sort of EMBRACING marginalization. At the very least, it doesn't look like we're Playing To Win, ya know? It's like when "Pirate Radio"— something tough, proud, and mysterious that captures the imagination—becomes "Community Micro-powered Radio"—something that makes me think of Wavy Gravy reading the *Slingshot* aloud for 3 hours. It doesn't seem like any way to get people to respect you. Even the flyers people use always seem to use some Eric Drooker drawing that depicts us getting beat up by a cop or getting kicked out of our houses or run over by tanks or something. Who wants to go on a march like THAT?

What I'm saying is that I'm more interested these days in organizing around building what we are FOR instead of what we're against all the time. This year, confronted with the widespread eviction of activist and art and punk spaces in SF, a zero percent commercial vacancy rate, and an unprecedented and rigorous crackdown and prosecution of graffiti, a bunch of folks got together to come up with a plan to decide what to do with what we had access to, to make The City look the way we wanted it to. We made lists of ideas, agreeing to coordinate efforts to make posters together around agreed-upon themes. We decided to quit doing "graffiti" and start doing huge murals in broad daylight, and simply act like we had permission to do them. And we decided we wanted to break into abandoned spaces and do huge shows. The end result of that (besides a lot of posters, stickers, and a block-long No More Prisons piece done one day on 3rd Street) was the huge squatted show space and free cafe we opened at 949 Market Street, right downtown. It was exciting to me because everybody was involved, not just the punks, and because, after several years of fighting gentrification, it was the first thing a lot of us had done that seemed like a statement about how we WANT to spend our time, about the power of what we all can do together, and not just about our status as potential evictees. It was a complete act of faith that what we dream about IS attainable and worth fighting for.

Now, I wonder about ways we can organize neighbors to feel that good about stuff in a way that's, incidentally, totally anti-war. Like, besides the numbers in the streets (which aren't even there yet), what can we do so that there's something besides the shouting and fighting the cops? Before I split SF for the winter, one friend had this plan to use this abandoned building in the projects next to her house in some way to maybe distribute all this free food she has access to and start something there. She was about to start having meetings about what folks there might like to see, if anything, in such a space. I don't know if her plan would work, or if the folks in the projects would just think she's some dumb white kid outsider. But I DO know that taking that leap of faith and putting our resources and ideas on the line beyond our limited scene is the only way we're really going to build anything to stop this war.

Ironically, like September 11th, the squat was an action intended to change the way people think about the world. We tried to do something that would make people feel hopeful, confident, and un-afraid. Now the Sept. 11th attacks have made the world a darker, more cynical place again, a place full of fear and failed possibility. What will happen now? Where ARE those protesters that filled the streets so recently? How can we find a way to relate our vision of the world to our neighbors when everyone on the streets seems like an enemy again and there is the dark, nagging thought that the American people, even if fully informed by the truth, may not in any way CARE that bombing Afghanistan GUARANTEES the winter starvation of a million or so innocent civilians?

I don't know, but my friend's still groaning in the next room and it's a long time before sunrise. Events still threaten to rewrite our past. What about our hopes and dreams? What will we have left if we just give up? The stakes are high. Anyone from protester to Hunt's prostitute felt a little swagger when the cops got their asses kicked in Seattle. But have you ever really considered what it really feels like to LOSE?

I have seen the seed of possible defeat in person at the A16 Anti-IMF protest last April in DC. The cops so completely dominated the protesters with brutal pre-emptive strikes and raids and dirty tricks that by the last day the whole affair had become so pointless that THOUSANDS of protesters arranged a deal for a media-ready mass arrest that proved or contested NOTHING. I watched in disbelief as the lines came forward, one at a time, to TURN THEMSELVES IN, symbolically crossing a line and stepping into the waiting handcuffs of bored cops. It was pathetic and depressing, the only time I've ever been embarrassed to be on this side of the line.

The next day, I was in a cafe with my girlfriend reading the paper. The *Post* featured a front page photo of a girl handing a rose to a grinning Chief Ramsey and all the people in the coffee shop were looking at their papers and at us, like, "Hey! You're a couple of those dumb kids who came here to get your asses kicked by and then give flowers to our cops!" It was horrible and the bad taste didn't leave me for some time, even after we had split town, safely hidden away in the toilet of an Amtrak train to Philly.

I kept thinking about the punks. The poor kids probably thought they were hitching to Woodstock or something—the next Seattle, HISTORY. Then they had to go back to their little towns and try to figure out what it meant when everyone gave up. There's not enough beer in town, sometimes, to live it down when history hands you a new worldview like that.

Well, Icky, this probably wasn't what you rang for. There's not a lot of comfort in this one. But have you tried the word of Jesus? What about heroin? Right now, I'd probably give just about anything to be asleep and dreaming in that sweet Sept. 10th bed, but here I am on Houston Street in downtown Chattanooga with the rain coming in and the groaning from the next room's getting louder, and not even a drop of good whiskey in the whole house. So, I'm going it alone tonight, cold turkey, with all the rest of them out there alone in the caves of St. Louis, Cincinnati, Detroit, where they're starting to feel a chill like they've never felt before. It's 5:20 AM and all I have for company tonight is the new Dead Moon record, so I'm listening to it again. "40 Miles of Bad Road"—a song with a sound that walks tall where others crawl, music so rare and true and unafraid that it gives you goose bumps to hear it, like a melody you heard once and lost. A melody lost but so familiar we know it by heart, and keep searching for it.

We keep searching for it inside ourselves.

Take care,
Iggy Scam
Chattanooga, TN
December 7, 2001

THE NEW WAR STARTS AT HOME:
ARAB CAFE DRIVEN OUT OF HYDE STREET
STOREFRONT IN THE NIGHT

On a day when the *San Jose Mercury News* headline announced "Congress to Expand Power to Detain Immigrants," the Berber Cafe, a Tenderloin social club run for and by North African residents, disappeared without a trace. The cafe is believed to be a victim of the rising tide of anti-Arab racism since the World Trade Center attacks on September 11th.

The cafe on Hyde near Turk opened earlier this year as an ordinary breakfast spot with Northern African decoration. They sold coffee to the general public, but I never saw anybody in there except a large group of Northern African men who gathered daily to drink coffee, smoke out of hookahs, and play some sort of game with beads. The men would be in there from early in the morning until late at night, talking and laughing, gathered around the small cafe's two tables. Eventually the cafe took down their "Berber Cafe" sign and remained open, but with nothing for sale. Still, the men came and they could often be seen heating up the coals used to light the hookah in the dirt area around the sidewalk tree in front of the storefront. They added more decoration to the window, including a colorful hat of an almost sombrero shape, covered in colorful yarn, that is a common decoration in the peasant restaurants in the mountains of Morocco. The *Turd-Filled Donut's* co-editor, Ivy, has visited Morocco and would stop to talk about her travels with the men, who it turned out, were from Tunisia.

Walking past every night, I always felt good about the Berber Cafe. It was nice to think of a small group of men, so far from home, who'd found a place to hang out together and talk their old language and display the customary decoration of their country. It was nice to think of the Tenderloin as a place where I really do meet people from all over the world every day—from the girl at the donut shop on Golden Gate who is from Indonesia to the guys at the Berber with their loud laughing and games.

In the week following the attack on the World Trade Center, President Bush called immediately for war, for retribution, for some sort of violent response to world terrorism. The media responded by showing footage of Palestinians celebrating the World Trade Center collapse—footage that was later revealed to be ten year-old footage of Palestinians from some completely different event that the media cynically used to help whip people into an anti-Arab frenzy.

The footage showed Palestinians dancing in broad daylight, but it was night in Palestine when the attacks took place in New York. All through this week, the men gathered as usual at the Berber Cafe, staying as late as ever. The last time I saw them, they were still in there at 11:00 PM. But, the next day, their front door glass was cracked, all of their furniture was completely removed, and there was no trace of them at midday. A branch clipping from the tree out front had been left in the security gate, its symbolism unclear.

The next day, a note appeared, slipped through the gate, that read, "Jamal! What happened? We are concerned for your safety. Your friend, Brian," with a phone number. The day after that a "For Lease" sign went up in the window.

I called the landlord about the sign. He was evasive, and said in broken, Chinese-accented English, "They go! They have family problem. They leave key with friend to give to me, but I no see them go. Now I rent it out."

Angelo from Angelo's garage next door sort of looked at the ground and stonewalled, the way you're supposed to when people you don't know ask questions in the Tenderloin. He shrugged when I asked him about the Berber Cafe and said, "They disappear."

One more week later, Bush is still calling for a "new kind of war." I don't think killing innocent people to teach that killing innocent people is wrong will work, but that doesn't matter to Bush and his supporters. It probably won't mean much to the guys from the Berber Cafe either. The war is here.

They're already fighting it.

SQUATTING THE GLORIOUS RUINS OF THE DOT-COM BUST

I left town for a few months and when I got back in early 2002, I came home to a ghost town. Suddenly, there were potential squats everywhere. Vacancy rates South of Market were as high as 40%. Newly constructed loft spaces faded, unsold, in the Mission sun, as the clock struck twelve for the dot-com economy and the briefly-hip former ghetto turned back into a pumpkin before our eyes. I found a cute one-story abandoned warehouse in an alley South of Market and used a cordless drill to get the door open. I was pleased to find that it had working electricity and was fairly clean, but I would have to figure out how to get the water turned on to make it my new squat. The day I started moving in, I was carrying in an old futon I'd found on big trash night, when I met my new neighbor. He squatted in the abandoned house across the street!

The next day, I checked out a cafe in my new neighborhood, taking a long, leisurely morning with the paper. The other patrons all seemed to have been stranded there in some arrested state of hipness, beached when some long forgotten wave of Cool from a previous gentrifying boom period had broken. There were middle-aged women, still with dyed pink hair and leopard-print creepers; there were sad-looking balding men with goatees. At the counter, I overheard a young guy, about my age, chuckle to the tattooed and pierced girl at the register. "Well," he said. "It looks like I lost all my money!"

"Let me guess," she sneered. "Stock market?"

"Yeah!" he said. "It's all true!" He shook his head, as if in wonder. "I was a day trader! Remember how I used to just sit in here all day? I was a day trader!"

But she'd already moved down the counter to the next customer. I got a refill and considered the sweet urban irony of me and the former day trader, now scrounging for refills in the same cafe, while me and my friends set out with crowbars to open up the now-empty places where his kind had worked.

Like many, I'd expected a dot-com collapse to give poor people and underground artists more breathing room. But as the summer unfolded, it seemed like somehow we'd gone straight into The Great Depression II overnight. There were no jobs and homeless people filled the doorways of now-empty office space. Our country, so we were told, was now engaged in a perpetual war that would last beyond our lifetime. With more people needing help than ever, rich kid mayoral candidate and Board of Supervisors member Gavin Newsom began efforts to slash welfare checks for The City's poorest residents, launching his candidacy for mayor by attacking the homeless.

Jobs fled The City. Reeling from the discovery of its role in the growing Enron scandal, accounting firm Arthur Anderson alone laid off thousands in San Francisco. Somehow I, of all people, found a job though. I'm the guy who sorted Arthur Anderson's trash! I got hired at SCRAP, a non-profit that accepts donations of used items that would otherwise be thrown into the landfill and then offers them for sale, dirt cheap, as art supplies. When I started working there, Arthur Anderson donated countless boxes of whatever had been left in their offices when they closed their doors. I spent nearly the entire three months that I worked at SCRAP sorting these boxes, full of huge piles of Arthur Anderson's old Post-It Note pads, transparent tape dispensers, staplers, envelopes, and pens that didn't work.

I still have an electrical power strip that says "Arthur Anderson" on it that I took from work one day to use at a generator show at 16th and Mission BART that I'd set up.

Arthur Anderson's closing left hundreds of people in the Bay Area out of work, but their office closure CREATED at least one job: mine.

47 CLARION

The warehouse at 47 Clarion was not only one of my favorite squats ever, but one of my favorite places that I have ever lived, period. Ironically, the first time I ever went inside the building was the last time most people in town went there, when I played in Shotwell at the last show ever there.

The eviction of Aaron Noble and the Clarion Alley Mural Project from 47 Clarion was a high-profile local news story, another sign of just how bad everything really had become in The Mission. It proved that even the most established neighborhood institutions weren't safe from the onslaught of dot-com cash. After the eviction, the 94-year-old historic building was to be torn down and replaced with—of course!—prefab lofts. I had heard about it and been bummed about it in an abstract way like everyone else. It wasn't until I actually stepped inside it that night that I could feel just what a special place we were losing.

The building was built in 1907 and all made of wood. It felt like it was from an older world, somehow spacious like an old barn, yet intimate like a cabin in the woods. There was something else. I can't explain it exactly, but the space just felt STRONG somehow, like a lot of great things had happened there. Now, the artists had taken a settlement and were moving out. They had been having huge parties for weeks. The show we were playing was to be the last.

It was packed. People were looking down from the upper floor, hanging over the railing, waving bottles. Sacrilicious rocked like hell first, and the big room was full of people dancing, especially Rigo and Carmen. Before we played, we had Peter Plate come up to read a piece he'd written in honor of the space's last night, a rousing speech where he declared that the space had once been the Mission IWW Wobblie hall and tonight, we were linked to them. The yuppies were knocking down our Wobblie hall and we were fucking pissed! It was a damn good speech.

We were playing, there was lots of dancing and it felt like a good night. All of a sudden, during our cover of "Thick as Thieves" I heard some weird sound coming out of the guitar. Mission punks know this is not uncommon with Shotwell. But I looked up from the drums to see a cop trying to grab Jimmy! There was another cop by the door. Jimmy shrugged off the cop and stepped away from him. Next, the cop looked at me and made the hand-cutting-across-throat motion, mouthing, "Off! Turn it off!"

I looked at Jimmy, who was still playing the song. I looked out at the crowd, still dancing. I looked at the cop, smiled, and mouthed, "No fucking way!"

As soon as the music was done, Buzz, the bass player, yelled, "Keep playing! Quick!" and we launched right into another song, before the cops could try to assert themselves in the quiet. The crowd danced harder. The cop looked pissed. Finally, Peter took the cops outside to talk. There's nothing that Mission cops love more than talking to Peter Plate. Peter kept them confused for long enough for us to play about eight more songs! And that was that, a really great last sendoff to a haunted old Wobblie hall. The end.

Or was it? What has been most remarkable about the last few years in San Francisco was the great speed with which events happened and whole eras came and went. In late 2000, I was attending tenants' rights marches seemingly every day. In the midst of this came the publishing of Rebecca Solnit's *Hollow City*, an actual hardcover book with the urgency of a flyer, full of photos of the marches I'd just attended in those past months. I had first read in the book—and not in a newspaper!—that the Clarion Alley Mural Project warehouse might be sold and the artists who lived in it might be evicted. In just a couple months, the artists had taken a settlement and were leaving The City and we had played the last party there. But by the time just another month went by, the economy was slowing down. The papers were full of declarations that the boom was now bust. And the expected demolition of the warehouse hadn't taken place. 47 Clarion was still sitting there, empty.

Maybe if I couldn't write another chapter in 47 Clarion's history, I could at least add an afterword. Late one night, Jimmy and I popped the lock off the front door and I moved in to my new squat.

It ended up being a great free place to live, with running water and grand skylights set in the ceiling (no electricity, though). To pay tribute to the building as a longtime home to the creative process, I decorated my kitchen writing space with rough sketches of Aaron Noble's murals that he'd left behind. I have a lot of great memories of the four months I lived there. I remember lying in bed with Melissa until late in the afternoon, when we first started going out, and how my tiny room felt snug like a ship's cabin. I remember drinking coffee and eating pan-fried toast while the glorious Mission sun flooded in the skylights in my kitchen on long mornings. I remember many nights spent writing by candlelight until late, safe in the ship cabin, while The City roiled like a vast sea outside.

There was still a lot of space inside to explore, too. Jimmy's friend, Mark, who had lived there, had also left a bunch of stuff behind. Jim and I went through some of it, looking for stuff to sell at the flea market. We came upon a big pile of these weird, huge Styrofoam replicas of human heads that Mark had left behind. One day, months later, we solved the mystery of the creepy heads when we finally watched some of the dusty VHS videos we'd found in the squat.

On one old tape, there was a very young-looking Mark from around 1982, out on the streets of the Mission, explaining to the camera that he was going to use this strong epoxy to cement one of these Styrofoam heads on to a wall. Then he turned and actually started gluing the head to the wall! It was Art! Jimmy and I recognized the façade of the building Mark was in front of. It was the building at 16th and Valencia that Epicenter used to be in. Today, the wall that Mark was gluing the head on to is not visible because there is a new building there. But at the time, that intersection was the home of the Gartland Pit—the big, empty lot where the Gartland Apartments had been burned down by landlord arson in 1975.

We watched the video in amazement. There were brief shots of the pit, the longtime site of guerilla anti-gentrification, anti-slumlord art actions, including many performances by Peter Plate. After the camera surveyed the art for a while, a Latino guy came into the frame. He was trying to get Mark to STOP. He kept saying, "Stop! Why you do this? Why you do this my building?" while Mark tried to explain to the man, "No, no. This is good! You see, this is ART!"

I couldn't believe it: here on video we were watching perhaps the very first interaction between a Mission Latino and this new race of strange white people, The Artists! The Latino man had no clue what he was a part of at that moment either, how things would one day turn out. He had no context yet to understand the strange behavior of this man with the heads, but soon more like him would come. Here, in a building that was to be destroyed by the changes in the neighborhood, we found a tape showing glimpses of the earliest days of the changes.

Unfortunately, the boom wasn't busted enough to stop the condo project from eventually being built at 47 Clarion. I went out of town after living there happily for four months and left the squat with Zoe. One morning in November, Ivy and Zoe were sleeping there when the wrecking ball slammed into the building with them in it! They got their shit and got the hell out, the last people to sleep there after 94 damn years.

Melissa told me about it while I was away. She said, "It's so weird. The room where we used to lay is just a space up in the air now."

As part of the settlement, Aaron got the right to do a mural on the back of the new condos and got in a pretty good last word, a brief

valediction on the whole dot-com story in a way. The new mural depicts comic book hero The Thing, from *The Fantastic Four,* crashing
out of the rear of the new building.

The text reads in huge letters, "Kaboom!"

INDIVISIBLE UNDER GOD?

Energy crisis? Stock-market crash? World terrorism? Bring it on!
Not much changes around here in *Turd-Filled Donut* land. We get
rolling blackouts every time the guy down the hall turns on his hot
plate. Half the buildings on 6th Street already look like someone flew
an airplane into them, and people still have to LIVE there. Now
everyone's talking about going to war. All I know is whenever I see
someone waving a flag, I know something bad is about to happen,
and it's more likely to happen to me than the guy with the flag. The
assholes leading this summer's huge "Clean Up the Streets" campaign with their brooms and police patrols get to try to clean up the
WHOLE WORLD now, and the media's right there to keep them
whipped up into a frothing-mouthed frenzy.

There might be so much "Clean up the streets" hype these days
that the homeless are getting self-conscious about their appearance.
Jorge, the homeless ruler of San Carlos Street showed up at Hunt's
Donuts the other night with a new haircut. "People were starting to
complain," he explained. To WHO?!? DPW?!? GOD?!? I also ran
into Gomez the homeless squatter and Jack out front of Hospitality
House shelter and they were both sporting brand new button-down
shirts and slacks, like they had a date or something. "Gomez!" I
said. "You've been kicked out of three abandoned buildings this
WEEK! Where'd you get a new jacket and tie? Is The City paying
homeless guys to stand around in suits now, so no one will notice
them?" Gomez explains, "There's been all this yuppie clothing given
out free at St. Anthony's lately. I think the dot-commers are leaving
this stuff behind when they move away." Funny how that works

out, huh? The yuppies evict everyone and then the homeless guys dress up in their old clothes when the YUPPIES lose their spaces. Its kind of like how the cops shut down all the bars in the Mission because Latino people did drugs in them, and they became white, hipster bars—where white hipsters do drugs... Speaking of stock market collapse, a year ago, when Tom's Grocery closed, I expected its space to get taken over by web design jerks who'd start another neighborhood watch to complain about pee, but now that the market has been "corrected," Tom's space has now cheerfully been turned over to the new home of the 6th Street Cannabis Club! "Best clone selection, lowest cost, most potent BAKED goods in town," says a flyer. I'm not sure it'd exactly make Tom proud, but it could have been worse.

THE SIDEWALK'S ALWAYS BROWNER ON THE OTHER SIDE: This reporter overheard two homeless guys talking in filthy, urine-soaked Clarion Alley in the Mission. One said, "I want to go see that new movie, The Planet of the Apes." The other said, 'Hey! They should call it, Planet of the 6th STREET Apes'! Huh huh!" Now, THAT hurts!

INDIVISIBLE?: OVERHEARD down on Mid-Market, under the flying flags, a guy says, "Spare change for a homeless United States Vet?" Two gutter punk girls walking past yell back, "Fuck off! We're homeless heroin addicts!" THE THRONE OF OUR LORD: Graffiti in a stall at the Hospitality House Self-Help Center men's room reads, "Thank you Jesus for everything." Someone added underneath it, "Like making me a crack head."

THE CAMPAIGN TRAIL: Supervisor Chris Daly was spotted on Turk Street the other day, holding a painting he'd won in the silent auction at the Coalition on Homelessness's Art Auction benefit. "I got a Drooker!" he gushed, holding up his print by artist Eric Drooker. I redirected Daly's attention to the parking meter next to us where a small, determined Asian man had put down his plastic bag full of aluminum cans and had started doggedly digging at the slot with some needle nose pliers and a long thing piece of metal. Right before our eyes, a shiny, new quarter came out in the grip of the pliers, still stuck in the slot. We watched in awe and anticipation, mesmerized, as the guy struggled to get it out, like a fisherman fighting the Big One. Finally, Daly just shook his head, and said, "Well! Got to go!" After he left, the guy finally got it out. Daly should have stuck around; THAT was art!

SANDWHICH HEIST AT H.H.: Speaking of "Self Help", Hospitality House Drop-In Center workers are still on the lookout for sandwiches stolen from a group of clients on an outing to the movies at The Kabuki. Miss Washington made a bag of 32 sandwiches and another bag of 32 drinks and the large group of clients set out together for a free afternoon movie, but halfway there they saw the guy entrusted with holding the sandwiches jetting off down Geary the wrong way! He was around the corner and out of sight before anyone could react. If anyone recovers the sandwiches, feel free to contact H.H., but my guess is he's halfway to Mexico by now...

MISSED CONNECTIONS? The other night this reporter watched a young, clean-cut guy sporting the undercover look approach a table full of black prostitutes taking a break at Hunt's Donuts at 20th and Mission and say, "So...how does a white guy get laid around here?" One girl shoots back, "850 Bryant's the only place a cop like you can get laid! You got to get it from us in the office!" and the donut shop broke up laughing, while the guy sheepishly backed out the door. Uh, does this mean we can't still be friends? Meanwhile, the Center City YMCA on Golden Gate has been wilder than Capp Street this summer. On the bulletin board in the lobby for members' comments, someone writes to ask, "Why are the bleachers above the racquetball court closed to the public now? When I hit a ball up there, it is now impossible for me to retrieve it." Management response was terse, but evocative. "If people insist on having sex in the racquetball bleachers, the bleachers will remain closed." Another member writes in, "If I have to see ONE MORE guy giving another guy head in the men's sauna, I'm quitting my membership and demanding my money back!" The YMCA—who would've thought? It's just like the song!

MISSION BLUES: Carlos Guitarlos, the famed 16th Street bluesman, has been on a roll lately with a new CD, *Mission Blues,* and a front-page story about his hard-time life and music in *The Guardian.* The CD's good, too. Carlos sings the sweet ones real sweet and the sad ones real sad. I went to find the lesser light of Mission District street acoustic rock, OMER—sometimes called Wolf Boy—on his usual Valencia doorway tour to ask him if he was bummed that Carlos was getting all the press, but before I could show him Carlos's CD, Omer showed me HIS! Yes, Omer has a CD out and now, for only $7, you can pretend that Omer's shouting his rambling, monotone, vaguely threatening songs at you in the privacy of your very own home! The CD, *Democracy is a Good Idea,* was sold out the night I saw Omer, so he advised me to check out his website! "Yeah, I went dot-com," he says. "It's not so evil." Be your own judge at www.spectacularopticals.com/OMER. As for Carlos Guitarlos, when we called him for comment, he was down in LA recording a new album with legendary punk bassist Mike Watt. Congratulations, Carlos... Adam Arms, the Coalition on Homelessness's staff attorney, has split town, too, but not for Mexico. Adam's now up in Portland, Oregon working at the Public Defender's office and planning his wedding. The COH had a big going away party for Adam at Herrington's at the end of June, and it was held on a Thursday afternoon, presumably so that getting drunk on a Thursday afternoon wouldn't interfere with the Coalition's long standing staff tradition of getting drunk on FRIDAY afternoons. With Arms's departure, the Coalition lost not only a dedicated attorney who fought hard for victories against The City in cases where The City had confiscated homeless folks' property, but also the star player on their softball team. This year, the defending champion Coalition lost the non-profit softball tournament, failing to win a single game, as 6th Street's Rose Hotel staff and residents took home the trophy...

Carlos Guitarlos is in LA and Adam Arms is in Portland, but, yeah, nothing much is new around here. When the World Trade Center was attacked, the whole city shut down—except the guys playing chess on Market at the cable car turnaround. They just kept playing as if to say, nothing's changed; the people just trying to get by in the world will always be here. A couple of days later, I saw Aesop, who used to write for us, showing off his new baby to friends on Mission Street. The flags were flying all around in the grey, cold SF summer wind, and he was coming back from buying a bag of shitty weed at one of those Mission Street businesses that pretend to sell, say, pizza, but are really fronts. While his baby gurgled and everybody smiled at it, Aesop mentioned the flags that are suddenly everywhere, even in SF. He said, "You know, no amount of terrorism is going to make me love this fucking country." On 6th, later that day, a cheerful, very drunk man grabbed me and said, "My friend! A plane full of explosives is heading to blow up San Francisco! We have ten minutes to live!" and he rambled off cheerfully yelling, "Ten minutes! They'll blow us up! In ten minutes!" all the way down 6th Street.

Yeah, nothing much is new around here and sometimes I think of how pretty it is up in Portland, the way the sun shines off the river and all those bridges downtown in the summer. All those trees, all the green and the open space. I think of Adam up there, working on a family. Sometimes when nothing changes I think about it a lot, but I just don't think I'd like it up there.

No matter how you look at it, the streets are just too clean.

TRENT HAYWARD R.I.P.
HOMELESS WRITER/ACTIVIST DEAD AT 34

When I heard that Trent had OD'd and died in the empty lot at McAllister and Larkin, I went there, past midnight, to drink a beer and pay my last respects at the little shrine of flowers, candles, and half-drunk beers that his friends had left there. Pouring out the last of a 24-ounce tall can for Trent, I thought, "DAMN! Who DIES staring right at fucking City Hall?"

What a drag. Trent had the kind of sense of humor that I could imagine him joking about kicking the bucket there and floating off to heaven in that rarified air over that golden dome, and seeing the angels at the pearly gates.

"Welcome to heaven," the angels would say. "It's only $2400 a month...FOREVER!"

Or maybe not. Trent hated City Hall and all that went on inside of it as much as anyone I've ever worked with. I remember long days last summer spent typing articles for this paper at the Coalition on Homelessness's office on Turk Street, while Trent worked on his own time, cranking out articles for the *Street Sheet* about homeless people's civil rights. He'd spend all day calling up mayoral candidates, demanding to know what they'd do for the homeless if elected.

But then, on some days, he'd just blow up a big photocopy of Supervisor Amos Brown's face and tape it to the wall, writing, "Darts, anyone?" on it in marker. This was Trent's apparent calling, something more than writing or reporting—something closer to what Paul Boden might call, "The fucking pursuit of social fucking justice."

Or, as one guy who used to stay at the empty lot on McAllister, too, explained at Trent's memorial, "Me and Trent was STP. That's 'Stop the Pigs,' 'Save the People,' and 'Start the Party'!"

A memorial was held for Trent on June 11ᵗʰ in the empty lot where he died, across the street from City Hall. About 75 friends, activists, writers, and street paper reporters showed up to speak about and remember Trent. Most of the speakers praised Trent's writing and spoke of what a great friend he was to have around on the streets with you. And, of course, a couple of speakers took the opportunity to point out that it's unconscionable that homeless people can die practically ON the steps of City Hall in this city with all of its unprecedented boom-time wealth.

While I of course agree that the city's treatment of its poor and homeless is a daily crime and I know there are countless desperate people dying daily for want of housing and health care, I don't think Trent was exactly one of them. Trent was hardly in line for a treatment bed. He liked to get drunk and he liked to get loud. When the National Coalition on Homelessness held their rally in UN Plaza and their shopping cart march on City Hall last October, Trent brought the beer.

I remember limping into a Coalition staff meeting one Monday afternoon, nursing my own hangover, only to find Trent there with big scrapes and bruises all over his face.

"What happened, man?" I demanded. "Did the cops beat you up for sleeping on the sidewalk?"

"Actually," Trent deadpanned. "I just got in a fight with the sidewalk."

Trent wanted to live life completely on his own terms. It was part of who he was, part of why you would want to read what he had to say. I remember when he and his friend, Jack, were living out at Land's End, hidden away in a tent with a beautiful ocean view and living off stolen dinners from Safeway. It always sounded like a lot of fun to me. That kind of freedom comes with a big price, though. I think Trent knew the risks, which is why it's hard for me to entirely blame City Hall.

Still, when one of Trent's teachers at his writing class asked the crowd to turn, raise our middle fingers, and yell, "FUCK YOU!" to City Hall, I gladly joined in. "Fuck you!" we yelled, one, two, and three times, while the passengers of a westbound 5 FULTON looked on, confused, and probably a little jealous. "Fuck you!"

We meant it.

City Hall, of course, was not listening. And, now, a month later, there's even a new fence around the lot where the memorial was. I'm guessing the memorial got enough publicity that PG&E, the owners of the lot, decided to finally do something about homeless people dying on their property. They built a fence to keep them out.

I can imagine Trent's bitter headline: "PG&E TO HOMELESS— 'GO DIE SOMEWHERE ELSE!'"

On the day that Trent died, his expertly reported exposé on Hospitality House was running, front page, in the *Street Spirit*, on sale for a buck on every corner in the Bay Area. The article—a caustic, indignant, and very well researched look at how the venerable name in Tenderloin social service has sold out their clients to keep their high management jobs funded—was a must read for anyone trying to understand how rising real estate values and social service funding cuts have caused agencies that were once the thorn in City Hall's side to water down their services, or cease to exist. Trent had also just landed a paying job writing a weekly column of his observations of life on the streets for the online edition of *The Bay Guardian*. Things were looking up for Trent, and his writing was getting a lot of attention.

But the most well known story Trent had done was "Blood on the Clown Suit," which he wrote for *Trash Talk*, which is put out by the Media Alliance *Raising Our Voices* class he took. In "Blood on the Clown Suit," Trent finds that a guy he always eats lunch with at St. Anthony's was once a well-known comedian in the 80s and 90s. Trent recounts his riches to rags story, following the comedian from HBO special fame to being the funniest guy in the soup kitchen line. It was a story with a lot of warmth, a story of the grudging friendship that develops between people who find themselves in the same shitty circumstances together day after day, and a story of perseverance. The story ends with the comedian still cracking 'em up at St. Anthony's and still working on new material and a comeback. I thought it seemed destined to be picked up and reprinted somewhere else.

And, what do you know, I pick up the *Chronicle* a month later and there's Trent's story, running as a "human interest" story, right on the front page. It was Trent's story, except it wasn't exactly. They'd changed it so that it wasn't about friendship, but about how tragic it was that a famous and talented person could wind up homeless. It was about how the comedian needed everyone's help to get off the streets. Still, much of it was ripped off directly from Trent's story. Yes, it was Trent's story but his name was nowhere to be found on it.

"Some human interest story," I thought, bitterly. "Some news."

The Chronicle steals a story from a homeless guy and then they take all the credit. They let him do all the work and then they completely mangle the point. I made a note to try to find Trent to see if he'd known about it, but then, a couple weeks later, Trent was dead.

A couple weeks can be a very long time. By the time Trent's memorial was held, the comedian's luck had changed. The story in the *Chronicle* had brought donations of money and clothes, contacts from old friends offering jobs, gigs, and places to stay—all the breaks a homeless writer with his career on the way up might have received if he'd gotten his name in the *Chronicle*, too. The comedian, in fact, no longer lived on the streets, and there was talk of a cable TV movie to be made about his life. When the comedian came up to the microphone to address the audience at Trent's memorial, cell phone in hand, he looked like a performer very much On the Way Up. This would be his last gig in such a small club.

"If it weren't for Trent," the comedian declared, "I'd still be eating Christmas dinner at a dump like St. Anthony's." And the crowd grumbled, uneasily.

Like the Wednesday dinner at St. Anthony's digesting in their stomachs.

The comedian paused. This was a rough room.

"If it weren't for Trent, I'd still be trying to scrape up cash to sleep in shithole dives like the Sunnyside Hotel." The comedian looked out to a sea of blank faces. Good riddance, I thought. I live in the shithole hotel next door.

The comedian was bombing. But, finally he seemed to remember that this was a memorial for Trent and not a press conference for himself. "If it weren't for Trent, that story in the *Chronicle* would never have been written," he explained. "But I want you to know, the reporter for the *Chronicle* DID try to find Trent to work on the story. He tried to find him for weeks but Trent would never call them back. When I found Trent and asked him why, he said he would never call them back because the *Chronicle* was such a piece of shit. Trent told the *Chronicle* to fuck off!"

And, with that, the crowd applauded at last. Not for the comedian, but for Trent.

Because nothing had been stolen after all.

PUBLIC ART REVIEW #3: THE BAYVIEW BANK ON MISSION STREET

The Bayview Bank faces Mission Street at 22nd with an enormous windowless wall, effectively a blank white canvas. But if you look at the wall, you can see, slightly faded but still clearly visible, a series of red, green, and white splotches where paint struck the wall years ago.

I remember happily that night years ago when three friends and I climbed to the roof of the former Leed's shoe store across the street from the bank with buckets of paint and a couple of bags of party balloons we bought on Mission Street.

In an event typical of the era, the dot-com company BigStep had bought the Bayview Bank building and evicted all the Latino community non-profits in it, so that BigStep could occupy the entire building. We had chosen red, green, and white, for the colors of the Mexican flag, and cheerfully fired sloppy wet balls of paint across the street for hours, laughing as they exploded, Jackson Pollock-like, across the bank's wall.

It was a fun thing to do. I heard it made TV news and I read about it later in various accounts of that time. Of course, not long after, BigStep went under and the dot-com economy disappeared. The non-profits started coming back to the building too. But no one ever bothered to clean the graffiti off the building and today it stands as a reminder of the day-to-day battles of the late 90s in the Mission, an unplanned monument to the struggle of that time.

I pass the bank almost every day and rarely think about the splotches of paint anymore, but sometimes I'll stop and look at them and the years reel past in my mind. How did it happen that we went from non-stop fighting eviction and gentrification to fighting against the president's visions of a perpetual worldwide war, without even a slight break?

TUESDAY AT NOON FOREVER

When I first heard the Tuesday at Noon civil defense siren, I was sitting in my SRO hotel off of 6th Street. I had a split second, almost déjà vu feeling, and I thought, "Well, here it is at last: the war, the End of the World."

Years of childhood terror from the Reagan years and the constant threat of nuclear war flashed before my eyes. I remember that hopeless childhood despair at the idea that the old white men who ran the world might just decide to blow it up before I could get to live my life in it. After a minute though, the streets had remained calm, and I noticed that it was exactly noon and I realized it must have just been a test.

Now that the momentary panic is gone, when I hear the siren my feelings about it have become more nuanced. The siren seems like a small marker of time constantly moving forward in a city where the seasons change so imperceptibly and the fog always seems to be rolling in.

Sometimes I hear it and think, "Another Tuesday at noon," and I feel a little anxiety. Life is what happens to you while you're waiting to figure out what you're going to do with your life. What must the siren have originally signified to the people hearing it when it was new, 40 or 50 years ago? The siren represented not just the threat of nuclear war, but the possibly more terrifying thought that the old white men in charge expected to be able to WIN such a war.

The siren was supposed to make people feel safe. But really with its dour, Cold War pomp, it was just another part of the war effort. The siren, with a straight face, was asserting a laughable pretense: in the event of nuclear holocaust, civil preparedness would keep our nation and government intact—possibly even in bunkers under the earth's surface, even after nuclear missiles had turned the world's cities to piles of toxic rubble.

The average citizen's patriotism, their anti-communism, was expected to remain steadfast even after the end of the world. What a drag. Now I hear the siren and think of 50 years of people going to work or school, people just trying to get by. I think of 50 years of the streetcars grinding on Market Street and the fog rolling in and everything's normal. But, there is always this threat and fear hanging over everything.

Ordinary people, who've had to live with the threat of the end of the world for some time now, know this fear, but it's largely suppressed. The siren must've been truly alarming at first but probably soon just became an aural manifestation of that fear, blending over time into the everyday sonic landscape of the city, along with grinding streetcars and foghorns on the bay. I think of 40 or 50 years of Tuesdays at noon and the siren becoming part of the inner life of the city. History.

The thing I love about the siren, though, is that it makes me think of fallout shelters. I've always sort of been obsessed with the mystery of the fallout shelter. I see those dusty, forgotten, faded signs on the old buildings downtown with that worn out yellow and black radiation symbol, and my spine tingles a little. Are the shelters really still down there in the basement? Or did everyone just forget to take down the signs? If they are down there, what's inside of them? And who would even have the keys now?

The Oddfellows Temple at Market and 7th had one of those signs up for years and years. And then one day, it just wasn't there anymore. Did some labyrinthine federal bureaucracy finally issue an inscrutable decree that it was now safe to remove the signs? Who knows?

Melissa and I snuck into the Oddfellows Temple and managed to get into the basement and poke around. We found a couple of creepy little rooms but none of them had the kind of formidable, steel vault feel that I would imagine a fallout shelter to have. Where did the shelter go? I wonder today if the Tuesday at noon siren is like the fallout shelter signs, except that no one has remembered to shut it off.

I decided to call someone at city government and get to the bottom of this. Where did the sirens originate from in the city? What are their relationships to the fallout shelter signs? How come I've never actually seen a huge siren speaker mounted on a pole? I had some questions.

I thought that it would be almost impossible to find anyone in city government to even know what I was talking about. I expected my call to be routed from obscure office to obscure office. Miraculously, on my very first call, however, I found the guy with at least SOME of the answers, Lou Canton of the city's Emergency Communication System.

It turns out that the civil defense siren is controlled from the Emergency Communication System Control Center on Turk Street, across the street from Jefferson Square Park. Some readers may remember that the last protest against the war in Iraq before the war started ended in Jefferson Square Park, and huge crowds of police with binoculars and video cameras gathered on the roof of the Emergency Communications building to videotape the crowd of protesters.

Canton said that there's supposed to be one siren per square mile in the city, which is why the siren is so loud no matter where you are.

Yet, he estimates that many of the sirens have fallen into disrepair and that less than 40 of them are probably still functioning. Speakers are mostly located out of sight on the rooftops of schools and government buildings. Canton recommends a fire station at Turk and Webster for a good place to hear the siren up close in its loudest glory.

Less, however, is known about the siren's origins. "It either started in the 50s or 60s," he says, "But no one's been in the office long enough to know." The siren was a part of FEMA's fallout shelter program, Canton thinks. At the time FEMA surveyed existing buildings in the city and requisitioned space in basements to be used as public fallout shelters.

FEMA would pick a suitable location, build a wall, and create the shelter in the existing basement. Then they'd supply the stockpile of canned foods and radiometers and that was that. The yellow and black fallout shelter signs went up on the outside of the buildings. And so the little rooms were left untouched until maybe '84 or '85, when Canton thinks that the program was discontinued.

He seems to remember that the Flood Building and the Union Square parking garage, for instance, had fallout shelters, though he's never been inside of one. Canton told me that an old timer named Frank Wilson over at FEMA in Oakland may even remember if there is a list of them. But then again, come to think of it, old Frank is probably retired by now. Maybe no one knows anymore.

Interestingly, this lack of an official history of the siren, of any sort of paper trail, seems part of a national split personality. Simultaneously planning for nuclear war while refusing to acknowledge its horror kept nuclear fear literally, architecturally, underground.

Canton says that the siren now lives on as a government safety measure in the War on Terrorism. Mr. Canton was a nice guy and I do believe that he is genuinely interested in keeping San Franciscans safe in the event of some disaster or attack. Still, the siren's history, and its reconfiguring as part of a new endless war, seems to be about anything BUT making the public feel safe. It somehow seems more closely linked in my mind to the police with video cameras on the Emergency Communication System's own roof at that protest.

The siren's grave, self-important weekly whistle evokes the cold technical engineers of the Cold War, sanely and rationally trying to carry out the directives of an insane and a totally irrational commitment to the nuclear arms buildup.

Seen like this, the siren is clearly the direct ancestor of today's ridiculous but always terse and inscrutable directives from Homeland Security, the weekly directives to stock up on duct tape or buy sheets of tarp. The siren gave birth to the arbitrary, almost top-secret differences between the so-called code yellow and code orange and a whole new theater of public fear. The Homeland Security directives are just starting to affect our lives in ways which we are barely able to understand. Yet, the color-coded warnings about terrorism are already presented as if they've always been in place.

A couple months back I was on my daily ride to Fort Point under the Golden Gate Bridge on my bike. I was dimly aware that an oblique communiqué from Ashcroft had seemingly overnight raised our new code to the ominous "orange." But when I got there I wasn't expecting to see the road to the fort blocked off. A gate was drawn across the road and a young, tan, white cop, fit from the gym, stood in front of his cruiser barring the way to the bridge. His arms were crossed and his face was set with grim, patriotic determination.

A middle-aged black guy, in a National Park Service rain poncho, leaned against a post off to the side. I went up to him and said, "Hey, what's up with the gate?" He shrugged, "Well, they put it up to code orange yesterday, and that's just about as high as it goes. We're supposed to close the road under the bridge." We both paused and stared off toward the bridge, watching the rows and rows of cars spinning effortlessly along, California's sun glinting off windshields as they crossed the famous span.

Finally I said, "So, do you think that this is going to keep people safe or is it total bullshit?" He grimaced and spat and said, "Aw man, it's TOTAL bullshit. There are cars already all over the goddamn bridge. You can drive a bomb on top of it anytime you want!"

I thought of that and I thought of the siren, too, the other day on the BART platform when I saw the computer sign flashing what must be the new San Francisco city motto: Bathrooms closed until further notice. All of a sudden I got pretty damn angry. Further notice, huh? Further fucking notice?!? Give me a break! Now that we're giving in to code orange, we're never going to see the insides of those bathrooms again as long as we live! What on Earth would have to happen for the top-secret command to bow down and give in and give us back the keys to the damn BART toilet? For all we know Osama himself is locked in the toilet at 16th and Mission, safer than he'd be anywhere on the damn planet! Further notice?

The whole thing is so ridiculous. But just like that it's how we live all over again. After a while, there will be no one anywhere who could remember the toilets ever being open or how they got closed to begin with. The origins would be a complete mystery, just like the siren.

I thought of 40 or 50 years of Tuesdays at noon. I thought of 40 or 50 years of people going to work or school, just trying to get by. And all the while everything's normal but there's this fear hanging over everything. I thought about life being what happens to you until further notice. Further notice? Who gets to decide when that time comes anyway? When do WE get to decide? When is it going to be up to us?

WE WANT THE BILLBOARDS!

Despite the collapse of the dot-com economy that had driven Mayor Willie Brown's neighborhood planning policies, the new "progressive" supervisors (that MAC's energy had helped elect) never seized the opportunity to forcefully articulate a vision for the city's future and implement a Left agenda. Supervisor Tom Ammiano, the presumptive progressive mayoral candidate in 2004, and the rest of the much-heralded new progressive Board of Supervisors elected in 2000, stood by and watched as Supervisor Gavin Newsom and his powerful backers from the Democratic Party machine made getting rid of homeless people the number one issue for the 2004 mayor's race a full two years before the election. Newsom's campaign started for real in 2002 when he launched his ballot initiative, Proposition N, the cynically named "Care Not Cash" plan, which, if implemented, would slash the checks of homeless welfare recipients in The City to $49 a month from the already insufficient $287.

Newsom was quite wealthy and in his 30s with TV news anchor good looks. He was the owner of a Marina District wine bar and a friend to the Getty family. His emergence was apparently the galvanizing force that a San Francisco Left, largely dormant since September 11, 2001, needed to stir itself. But there was a sense of a bitter déjà vu. In a way, Newsom was Dot-Com Man all over again—the straight, white, rich guy who was coming to suck the soul from our funky, diverse city. But what was our city all about anyway? What did we want? We'd lost the moment and all we could do was react.

My old SOMA squat became a base to plan alterations of the Care Not Cash billboards. The billboards, paid for by Newsom's backers in the Golden Gate Restaurant Association, showed well-dressed men and women holding cardboard signs—like the panhandling signs of the homeless—but the signs said things like "I am tired of having to step over people on my doorstep." My friends and I spent the summer of 2002 riding around on our bikes all night, gluing our posters over Newsom's billboards. I was proud that, despite everything, we'd found a way to carve out some space for ourselves. When our alterations were taken down after a few days, though, I'd just feel desperate using street art to fight a multimillionaire. After all, even the billboards were owned by Clear Channel!

GAY SHAME! AN INTERVIEW WITH MATTILDA
AKA MATT BERNSTEIN SYCAMORE

Started as a radical queer reaction to the corporate dominance of so-called "Gay Pride," Gay Shame has evolved into a loose knit organization of folks that consistently put on some of the most fun and fearless protest events in The City. I was blown away by 2002's Gay Shame Awards, an illegal rally at Castro and Market that featured free food, banner drops, a zine, burning rainbow flags, stilts, and a wild dance party that completely took over Castro Street! I talked to organizer Mattilda AKA Matt Bernstein Sycamore, later that summer about the group's ideas, origins, and tactics.

What was the origin of Gay Shame?

Mattilda: Disgust at mainstream gay politics that center around assimilation over everything else and at Gay Pride celebrations that have become nothing more than opportunities for multi-national corporations to target market to gay consumers. Gay Shame wants to create a space for radical queer community building and a space where people can celebrate their differences rather than rallying around this Pride for assimilation. I think a lot of radical queers feel really hopeless about the radical potential of queer identity. We want to bring all those people together, all those people who look at The Castro and say, "Oh God! There's no place for US there!"

Pride today seems all about joining the army and getting married.

M: Right. In NYC, Gay Shame was centered around a queerish Anarchist collective space called Dumba. There was a whole range of stuff, like drag shows and performances and people tabling and talking about political issues, especially needle exchange and crackdowns on public sex and issues of class and poverty. The idea was to not separate culture from politics, because it's all intertwined.

How was it different in San Francisco?

M: Here in San Francisco, the first Gay Shame event was similar, except we took it a little further into the public domain because we did our first event outside, in public, at Tire Beach in 2001. The whole idea was to create this queer Temporary Autonomous Zone for the day for the freaks and outsiders and queers who didn't feel part of anywhere else to have our own space. We had childcare and people were making out. Someone poured cement and we made mosaics on the ground. There were political speakers. There were way too many bands, of course.

How did that show lead to Gay Shame as political organizing group?

M: It was successful in a lot of ways of bringing people together, but one thing that we didn't like was that it became kind of like a scene for a certain group of people who weren't really interested in politics, but just thought it was cool. This year, we wanted to do something where the politics were so intertwined with the spectacle that it couldn't be separated. People would have to participate.

At the Awards, I was just standing around and someone came up to me and yelled, "Hey! Help me push this couch into the street in front of this bus!" That was some rad participation!

M: The Gay Shame Awards were definitely our most successful event. We got to be really theatrical and really crazy. We got to be very political too, while at the same time not being dogmatic or formulaic.

How did you plan all the free food, speakers, banner drops, the zine, etc. into one event?

M: Originally we conceived of the Gay Shame Awards as a way to get people excited about confronting the Pride Day parade. In terms of meetings, I'd say there were usually 10-30 people, and maybe 50 people involved all together. We had a food committee, logistics, props, wheat-pasting, and propaganda. We did A LOT of wheat-pasting—at least 10 trips on different nights, especially in The Castro and The Mission.

Was the wheat-pasting a way to let people know about the event or a way to recruit people into the group?

M: Both... Wheat-pasting, for me, is really important as a visible, semi-permanent, radical queer presence on the streets. Sometimes you can wheat-paste stuff and it'll be up for like a year, especially here in the Tenderloin. There are still Gay Shame flyers up around here from last year!

Yeah, I love how, here in S.F., you can still see all the stencils for old political events on the sidewalk years later... "Dyke March '98"...

M: Totally! The point of the Awards was to reward the most hypo-critical gays for their disservice to the community. We wanted to call people out in the center of where these people all are, The Castro.

So this is at Harvey Milk Plaza at Castro and Market...

M: It was also very important to have it in public where people who weren't expecting to see it would have to be confronted with it.

What actually happened at the event?

M: We had a stage to give out awards and planned that each award was going to be a rainbow flag that we would light on fire, which was harder than we thought it would be, because they were all plastic and it was very windy. We made a zine in which we talked about all the people who were nominated. We wanted to make sure our message was really clear. Some other folks planned the banner drop that would hang behind us on the empty building on the cor-ner, which is now the Diesel store (laughs).

We encouraged people, as the flyer said, to "dress to absolutely terrifying, ragged, devastating excess." Some people had real great outfits, like the woman who made the outfit out of Starbucks bags and rainbow flags—a full dress that she'd sewn! There were people on stilts. The food came on silver trays and there were other people handing out patches and art that they'd made, and zines. That was an-other thing that was important for us, not just that everything would be free, but that it would be given away, because Pride is where you have to BUY your pride. You BUY your $9 Pride Budweiser and you

BUY your rainbow flag and then you can be proud. The thing that was really exciting about it was that people were really excited by the politics of it and some of the crowd was even more informed on the issues than the organizers. Then, we blocked off Castro Street with sofas and threw a huge dance party in the middle of the street.

Were you counting on the cops not wanting to break up a queer event in the Castro, no matter how illegal?

M: No, not really. We just figured if we had the right number of people on hand then we'd go ahead with that part of the plan. We had police negotiators in the group whose basic job was just to tell the cops that no one knew what was going on. They were good at confusing the cops.

One of my favorite things about the Awards was watching the cops try to figure out who was "in charge" so they could tell them to stop the party. We all just shrugged and pointed off into the crowd in the other direction…

M: The sofas worked really well, because they blocked the street in this really relaxed, glamorous way. Like, FORGET about CHAINING ourselves across the street!

What were some reactions to the Gay Shame Awards?

M: We got so much press that we were shocked. The *Chronicle*, *The LA Times*, the editorial for the *Guardian* got syndicated nationally… A lot of the reason for the Awards was to get press and to make the award winners accountable for their hypocrisy. The *LA Times* had a well-researched paragraph about Mary Cheney in the article about us…

Now you're kept Gay Shame going as a year-round group, organized to fight more than Pride. What's the new plan?

M: It's become clear that we wanted to organize together, and we've built this group of people that wanted to do similar types of actions, so we've decided to keep it going. Next up is our event at the Gavin Newsom campaign headquarters. We're going to build a shantytown in the Marina in front of his businesses!

SCUMMY MISSION FREAKS INVADE THE MARINA!
GAY SHAME PROTEST, FILLMORE STREET 10/02

Joey and I rode out to the Marina together, going out of our way a bit to take photos of all the Care Not Cash billboards we'd fucked up the night before. Out in the Marina, our crew of freaks stood out pretty hard, like someone had hijacked the #14 Mission bus and drove it out here instead. This was one of those times that being prompt and prepared for a surprise attack would have been really smart, but the protesters seemed more like they were arriving fashionably late at a great party, standing around comparing outrageous outfits. Still, it was in full-on Gay Shame style and it was fun watching the Aryan Marina dwellers freaking out just because they had to look at us. While we were waiting for the full crowd to arrive, cops were coming over to us and saying things like, "It'd be a shame if everyone had to go to jail tonight just because they didn't stay in the crosswalk when they were crossing the street. Know what I mean?"

We knew. It was clearly going to be a heavy scene with the cops. They were saying, basically, if we marched we'd get arrested, but if we didn't leave this very spot in front of the Marina branch library in exactly ten minutes, then we'd be arrested, too.

So we marched, but on the sidewalk, as ordered. I was surprised by the small turnout. There were probably only 40-50 people, even less than our barely-planned Mission Street parade. Nonetheless, marching on the sidewalk was still fairly terrifying to the Marina residents and it didn't feel too defeated, because we were still planning to take over the street. Not that conspicuously carrying one of the six pink spray-painted Bob's Barricades we were going to use made me feel much better. But I hate Gavin Newsom and had already made my internal peace with the idea that this event could turn into some full-blown riot or that I could end up spending a couple days in jail. I wasn't dressed warmly enough for jail, I noted sadly to myself, but, then again, I suppose none of the Gay Shame crew really were.

When we got to the Fillmore and Lombard Streets intersection, where Newsom's restaurant and campaign headquarters were, there awaited what could only be described as a phalanx of cops, guarding the entrances to both. Here was the whole police/civilian relationship laid bare for anyone who was paying attention: heavily armed cops escorting the very wealthy past an unruly mob of the angry poor and into the safety of five-star restaurants. The burning question of The Zero's is already shaping up to be, "Which side of the line of riot police are you going to stand on?"

Seeing these cops and sensing the, uh, HOSTILITY of the neighborhood to us, some of the people with me in front of the line started to have second thoughts. One girl started trying to get us all to march down this tiny alley and then come back around the block to "surprise" the cops. The idea of surprising these cops was ridiculous, of course. This was like football now—a goal-line stand. Everyone on the field knew where the ball was supposed to go. I said, "No way! If we go in that alley, they'll seal us in there and shut us down!"

There was some hasty debate. Most of us up front were obviously, to varying degrees, afraid. But then, in a moment that I'll never forget, Mattilda fearlessly walked to the front, face painted red, with huge green eyelashes and blonde wig, wearing a "dress" and "shoes" made out of duct-taped Prada shopping bags. Mattilda calmly announced, "This event is going GREAT! They all know where we're going, so let's just go over there and take over the street." That settled it. We veered suddenly across Fillmore and into the street and started putting down our barricades. The Marina street party was on.

Surprisingly, it all worked. At first, there was the feeling that the cops would descend upon us at any moment and the ultimate street war would begin. But the organizers went ahead anyway with the Gay Shame program, rolling out a strip of white carpet that they called "The Exploitation Runway." Protesters dressed, unconvincingly but amusingly, as rich assholes would strut up and down the runway, narrated by Mattilda and Reginald's sarcastic commentary. The Gettys, Dianne Feinstein, Newsom, and the other usual suspects were represented. Zara would later say that he thought this was the whole problem with the event, that it was a sarcastic comedy routine for us, and not a clear statement to the passersby about why they should vote "no" on Prop N. I tend to agree, though I would point out that the show being surrounded by cops didn't encourage people to come over and check it out.

Either way, I quickly got bored, and went to the sidewalk to try and pass out "No On N" flyers. Maybe one in every ten people walking by was even mildly interested in why the streets were filled with cops and freaks and an extremely loud sound system with Friday rush hour traffic at a complete standstill. Everybody else rudely shoved me out of the way, cell phones in hand, not wanting anyone to tell them shit. I guess it was nice to think that we might influence voters, but this was still the Marina.

The all-out street takeover dance party of the Gay Shame Awards back in May never developed. The scene was just too tense. When the planned presentation came to an end, there was some discussion as to what to do next. I think there was a genuine concern about what might happen to us if we broke up and straggled off into the Marina in small groups. The hills of Pacific Heights, the unassailable, symbolic Everest of local power, loomed over us, and I suppose some combination of inspiration and nihilism made this the obvious way to go. The crowd started marching in that direction, in the direction of Newsom's house.

As I trudged up the hill, carrying an enormous cardboard house that had been part of the "shanty town" we'd erected in Fillmore Street, I remembered my only other trip to Newsom's house. It was the "modern, tasteful, hip"-looking small loft/condo type place on a street of immense mansions of brick and stone, almost like a clubhouse for young Gavin to play in until he'd proven responsible enough to take the keys to the old money. I had ridden my bike up there, just to see where the enemy lived, and had shuddered a little looking at the mansions. There was violence in this street. I had dreamed of a poor person's march up these hills to confront these pigs where they live. I could now see that it was inexorable; if not today, soon; people would climb these hills with anger and rage. The retaliation would undoubtedly be brutal.

I thought of the Bonus March during the Depression when the World War I veterans marched on DC to demand their pensions early. They set up squatter camps on the Anacostia Flats and thousands came from all over the country to live in tents and protest. They had fought for their country and now, wouldn't their country take care of them?

The US military was called out to burn the tents and attack its own veterans. The routing of the homeless veteran forces was a success and it put the names of the two young officers in charge—Dwight D. Eisenhower and Douglas MacArthur—on America's front pages for the first time. Now, young Newsom, too, is learning what it will take to get to power.

As it turned out, tonight wasn't the right night, though.

After marching for blocks, assuming we were going to Newsom's house, someone told me that we were actually headed to that big church at Webster and California where Newsom was supposed to speak that night about Prop N. Then, when we got there, the cops wouldn't even let us have a shrimpy, completely legal, moving sidewalk picket out in front of the place. Of course, we were way up the hill, now, in some pedestrian-free area where no one would be likely to see or care what the cops did to us. When they started trying to seal us in a little square and move in and arrest us, we all got away as best as we could.

Many of us who had dispersed ended up down at Yerba Buena Museum, where Zara's painting was in the "Bay Area Now" show. Zara had, of course, made hundreds of counterfeit tickets to the show, so none of us punks, queers, or activists had to pay the $15 or so to get in to see his work. Inside the museum, surrounded by art patrons—at ease and self-assured in this upscale environment—I felt like my night had gone full circle. I had gone from the protest outside of the expensive restaurant to looking at art with the kinds of people who had been inside of it. Still wired from the night's confrontations with the police, I raced around the museum until I came around a corner to find myself unexpectedly alone and face to face with Zara's painting. I stopped and stared for maybe 10 minutes, all alone with the painting that spoke so quietly yet forcefully about everything around me. It was at least 20 feet long, maybe 10 feet tall, and depicted a demoralized landscape of tree stumps and bleeding, eviscerated horses. Multi-colored planes and bombs fell from the sky into the lifeless scene that was captioned with the blazing banner, "If this is what we're for, this is what we'll get."

As for Newsom's house, if not today, then soon.

WHAT 2002 FELT LIKE

The morning we were supposed to record my band's new record, my squat got busted. When Paul came to pick me up, we used his car to move all my shit out of the squat and into the practice space. I would just have to deal with it days later, after we recorded.

I started sleeping in the practice space. It was better than living with Cinque and Greg in the van. They had to worry about getting busted by the cops. I just had to try not to get busted by The Quails, who shared the space.

The problem was we had a Submission Hold show booked for the squat. We had to break back in, because there was nowhere else to do the show. Luckily, instead of boarding up the squat again, the property owner had just closed the door, apparently assuming it was now locked. It was, but I was the one who had put on the lock, and my key still worked. We went in easily and went ahead with plans for the show.

The Submission Hold show ended up being great. A lot of people came early to eat free food and watch Kat and Anandi's movie in which they had interviewed people in the scene about activism in punk. My dusty, lonely old squatted garage looked great, full of dancing punks. I went ahead and booked another show there, and Anandi and Kat used the space for a free, weekly movie night.

Unfortunately, just a couple days before the show I booked, the squat got busted for real. The doors were now completely covered with thick plywood. Breaking in would be noisy and would take a while. It would blow our whole cover on the block, revealing that the story we'd told the neighbors about renting the space was a lie, and therefore making any show there a certain bust, even if we could get in.

There was nowhere to move the show. Cops had even started showing up and busting generator shows at 16th and Mission. It was time to find a new squat.

Ivy and I got out the bolt cutters and went to work. But, there weren't many good options. After cutting the lock, only to set off a silent alarm at a great storefront at 1st and Mission, we gave up. Fuck it. The show would just have to happen in the park with a generator. If the cops wanted to try to stop it, we'd see how things turned out. I wasn't excited about the possibility of a police riot in the park, but, if it came to that, I just hoped nothing bad would happen to the out-of-town bands.

The night before the show in the park, at band practice, Ivy and Cinque told me all about how the previous night had ended up with a huge crew of our friends destroying the plate glass windows at the shiny, new chain store in the neighborhood. I had gone home early and missed out, I guess. As it turned out, though, I had invited most of the same crew to come meet us after practice to go walk around and drink beer.

"One night of rage," Jake Filth once sang, "is all I need!" But have you ever felt like you might actually need TWO, two whole nights of rage? That's just how that whole summer felt. We would try to just go out and drink beer and walk around, but we'd just end up breaking stuff.

By the time we left the practice space, there were about 12 of us, including some kids from out of town who most of us had never even met before. I had thought it might be nice to sit on a hill and drink beer, looking out over The City, but it was soon clear that the night was headed in a darker, surlier direction. Someone suggested we go to the new yuppie hipster bar on skid row and fuck with the owner, who used to be a punk. As we walked up 6th Street, I noticed people in our group gathering garbage and bottles off of the street. When we arrived at the bar, the ex-punk, now proudly gentrifying the neighborhood, invited us in for free drinks. Instead, I watched as everyone strode past him into the bar, where they dumped all the trash. Fuck that guy. It was time to get more beer, but not there.

By the time we made it to Nob Hill, no one wanted to sit and look at The City. Instead, everyone suddenly had pulled out cans of spray paint, and was writing on any available surface. Someone else pulled out a radio and we started blasting the Spawn Sacs tape. Spray painting on mansions and blasting music with 12 people at 1:00 AM in one of the richest neighborhoods in The City probably isn't the best way to avoid arrest, but who wants to worry about the cops all the time? We marched on towards Russian Hill.

I remember seeing four or five of us, simultaneously spray painting different walls, without even looking around for cars or people on the street, and thinking, "Hmm. This seems sketchy," right before the cops finally came. Greg was spray painting this wall when, down the block, this guy leaned out of his upstairs window and yelled, "Hey! Cut that out!" Of course, for some reason, the cops happened to drive by, right then. The guy started yelling for the cops to stop. Everyone chucked their cans and scattered in different directions, but the cops doubled back and cornered Greg in an alley. Ivy, Cinque, and Squirrel got away. Come to think of it, I never saw those kids from Memphis ever again. I was in the clear, a block away, but decided to go back and face the cops with Greg. He was new in town, and I didn't want him to have to go to jail alone.

The cops actually had a couple other folks, too. In the alley, they lined Greg, Paul, Mike Taylor, Sara, Anandi, Arwen, and me up against the wall. One cop had been looking around out on the street and he now came back. Apparently he only had been able to find one of the paint cans. He now held it up, demanding, "Whose paint is this?"

I said, "No one was painting. You just found that in the street. It could belong to anyone." The cop was furious, yelling, "Just tell me who it belongs to!" but everyone followed my lead and no one admitted knowing anything about it. You might think it is bad to refuse to talk to the cops and that if you tell them the truth, they will go easy on you, but it's just not true. In situations with this large a group of people and cops looking to charge someone with having spray paint or some drugs or something like that, it is best to deny everything and say nothing. We couldn't ALL possibly have been spray painting with that one can of paint, right? Now the cops would have to decide if it was worth doing paperwork on eight people to haul us all in, only to be able to really charge one of us.

The guy who was yelling out of the window came out and started telling the cops his story. He said he'd been asleep but the sound of the music woke him up. He looked out and saw us in the street. "It was him!" he said, pointing at Greg. "He was the one who was painting!"

I yelled, "Why do you think it was him?"

The guy yelled, "Because of his haircut, that's why!" Greg had a mohawk, it was true. But so did Sara and Ivy. His positive I. D. on Greg would get Greg the charges tonight, but would it hold up in court?

We all got taken down to the Tenderloin station, where only Greg was charged. They split us up, guys in one tank, girls in the other. We were still pretty drunk. In the holding cell, we joked around, trying to see if Paul could take pictures of us with the camera he still had in his pocket, while his hands were cuffed. He could. By the time that got boring, we had been let back out and were standing on Jones Street—all, sadly, except Paul, who they kept on a warrant for an old skateboarding ticket.

It was 2:05 AM. The cops had apparently decided to hold us until just after the liquor stores closed. Fuck them. There's always more beer! I had the key to the Coalition On Homelessness offices, nearby on Turk, where there's always a six-pack in the fridge. Within minutes we had beer and were on our way back to the practice space to see if we could find the rest of our crew.

We found Cinque and Squirrel at the practice space and they had tons of beer. We wound our way back towards the Mission, blasting our radio, still laughing about how we'd managed to get out of jail so fast. We were still drinking past 5:00 AM, as the sky turned light in the east.

I was particularly happy about our jail solidarity, the way no one had talked to the cops. Now, I excitedly briefed Greg on his future court date. "So this guy WAKES UP at 1:30 in the morning and looks out from a second story window at a crowd of eight people down the block, and he I.D.'s you based on your haircut, even though it's the middle of the night and even though Sara is the same height, is also wearing a light-colored hoodie, and also has a blond mohawk?!?"

I was feeling good now. We had plenty of beer, the case was a sure thing, and Paul would be out of jail in time for the show in the park, too. As the sun came up for a new day, I waved my beer in the air and snarled, "We can beat this thing, Greg! On that evidence, no jury in the WORLD would convict!"

HOMELESS HOME MOVIES

I first had the idea for what would become the Homeless Home Movies project early in 2002 when it became clear that Supervisor Newsom was trying to whip the entire city into an anti-homeless hysteria in order to march into the mayor's office on a road of homeless people's bones. Suddenly, it seemed like every letter to the editor in the *Chronicle* was about The Homeless, now portrayed as this monolithic population of unfortunate, half-dead losers who had descended on our over-compassionate City to soak us for easy welfare checks, so they could spend their carefree days living high on the hog, shooting drugs, and pissing happily into our doorways. I was damn sick of hearing about it. How come no one ever asks homeless people anything? You'd think people would be ashamed to talk this way about other grown adults, about people who, though lacking in housing, still had hopes, dreams, aspirations, joys, pains, and the whole range of a lifetime of human experiences that were now dismissed so easily with one word:

Homeless. What would homeless people say if you gave them the forum to talk back to the society that was always plotting "what to do about" them?

The idea was to film homeless people talking about anything they wanted to and then to play the film every night for a month in the window of ATA on Valencia Street.

Artist Television Access at 21st and Valencia lets artists exhibit works in their storefront windows for a month at a time, and all you have to do is sign up to get a month. I thought it would be a nice counterbalance to the current tenor of the anti-homeless news and activist response if I could tell homeless people I would film them talking about ANYTHING they wanted to talk about and then put the results on display for a full month on a looped tape in the ATA window. If you had a chance to say anything to all the people walking by, what would it be?

It wasn't motivated specifically by a desire to influence the election by countering Newsom's anti-homeless lies. It was more complicated than that in my mind. I didn't want to coach people to talk against Newsom or his legislation. I didn't want to try to get people to tell sad stories to seem more deserving of help, or to not talk about drugs or anything crude. I literally wanted to get people to talk about ANYTHING. I wanted to point out that the only thing all homeless people have in common with each other is that they don't have a house. Other than that, they are just people. How did it come to seem normal to classify, categorize, study, and plot the elimination of a whole segment of the population simply based on economic status? This was unlikely to affect the election results positively, but if it did contribute to the greater good, it would be in a more truthful, more satisfying way than by some anti-Newsom propaganda.

As it turned out, it wouldn't matter. When I signed up, the first month available was in December, after the election would be over. I signed up and promptly forgot about it until, oh, about two weeks before December 1st. When the time came to work on it, I was feeling so saddened by the passage of Newsom's cynically named "Care Not Cash" at the polls and so numb from the year of bitter defeat that it was hard to get excited about working on it. It seemed too soon to pick at the scab, right after the election. Luckily, Sarolta, who I had asked to help me film people and edit the footage, was really excited about it and she forced me to work on it with her, or it might not have ended up happening. Now, whatever footage we finally got would end up being an unintended reproach to a city that had turned its back on these folks.

We put out a flyer and spread the word among homeless friends that we were doing the project. A couple of folks came forward through these connections. We tried to go to UN Plaza and ask homeless folks if they wanted to be in it, but in the post-election environment, no one wanted to do it. You could see anger and distrust in the eyes of people we'd ask, and who could blame them? People had been filming them and using the footage and their very stories against them all year. But we got some good stuff. A couple of guys in the Plaza talked about why they'd moved to San Francisco. One guy, Robert, talked about why Mission Bay was his favorite part of SF. But my favorite stories, by far, were from my friends, Willie and Randall, who explained, among other things, how to cook a chicken in a coffee pot.

We edited the footage and made a segment of stories that would repeat every twenty minutes or so for hours. Sarolta came up with the idea to display the footage by having it projected from within a tent that we'd have in the ATA window, so that it showed on the front of the tent. It was a nice idea. The tents or bedrolls or cardboard boxes that you passed on the street were literally full of these stories. The audio would play out of the ATA's own speakers, rigged to play directly onto the street. We put up a flyer with an explanation on it and a number to call for any homeless people who passed by who wanted to talk on film and be in the next round of segments. We'd envisioned changing the tape later in the month if we could get more people to talk.

When we finally got it up and running, it was so great to hear Robert's voice booming out across the empty, late night intersection, telling his story to the city. While we worked out the kinks, another homeless guy came and watched the tape and told us he loved it and it was a great idea.

Unfortunately, he may have been the only person who liked it all month. After a week went by, our friends kept telling us that every time they went to the ATA to see our exhibit, the workers there hadn't turned it on for the night. I never saw it running, either. Finally, when we checked with ATA, it turned out that the neighbors complained every time they turned it on, because they said the sound was too loud. The ATA people and other artists who had done exhibitions there all said it was no louder than any other exhibit they'd had and no one had ever complained before. It was sick and sad, but apparent that the neighbors simply didn't want to hear homeless people talk any more than they wanted to have to look at them on the street. The whole thing made me exhausted. Even on video, their voices were still being silenced.

PUNKS AGAINST WAR!
THE MISSION STREET ANTI-WAR PARADE
10/6/02

As Election Day in November 2002 neared, so too did war with Iraq. I grimly sorted through Arthur Anderson's old trash at work while listening to news on NPR of hundreds of thousands protesting across the world against the potential US invasion of Iraq. Many of us who'd been involved in 949 Market had now morphed into a group calling itself "Punks Against War."

In October 2002, a group of about 60 loud, costumed, and slightly drunk punk rockers took over the streets of the Mission with an anti-war parade. The parade, following a truck pulling a U-Haul trailer with bands playing on it, went from the 24th and Mission BART station up 16th and then to Dolores Park, via Valencia and 20th Streets, in an effort to bring anti-war protest information directly to the people of the neighborhood we live in in a fun and exciting way. People danced like hell in the streets, the cops couldn't shut it down, and thousands of bilingual anti-war papers were distributed along the way! Here's how we planned it and why:

Though it was five months before the war in Iraq would start, it was already clear that Bush wanted the war to happen no matter what. I was starting to feel hopeless about it, wondering, "What are we going to DO about getting people together to try and stop this?"

When my band, Allergic to Bullshit, played in late September at the Balazo Gallery, I was hoping to use the show as a chance to get everyone there to start talking about ideas of how to fight back. That day, I went to the library and photocopied old articles from the *Chronicle* from the day the bombings started in the first Gulf War. At the show, between songs, I read the news reports to the crowd—front page stories about huge, spontaneous demonstrations that had broken out all over San Francisco when the war started. Then, people had shut down the Bay Bridge and the Federal Building and, according to the *Chron,* "5000 protesters marched from 24th and Mission through the Mission, Castro, and the Haight" setting cop cars on fire and all that.

Before we played our cover of "Courage" by The Minutemen, Ivy and I passed out a big bag of freshly stolen spray paint cans that we'd racked that afternoon, saying, "I know everyone's got a lot on their minds about the war, and there are a lot of blank walls out there, so here's some paint." It was, at the very least, an attempt to put spray paint in the hands of the drunkest and wildest people we know, but was it something more? I don't know, but everyone I talked to that night was fed up, too, saying, "We have to DO something." A couple days later, Anandi and I came up with the idea for an anti-war parade on Mission Street, and in a few days, we had a flyer on the streets.

Why a parade? Or, even, why did we feel that we, as a punk community, needed to do something specific to protest the war, when, in SF, there are always plenty of huge anti-war marches? Not In Our Name was, in fact, doing a peace march downtown, on the 7th, the day after our proposed parade, and there had been 20,000 people at the last one. Did there need to be two events?

I really think so. I've been to a million of these enormous Bay Area protest marches over the years, and some have been truly inspiring. But, I've come to think that there are a lot of problems with the tactics, or just the overall template of the traditional SF march. The marches are always downtown and early in the day, on weekends, when no one is on the street but tourists. The marches are frequently so identical in size, look, attitude, and location (Powell and Market! Emergency Rally! Again!) that they seem almost like weekly occurrences, which obscures their meaning: "Why are all those people marching? Oh, they're just the people who march around here all the time."

When you're shouting at deserted buildings in the financial district on a Saturday morning, it's clear that the event is intended to be only symbolic and for media consumption. But the media rarely cooperates, usually deliberately ignoring or undercounting the protest, reporting the message wrong, and choosing to interview the one most obvious wingnut in the crowd to fill in a quote or two.

I do think it's important that the big peace marches happen. I realize it is important to create a safe space where everyone, young or old, can feel they can come together to say that they are against war. Not everyone who is against the war, of course, is also against capitalism, or wants to free Mumia, either, but they still want to have a space where they can go and be with other people and stand for peace. Most people want to do this without breaking the law or getting arrested. I recognize all this and understand why the big downtown demos are the way they are.

But I think we need MORE and not fewer anti-war voices, happening in all parts of town at all different times in all different ways. I think of the spontaneous marches after the Gulf War I and think that if we tried to take the bridge at a peace march now, the ORGANIZERS would turn us in to the cops. Why not have MORE chances for people to be directly involved in the planning of how protests will look and feel? Why not have events where you try to talk directly to your neighbors about the war, instead of trying to talk to them through the media? I think it would be so beautiful to see spontaneous anti-war marches throughout The City, on Mission Street, on 3rd, Castro, or Haight Steets, with thousands of people marching all at once!

I was taking inspiration for this from the marches that the Latino day laborer program had been doing on Mission Street to protest the way the cops harass them as they line up to be picked up for work every morning. The marches are generally small, ragged-looking marches of less than 100 people, but, when they march right down the center of Mission Street on a weekday during business hours, they are completely unexpected. People run out of their shops to see what is going on and to cheer on the workers. The out-of-the-ordinary protest style gets people's attention. We were hoping the parade would be a good way to surprise our actual neighbors, instead of the media, into paying attention to what we had to say.

We decided to make it clear in our flyer that our parade was in support of and an invitation to the larger rally downtown the next day, and we put the flyer for the Not In Our Name rally on the back of ours. Our main goals were to 1) make something loud and festive that would make the late Saturday afternoon, family-oriented crowd happy on the working-class shopping drag, Mission Street, 2) distribute a large amount of strong, bilingual information against the coming war as we walked down the street, 3) pass out free food at the beginning of the parade to get people to foster the parade-like feeling, and, 4) be able to illegally hold Mission Street for at least the eight blocks between 24th and 16th Streets.

The problem was that there were only 9 days to do all the work leading up to it. That's where the PARADE part comes in. It was up to whoever wanted to come to make it look however they wanted it to look. Instead of trying to centrally organize the event, we told people to try to work with small groups of friends to come up with signs or costumes and parade themes. Like, Ivy owns about five animal suits, and Anandi wanted to have people wearing them with signs that said, "Animals for the ethical treatment of people." Paraders could, at the very least, show up with a sign saying where they lived, like "24th/Folsom Against the War." It was an experiment, counting on there being a lot of people out there who were mad about the war who would be excited to have a completely open space where they could creatively protest. We decided not to put an ending spot on the flyer so that we could wait and see how big it ended up being and let the people on the parade take it where they felt like taking it.

But the best part of the plan was the flatbed truck! The idea was to have everyone meet at the 24th/Mission BART and then follow a flatbed truck that would have live punk bands and speakers right on the truck as it drove down Mission! Fuck Yeah! It would be the low rent version of that Sex Pistols boat show, except we would have Shotwell instead, of course. Jimmy assured us he could get us a flatbed and we spent the rest of the week stealing huge bags of beans, rice, and tortillas to make the free burritos, making banners for the truck, making signs to carry, and trying to find party hats, since I had put on the flyer, "Free party hats for dogs."

In the week before the parade, I went back and forth between being totally stressed out about the parade and totally certain that it would work. I had never been involved in setting up a protest march before, let alone a potentially illegal one. On the one hand, it seemed like the worst thing that could happen was that not many people would come and we'd just end up walking on the sidewalk in costumes, passing out anti-war literature in Spanish, which is something we felt was missing at the moment anyway. On the other, though, I was worried that it just wouldn't come off; it wouldn't be parade-like enough and we'd look like dumbasses.

I want to say that none of us who came up with the flyer for this entered into this lightly, as a total irresponsible lark to go raise hell on Mission Street. We were really concerned with trying to come off respectfully to the Latino families who would be out in full force on Saturday. I was worried at first that it was too audacious for white punks to do a big event on Mission Street, that we would show too much of a sense of ownership of the street with that. But then I thought about how Latinos in the Mission are now treated nightly to a parade of overdressed white yuppies who drunkenly hop taxis from bar to bar and piss in the doorways, and obviously our event, with people in animal costumes throwing candy to kids on the sidewalk, was different. I thought our event would be generous and also a sincere attempt to invite Latino folks to the next day's rally.

Plus, we live in this neighborhood, too. Our illegal generator shows at the BART have been popular with folks, young and old, since we started doing them. We wouldn't have showed up and done it somewhere where we didn't have a lot of personal history already. I felt like it was worth it to take a chance to reach out to folks we live and walk alongside of every day. and I felt like we could assume that the Mission population, many of whom had come to this country to escape Central American death squads, already knew plenty about how Bush's war sucked, and would appreciate the free food and information.

Of course, everything seemed like it was going to fall apart all week. No one had any money so we had to steal everything connected to the parade all week. The flatbed fell through hours before the parade. But, on parade day, we sent the free burritos and stacks of info over to the BART on time, just as Kat was renting a U-Haul trailer that we would pull with the bands on it behind her pickup truck. The trailer was the savior. Seriously, for only $35 you can rent one and have a band play on it in the streets of YOUR town!

When we pulled up to the BART, a full hour late, a huge crowd of anti-war animals, cheerleaders, and people with clown noses all raised their signs and cheered at the decorated tuck. They also raised their beers. Jimmy, dressed as a black and white spotted cow, was passing out cold beers from a keg he had on ice under a rug in a shopping cart. "Cerveza Alto Guerra," he growled at strangers, as he passed out cups of foamy brew to curious strangers on the street.

The free food and costumes had worked. A large crowd of bystanders was already waiting excitedly, to see what the hell we were going to do. Someone from the parade had already had to go out and make 500 more of the anti-war flyers! The parade pulled in behind the truck, and, as the truck lurched out into traffic, Running Ragged started playing the first notes of their set. When we had all finally caught up to the truck, I looked back and traffic was totally stopped. The parade had filled out across a now empty Mission

Street and music was echoing off the buildings. People were dancing in the back of the truck and people were lined up on both sides of Mission, smiling and waving and running up to take our literature. Everyone in our group had signs. Everyone was loud. It felt great!

The best thing about the parade, among many good things, was just the overwhelmingly positive response. People on the street were holding up their kids to look at us, and laughing. People were hanging out of apartment windows and waving. Periodically, we would move over a little to let some traffic get by, and a lot of the cars honked and gave us the thumbs up, some rolling down their windows and yelling, "No War!" I felt like the wording on the flier had turned out to be justified: "This community is against Bush's war." Bands took turns for a while. Allergic to Bullshit took over for a bit as we stopped in front of Mission Records to fill the street and let the punks at the show there come out and hang for a bit. Then Shotwell took over as we hit 16th Street.

We had made it to our established goal of the 16th Street BART and we were talking over our new plans as we walked. By now it was clear that though we had a lot of people, there weren't enough of us to, say, go all the way down to City Hall or to leave the neighborhood. So we decided to double back on Valencia. At 16th and Valencia, the cops showed up and started trying to tell us we couldn't block traffic. Of course, their own stopped cars across the intersection now ENSURED blocked traffic! We took advantage of this and stopped the truck for a while. Shotwell started playing the Dicks song, "We don't need your fucking war," as the rest of us shrugged off the cops and ran up to flyer stopped motorists. The cops started getting more persistent, so Jimmy announced the next song, an anti-cop song. It was starting to be clear that we couldn't entirely defy the cops, though, so we told them we were going to go to Dolores Park and have a show there. The cops accompanied us the rest of the way, fanning out in front of us and blocking intersections for us, so that we could safely make it to Dolores Park to finish out a couple sets on 18th Street while a big crowd gathered around, yelling at the bands to keep playing. That day still sticks out in my mind as one of the few times I've really felt the barriers between different communities slip away, and the possibility that we could all work together against a war felt real.

It was pretty funny, too: I guess we DID have enough people to make it a legal march after all!

MATTY LUV R.I.P. 10/6/02

People have been telling me all week about how Matty's songs changed their lives. It's funny to me that when I first started playing a band with Matty, I'd never even heard Hickey or The Fuck Boyz. My first clue about what Matty and Aesop were all about came after the cops shut down all the Mission's all-ages clubs. I went to practice and said, "Look, we have the numbers. The cops can't stop us. Let's just get a generator show and start having huge, free, illegal shows out on Mission Street." I'd only been back in SF a few months and sort of expected the 10-year Mission veterans Matty and Aesop to tell me why you couldn't do it or why it wouldn't work. Instead they matter-of-factly said, "OK. When?" And we started planning out the specifics right away. That summer, we played shows on the street under threat of arrest all the time and I'd always look at those guys and think, "I love this band! Matty and Aesop aren't afraid of anything!"

The cops weren't just shutting down clubs in that heavily gentrified year of 1998. Thanks to the efforts of Officer Ludlow, they had pretty much shut down all the Latino bars in town, too. As the Latino bars all quickly were changed into dot-com, yuppie bars, we heard rumors that Ludlow was taking a cut of the profits for making it happen. Mission bar door guys told us that Ludlow could even be found getting drunk at various yuppie bars he'd helped open and bragging about his whole operation in public! The arrogance of these crooked, racist pigs was so disgusting, but we were helpless to PROVE that anything corrupt was really happening.

But then our friend got a job as a barmaid at a new "upscale" bar on 24th Street. She told us that not only did Ludlow come in there, without fail, every Saturday night, to get wasted and brag about his new empire, but he also had a sort-of crush on her and he would try to impress her with his pathetic story every time! It's a tribute to what a badass Matty was that instead of just thinking, "Damn, what a fucked up story," he instantly thought, "Now's our chance to get this bastard on tape and take him down!" Not only that, Matty promised, we would get very drunk, for free, while doing it! We went to the bar with a tape recorder hidden in a bag. We'd tried to look more "normal" by putting our hair under hats so that Officer Ludlow wouldn't freak out if we actually sat at the bar next to him, but it didn't really work, because Matty's huge dreads stuffed in a cap still just looked too weird. Still we gave it a shot.

We drank steadily for free, for hours, giving each other knowing, inscrutable, secret-spy glances until suddenly, around 11:00 PM, in walked Ludlow. With his gray hair cropped short, his new leather coat, and his eager entourage of twenty-somethings, Ludlow looked like an aging hipster mentor gone slightly to seed. Yet he still had the inscrutable Mission Station, police-issue face. He sat down the bar a bit and started talking on a cell phone while drunk rich kids came out of the crowd and greeted him warmly. We couldn't believe it! Here was our chance!

I still don't know exactly what happened that night, but it proved to be really difficult to get through the entourage and actually get close to Ludlow. Matty kept getting up and going to try to stand near him, awkwardly holding this weird bag—the bag with the tape recorder in it—out towards Ludlow. But there was no way to know if we were actually taping Ludlow's conversation or not.

In the end, we were very drunk, back at the Hickey Hotel, realizing we now had a whole tape of the bar's jukebox blasting Van Halen's *Fair Warning* LP over unintelligible sounds of a bar full of drunk people talking. We listened in silence for a while as it sank in that our sting operation had failed. When "So This is Love?" came on, I said, "Well, you have to admit, this is a great record." Matty nodded in full rock agreement.

Taking out the gate at Leed's, hanging out at Hunt's, arguing with cops at neighborhood meetings in the Haight... Matty and I used to do fun shit like that all the time, and then I went out of town for five months and came back and he was using and we didn't do much of anything fun for awhile. Come to think of it, not much of ANYTHING seemed like fun that next summer at all. It's part of our secret history: when Matty Luv quit doing speed and started doing heroin, it was the end of an era in the Mission.

He was crabby all the time, the way junkies are. We argued in subtle ways about him becoming a junkie, me being a drunk. When he nodded out while recording my new band, I felt like crying. What was weird was that, in many ways, he was even more accomplished than ever, but it didn't make him happy. When I interviewed him for *SCAM* about the needle exchange program that he and Ro started, he was high as fuck, slurring his words. He was telling me how they'd just gone out, Black Panther-style, and started doing illegal exchange in the Haight. They had gone to jail for it, but had never given in and had forced the city to eventually recognize their exchange site, to make it official despite neighborhood controversy, and even to eventually fund it. It was such an inspiring story of a completely selfless and principled effort to force public health officials to try and help these strung-out, runaway kids on Haight Street, but his detached, slurred speech gave the odd impression of an old drunk talking about something he had done years ago. Or maybe it was that he was thinking, "Well, of course, we beat the cops and got our exchange recognized, but what I really want to know is how can I be so good at so many things, so well-liked and respected, and still be so completely unhappy?" It was like he could have so much, but it was never enough.

Matty and I became good friends again, though, after the horrible incident at Ro's. I went to visit him with Ivy in South Florida, where he'd gone to live with his parents while he awaited trial. He was like a teenager again. His dad dropped him off to hang out with us, even. We rode bikes and explored Miami's weird neighborhoods all day and he seemed so excited. I was, too. He was clean then, of course. It'd been a while. Later, he wrote me funny letters about how he got a minimum wage job in the deep South Florida suburbs where we're both from. He was working at a car wash, a 35-year-old white guy working with a huge crew of Dominican teenagers who spoke no English. He told me how they'd sort of all come to really like him in this weird way, and I think he appreciated the humor of the San Francisco guitar hero returning completely to his roots.

In a way, it was like he was starting everything over. When he came back, he told me he hadn't played guitar in a year and didn't think he even knew how anymore. So we started playing music together again. Once a week, we'd try to play the entire first Ramones record together, with him on guitar and singing and me on drums, at my practice space. It was true: he HAD fallen off. But watching him trying so seriously to learn all those old songs was so sweet. He worked hard at it. Soon we could play the whole first record and part of "Leave Home" in order. If I fucked up a part, he'd stop and yell at me and we'd start the whole song all over again. *Beat on the brat! Beat on the brat!* He'd have this huge grin on his face the whole time.

Matty threw himself into trying to save Mission Records, into

making the punk record store profitable. He gladly sought out the
least glamorous roles in any club—trying to make the shows actually start on time and sound good and making sure flyers got made
for each show. He soon became the hardest-to-fool doorman in SF
punk history, since, after all, he already knew—and had personally tried—every possible way to scam your way into a show. When
Matty died, he was working so hard to come back, to be a part of
this scene.

You can always come back, but you can't come back all the way.
Soon, he quit taking the shitty, creepy prescription meds that made
him feel apathetic and just went back to heroin. What's the difference? He was still just unhappy. For a long time, I could never really
tell how he was doing. Some days he was so fun and happy. Most
days, though, I'd see him from a distance, walking down Mission to
16th to score, and he looked like a ghost that was haunting himself.

It would give me that creepy feeling I get when I look at a star
in the sky and think about how I'm only seeing the light it gave off
thousands of years ago—that somewhere, in a cold, distant, and
horribly alone place its light may actually have gone out. I'd wonder
if Matty's light had gone out.

But, fuck it, right? In the end, all we have is the battle we all have
with our own hopelessness. We all have to find our own reason to
get out of bed and walk down these same old streets, every day a
little more in the shadow of our older, better selves. A bunch of
my friends and I were feeling pretty hopeless lately about the war
coming up, so we organized an anti-war parade and took over the
streets again. It felt good, necessary. The flatbed truck from the parade stopped for a while in front of Mission Records and everyone
from the show inside came out to watch our show in the street for
a minute. The door guy, Matty Luv, came out to cheer us on, too,
flashing us a big grin. It was the last time I would see him alive. He
OD'd later that night, alone in his house, while we were all celebrating the parade's success, drinking beer in the park.

This week, after Matty died, some people who'd been on the parade and felt the freedom that day said, "It's so sad that some people
can find the inspiration to fight back, and some can't."

But I don't think that's fair. I think of Matty working at the
carwash, going from guitar hero to door guy, but still working so
hard to play those Ramones songs. I think of him getting up every
day to fight his way back. I think of how he had to come up and

tune my guitar for me before my new band played a couple weeks ago, just like he always did in our old band. Matty was better than most people at most everything he did. I think of the last time I saw him, walking and laughing with Sarah on Capp Street, just last week. As I rode past, he lowered his head and looked at me over his glasses. As our eyes met, he thrust out his fist, a gesture that plays again and again in my mind, now seemingly full of hidden meaning.

The light never went out.

But it was never enough.

INTERVIEW WITH PAUL BODEN, DIRECTOR OF COALITION ON HOMELESSNESS S.F.

I did this interview with Paul the night before the November 2002 election when Gavin Newsom's "Care Not Cash" initiative, Proposition N, was going to certainly pass the next day. Like a lot of folks, I was crushed by that election loss after the long, bitter fight. But in this interview Paul puts that loss—and electoral politics in general—into perspective. Paul was mad and cussed non-stop as usual that night, but, unlike me, he wasn't worried about the Coalition's future and gladly talked with me long past the Coalition office's famed "Three Beer Rule."

So what's going to happen with Prop N?

PAUL BODEN: I think there's been a fucking hellacious campaign to try to offset the millions of dollars that Gavin Newsom's going to end up spending on this. Whether or not it's enough to overcome the media blitz, it has still been enough to discredit Prop N. It'll be close, which is a hell of a lot more than anybody anticipated when we started out. But to a homeless person trying to get GA (welfare), close don't mean shit. We still lost.

Are the polls looking any better?

PB: "The polls" have gone from 74% to 55%. But I remember when I was ass out, one year they were going to cut the AFDC money by 17% and the "homeless advocates" got together and got them to cut it only 12%, and I'll never forget, these guys put out a statewide flyer...

Saying "We Won!"

PB: Yeah! "We Won!" Well, you didn't fucking win! You CUT BACK the percentage of damage that was done but you can't call that a victory. If we lose by 1%, we fucking lost.

Do you feel the campaign's had an impact?

PB: Yeah, because when 50 or 60 thousand bucks goes up against a million and they have all the airwaves and all the mainstream media, the ONLY way you can get your shit across is through word of mouth and talking to people. When people realize that one person is really passionate—maybe not the most articulate, and I'm talking about myself, right?—but knows what they're talking about, then they start to feel like, "Well, maybe I trust THIS because that Newsom is so polished, so chrome, so SLICK, and so...full of shit!" And he says the same little polished shit every single time, like 150 times, but he's up against 150 different people who AREN'T slick. I think it has resonated with the people. We've been out talking in the neighborhoods and we've called 9,000 people on the phone banks, all with volunteers.

Do you see any changes in the organization if Prop N passes and the COH loses?

PB: I don't see how it's going to impact the Coalition, because COH doesn't get any government money. We're going to be here regardless of what happens. Just like effin' Newsom and Ammiano (progressive Supervisor, running against Newsom for Mayor). Two rich, white dudes—and Ammiano ain't as rich, but he's a homeowner—are going up against each other over the issue of homelessness. Homeless people are going to be impacted, but Newsom, Ammiano, and the COH ain't. What's going to happen is that homelessness is going to increase at a greater rate and the anger and frustration of fucking cops and homeowners and real estate companies and business owners are going to come out, like, "We passed this Prop N and this is supposed to be solved." Well, it ain't gonna be. No governors are talking about homelessness, no senators. It's always talked about as a local issue. Arresting people, incarceration, closing public parks, stopping food programs, stopping sitting on the sidewalk—this is all they talk about, and every single one of them wonders why, twenty years later, shit's worse than ever!

Can you talk a little about the start of this place and your past?

PB: I'll give you the *Reader's Digest* version. I'm 15 years old, my mother dies and I end up ass out on the streets when my father sells the house. I bounce around for 5 or 6 years and end up in San Francisco in the Tenderloin on Leavenworth Street. I walk past this long-ass line of families, single adults, seniors, youth—a long-ass line around the block and everyone was in line for a shelter bed. I'd spent over a year in Europe and I'd been in squats in Copenhagen and Amsterdam and I was homeless here in SF, like, "Fuck this shit!" It was like 1982 and I started talking to people about squatting and how cool it was over there, not knowing anything about organizational structure or all the hard work that enables you to get away with that shit. I was a 22-year-old toothless burn-out and they were like, "Come here, man, why don't you help us out?" I was still homeless, but I was seeing these seniors and started thinking, "Get over it, Boden. These people are a lot worse off than you." I had been out there on the streets for seven years and all of a sudden I was hooked up to something. It wasn't squatting or The Revolution that I was looking for, but it was something that was really helping out some people. Six months later I actually got $10,000 a year to WORK in the shelter.

Around '87, me and a bunch of frontline staff at shelters and homeless people spun off of what was the status quo at the time and started the Coalition. We formed the COH to say, look, let's learn the lessons from the War on Poverty. When you can divide the service providers from the clients, then you have overseers and slaves. That way they were able to kill the War on Poverty and say, well, we're not funding CETA, VISTA, day care, and jobs programs anymore because the staff and clients saw themselves as separate. But if we saw ourselves as one, like, one month you're on payroll, and one month you're not, or we come from the same neighborhood and the paychecks we earned were spent in the same neighborhood... then we're both together. It's a fist. Whenever there's a division between service providers and receivers of services, there's the ability to just kill the programs.

When I first showed up at the coalition I was disappointed. I wanted to see homeless people storming City Hall with crowbars. Then I realized that's pretty far from what's on most homeless folks' minds...

PB: Yeah, we have to listen to what homeless people are talking about. Not that they'll never be at that place, but they're not right now. If homeless people were saying, "Let's bomb banks!" that's what we'd have to do. But if WE say to homeless people, "Here's what you should be doing," then the only ones who are going to get involved are the ones who agree with us, and then we're elitist. Then the "WE" means the staff deciding what this organization does instead of the clients. Yeah, capitalism directly impacts the life of homeless people and, yeah, a lot of homeless people want to BE capitalists. We can't get too far ahead of the people we represent. I think that in a lot of organizational groups, the staff get a lot more quickly educated on the issues and the connections between all this shit then the people they're representing, and then they end up trying to educate people instead of LISTENING TO the people. They get ahead of the people and then they start getting frustrated and then they become elitist. Membership gets smaller and smaller and all of a sudden it's like a fucking cell. Meanwhile, the education isn't getting any better, the drug treatment isn't getting any better, and the housing isn't getting any better.

Any advice for people organizing campaigns?
PB: Yeah, don't do a campaign; start an organization.

The news media has been giving the COH more shit than ever lately.
PB: They called us a "one plank platform." They say, "All they want is housing for homeless people." Yeah! Think about it, asshole! The only common denominator that all homeless people have is a lack of housing! One of our best compliments, that came when we were ten years old, when we could still get compliments from The City, was that we were compared to a pit bull grabbing onto your ankle. We don't let go. We never bought into the concept that it was important that they like us, because we started with the attitude, "We're homeless. They don't like us." There were four homeless people in a storage closet, converted to an office. They didn't like us then and they don't like us now. But that's not the issue, because we've created over 3000 units of housing, a treatment program, service provider programs like McMillan's Drop In Center. We created *Street Sheet*.

I was here way past the three-beer rule time, and I heard you telling

210

the story of the Street Sheet to a new guy...

PB: As of this month, 5 million issues! So, that's like, what? Three million bucks directly into homeless people's pockets? I don't know too many non-profits that can make that claim!

Say we had some time where we didn't have to be fighting back at some fucked-up proposition... What do you WANT to see happen? What would you be fighting FOR?

PB: Well, shit is just so far off course. In order to get back to where we started, a WPA program of some kind is going to be necessary. These guys out here sweeping our streets need a goddamn paycheck, not a welfare check. Now they want people in public housing to go out and sweep streets. There is not a motherfucker in this country who has a tax credit or a mortgage interest deduction off their taxes who has to take a piss or have a felony warrant check, but to get a subsidized room you have to do all those things. So the pendulum has shifted so far into the repression, that, short of fighting, I don't know.

MARKET STREET NEW YEAR

From the window of my new room, I can see the rain falling on Market Street and hear the steady drag of streetcars marking the steady drag of time, the red light/green light march of crowds. Past newsstands, huddled in doorways, past the darkened bar. There is an inner life of crowds, the murmur of late afternoon headlines, but also something more. An ache, a pain. The clang of a streetcar trolley bell that still brings back memories even as the newsprint of election results and war yellows and fades.

This is my favorite time of year in SF, the time when the rain comes. It was raining when I moved here, when I walked until dawn every night, up and down all the hills, exploring the new city, my duct-taped shoes flapping and dragging a hi-hat and snare beat as I walked. The rain started the night after the election this year, howling down the streets, warm and angry and wild, an actual thunderstorm that bent trees in half and overturned trash cans, that downed power lines. The rain raged through the streets the way I felt like we should have, those who lost, taking to the streets, solemn and true. My friend told me that ever since she worked as an outreach worker, she can't see the rain without getting sad and thinking of wet, homeless kids. I thought of that, too, but I was still relieved when the storm came. There are things that elections cannot solve. There are things that have no political solution. The storm came and I was glad to look at the world as it is again. There are elections and wars and the rain comes anyway to this place, aching and covered in concrete, and somewhere in the cracks in the cement, something grows.

My new room is in a haunted, old pre-earthquake building at 7th and Market—not a fancy place, but a place with some style. A clacking, old typewriter and whiskey bottle in the desk drawer kind of place. A walking in the rain kind of place. I spend a lot of time, now, walking in rain in the Tenderloin. Maybe it's because SF is such a small place, but sometimes the layers and layers of history seem so overwhelming to me. I can remember not just what I read in books and what happened to me, but almost every story anyone ever told me about something that happened to them in a specific location in the city. When I walk, I can see all these things happening at once on that very spot, the street corner where the tranny riot was in the 60s and where my friend also got stabbed by a skinhead at the punk club in the 80s; where Dashiell Hammett once walked, and where I once looked at a storefront space for rent.

My new favorite thing is just looking at 7th and Market. The office building and the old post office, now the Federal Court House, were among the only buildings that survived the earthquake of 1906. In old photos, you see rubble and ruins everywhere, City Hall ripped angrily in half, and these two buildings standing, untouched. Today, there is a new, huge crater there, rubble and ruins, the site of the old Greyhound Terminal, and the future site of a new Federal Building. I love to go there in the rain and watch the bulldozers push the dirt around, to see the graffiti on the pillars in now unearthed basement rooms. It is so perfect, a crater downtown, just like the old earthquake pictures. It is a healthy thing to be able to imagine all these buildings in ruins. The crater is a monument to a failed ambition, oddly comforting like a can of malt liquor in a brown paper bag.

There are certain things that sustain me in this city. Some are deadly serious, like the dream of having community spaces available everywhere where people can come together to create and organize and talk or whatever. Some are just frivolous like the wonder in old hotel halls and junk stores on rainy days, the lost art of watch repair. I wish more people wrote on stuff with chalk. I had a girlfriend once who left me notes in front of my door in chalk on the sidewalk, and even on rainy days I can still see them there but in my mind and that is sweet. But what sustains me now is to stare at this crater, this monument to failed ambition, and wish they'd somehow run out of money and leave it empty. Empty to fill up with graffiti and trash, empty for the rain to come and grow stuff in it. If I could get a huge art show at one of those fancy museums South of Market where the old SRO hotels used to be, I'd just do an installation and fill a whole room with dirt and rubble and call it "The Lot." People would be free to come and drink beer or spray paint or have generator shows or have picnics or build shacks or whatever in it for the whole duration of the show's run. Staring at the lot, I think how the crater seems to prefigure the eventual destruction of the federal building even before it has been built. One day this crater will be here again. Do I really have to wait 40, 50 years to see it?

When I look at the crater, I remember everything I know about the Greyhound Station, all the trivia, like how it was squatted by punks for years before it was torn down. I think of how it must have looked, Market Street, the Big City, to the crowds leaving the station, the young and hopeful and the desperate all together. In the bustling crowds there is the promise of a place for everyone, the nostalgic lore of a better time, wistful and sentimental Herb Caen stories on yellowing newsprint. There is the hope of a new start, and the immigrant success story: the young Art Agnos arriving at 7th and Market by Greyhound for the first time, 25 years before he became Mayor of SF. I love how the liquor store next to the lot is still called "Traveler's Liquor," even now that the bus station is gone. I buy a bottle of whiskey and think of long night drives, full moon on cornfields and deserts, seen from the back of the bus, and wonder about the crowds on Market, the men standing around looking like sailors whose ships left them behind. I think of all the buildings lining Market Street, and the crowds that have filed between them over the years, marching against wars, cheering sports teams, or just running the gauntlet of buildings on the way to work every day. The buildings seem so permanent. Are we just passing through?

Inside City Hall, a couple blocks away, there is a permanent photo exhibit in the cafe, huge posters on the wall of the North Light Court. The pictures are of crowds. Rows and rows of faces, all turned to the camera, faces open and expectant, or faces all turned away, all eyes on something just off camera in the distance, a fleeting moment in history captured in black and white. There is the buzz of a 1951 crowd, craning their necks to get a glimpse of a celebrity of the day, General MacArthur, and there is the sleepy, long-afternoon crowd watching a parade. There are civil rights protesters draping the Abe Lincoln statue with placards in 1963. Cannery workers on strike gather in a crowd in Civic Center in one shot to receive free food at the height of the Great Depression. The photos are lovingly shot, democratic. What is a city, they seem to say, but a monument to the aspirations of the people who live there? What is a city but a dream, a dream murmured in crowds, of what we might be?

The crowd of demonstrators at the 1960 HUAC protests are pictured here, too, ironically making it up the stairs at last to be enshrined under the Golden Dome. When the House Un-American Activities Committee held hearings in City Hall to "expose communist activity in the Bay Area," a group of UCB students organized a protest. When the 100 or so demonstrators were denied entry to the hearings, they simply held a sit-in in the rotunda. Without warning, the SFPD used the building's own fire hoses to blast the protesters down the marble steps, where they were set upon and arrested by police. The next day, about 5,000 people showed up at City Hall, surrounding the building, chanting "Seig heil!"—a turnout so large that it signaled the end of the witch hunt 50s, the era of blacklist fear, and a beginning to what we now know of as "the 60s." Non-violent students challenging police was the one idea that ricocheted like a rubber bullet across the crowded campuses of the nation, bringing about the era of civil rights and anti-war protest to come.

Sitting in my squat on Market Street this summer, I would drink coffee and stare out the window at the crowds and at City Hall, at the golden dome, plotting, feeling sneaky, loving how I could plan an illegal show while staring right at it. What could be that one idea today? I lived deep inside the enormous, almost-block-long squat, in a hidden, locked room, and walked the streets in crowds like the Invisible Man, plotting. My friends and I met secretly at night in abandoned buildings to show movies or make posters that we'd take out and put up over billboards. We painted illegal murals and planned to take over the streets and have dance parties. I'd stare at City Hall and wonder how we could make The City ours. How could we make it look like the place we wanted it to be? How could we get our ideas inside that golden dome?

Tellingly, the photos in the North Light Court stop after 1960. There is no evidence here of the great crowds who filed past, year after year, in marches against the Vietnam War, or of the angry crowds breaking out the glass on the front doors of City Hall after Dan White got off, no evidence of the dream deferred. The very gold in the dome itself now seems like such an affront. It has gone from being a symbol of the casual waste of the dot-com boom time, to more of a symbol of the very arrogance and intractability of power, the unassailable dome a place to be defended from the crowds at all costs. I look at the photos and remember the times I myself have marched up the marble steps with a crowd of angry, homeless men to take our protest right to the seat of power. I thought of how Harvey Milk, who was killed in this building, always loved it and said it was the perfect theater, that a man who was despised for sleeping with other men could walk up these sacred steps in this ornate rotunda to take a seat in government. It seems inevitable—the perfect theater—that the angry poor will march in here again, our shouts echoing in the rotunda, a murmur in a crowd, a dream of what we might be.

But when I leave the cafe, I see not an army of the poor on the marble stairs, but a wedding procession coming down, and I am oddly moved. As the young bride and groom pose for pictures, they smile directly into the camera, their faces open and expectant. Outside, a streetcar trolley bell clangs and I remember myself when I first moved here. I see myself in the crowd, looking ahead at something just off camera. I've left so much of myself in every corner of this town. In the alleys, on the rooftops. In the darkened bar. In love in late afternoon beds. In jail. In the streets. In rented rooms and rainy streets there were first kisses, eyes closed, wishes. Somewhere in my mind it feels like it's all still happening at once. I see myself on the Greyhound riding to the Big City. My only regret is that I came here all those years ago to do certain things and now I find myself doing them. My only problem is that I've seen just enough pure, uncontrolled freedom in my lifetime in these streets to never be able to live without it.

Outside, it is raining. In the crowds there is a bustle, a promise, a place for everyone. There is the murmur of late afternoon headlines, but also of something more. An ache, a pain. Whiskey bottles forgotten in dusty drawers. Rain falling on graffiti-covered pillars in unearthed basement rooms. The men are standing around. Their ships have left them. The port is closed. The election is over. Grain is rotting in the holds. The riot cops are guarding the gold on top of City Hall. There is a shadow cast over the day, the disappointment of the times, solemn and true. The crowd is looking at something just off camera. As the New Year comes, their faces are open and expectant. Is there an idea that will sweep across the nation like an angry wind and change things, or are there just these layers of history? Can we make this city ours or are we just passing through? Will this be the year? The year for what?

THE SAN FRANCISCO SHUTDOWN OF 2003

The day the US invasion of Iraq began, tens of thousands of protesters in SF took to the streets in a full day of planned actions, occurring simultaneously throughout the city, that brought San Francisco to a standstill, slowing traffic to a trickle and shutting down the entire downtown area for most of the day. Protesters held Market Street well into the night and Chief of Police Fagan was moved to declare that The City was "in the grips of total anarchy." After five years of grinding war, that day is almost forgotten. I want to go back and look at the incredible organization that made it happen.

In early 2003, as it became clear that a US invasion of Iraq was inevitable, the call went out to protesters to shut down The City when the war started. This was not the usual "The Day After The Bombing Starts" demo announcement that counts on a spontaneous outpouring of rage from people; this was to be a publicly announced shutdown of The City that would be planned openly for months, right up until the moment the war actually started! Flyers around town were encouraging a citywide work stoppage. Everyone was to stay home from work, and, instead, go downtown to protest. Affinity groups were encouraged to take over key intersections throughout The City to "impose real economic, social, and political costs and stop business as usual until the war stops."

I was excited. This was the first time in ages I'd heard people talking about what they were going to DO together to demonstrate the power of their community. It seemed like almost anything would be possible in conjunction with the shutdown, from traditional lockdowns in the heart of the financial district to street parties, food servings, and group bike rides filling the streets all across The City.

What strikes me about that time, writing this now, is how long this war has been with us, how long into the future it threatens to be. Even then, we had already been waiting for 8 months to see what would happen. The waiting seemed to put everything else in my life on hold.

I went to check out a planning meeting at New College and was amazed to see a crowd of people calmly discussing bringing a major US city to a standstill. The map soon was dark with colored-in street intersections that various affinity groups had taken responsibility for shutting down. The Anti-Cop Cluster stood up to claim the protest at Citicorp and the UK Consulate. Some kids from UC Berkeley offered to take care of Market and Franklin. Puking for Peace announced plans for an, uh, action at the Federal Building. The confidence, the feeling of freedom in the very planning reminded me of the days leading up to the opening of 949 Market.

Zara made his yearly art calendar at the beginning of 2003, asking twelve artists from our immediate scene to contribute art to decorate each month. The waiting for war preoccupied the art in the calendar. The spring months of March and April were decorated with Kyle Ransom's painting of armless, mutilated-looking bodies. The word "bomb" appears ghost-like, again and again in Sahar's silk-screened images for July and August. Ivy's painting for the winter months declares in painted text, "Let the bombs fall! I'm not afraid!"

The possibility of a shut down city inspired a vision of what might be possible, what we could get away with. Some of us who had been involved in 949 Market started talking about what we wanted to do for the shutdown. Zara said that our friends in Gay Shame were talking about just rioting and looting after the war started, but it didn't seem like what we were into. I mean, smashing all the windows at Starbucks is a fine, if somewhat cliché, thing to do, but I wanted to do something that took advantage of The City being shut down. As Zara rightly pointed out, "We can steal a VCR any day. This day should be special."

It's not clear if it's defiance or just a total nihilism that Ivy was getting at. Either way, the art anticipates the war still being relevant, even dominant, a full year from when she painted it.

We wanted to do an action about what we were FOR instead of what we were against. The billions of dollars spent on the war necessitated massive budget cuts in health care, housing, and education spending—a very real war against communities here at home.

Could we do an action that was not just against the war, but one that could call attention to what we WANT in our communities?

At the spokes council meetings at New College, I was inspired by how many older folks were there, still fighting for peace. These were veterans of peace movements going as far back as Vietnam. I think how the waiting, too, was not just those months for this war, but spread across the time of our whole lives.

After many meetings, we decided to once again occupy a squat in a highly visible location downtown. The theme for our action would be, "It's not the war; it's the way we live." Opening the squat would not be a symbolic act where we called the media and waited to be arrested for civil disobedience. We intended to take the building and use it to demonstrate ways people could create the world in which we want to live. We would provide free food and first aid, and have a safe, free space for people to meet, discuss the day's events, and plan for the next day. Then, on the second day, we would have a big free meal and a show. We were counting on a huge turnout for the shutdown, which would likely include thousands of people whose only idea of anti-war protest was to join a march. We wanted to try to expose those people to ways that people could actually work together to DO something.

I went to the last march—the last big, legal one before Bush's deadline. Now that the war was really inevitable, there was such a disconnect between the way I was feeling and the mood of the Bay Area liberal crowd. Everyone was milling about in Jefferson Square Park, buying overpriced organic snacks from the street vendors that had sprung up at marches in those few months. People were still trying to sell their irrelevant commie newspapers. None of ye olde black clad anarchists showed up to flyer me for any breakaway march, so I split.

For our squat, we chose the former site of Dennis Peron's pot club—a 4-story abandoned building on Market Street at 10th. You could enter it fairly easily by climbing up the fire escape to the top floor and kicking in a window. The plan was to prepare the squat before the start of the war and then open it to the public the night of the big protest, presumably after the city had been brought to a standstill all day.

Later, I wanted to walk to the store, but I could see police helicopters hovering over what looked to be around Union Square. Impulsively, I turned that way to see if anything was going on over there, but when I got there, there weren't protesters anywhere.

We were counting on the city being so out of police control that our squat would fly under the radar for a couple of days, long enough for many people to know about it. Then we'd announce that we were going to serve free food every night in the squat and hold the building until the end of the war. If we could get large crowds to come, the space could develop a life of its own. People could propose ideas for the space and make their own plans there. If enough people were coming to eat, after a few days, there might be enough people who took it seriously enough to try and defend the squat from arrest.

Back in my room, I kept hearing the helicopters. I had the distinct edgy feeling that the march had not ended, would, in fact, never end. The sounds of sirens and shouts echoed up to my window. The Saturday night streets seemed to seethe with undeclared war.

Or it could just get busted right away. Who knew? But even if it only lasted a day, I'd feel pretty good about taking back some space and feeding a couple hundred folks in it. We had nothing to lose.

I saw Marco at the spokes meeting, and marveled at the coincidence. I had found his old band's tape at Thrift Town that day for only a dollar and had been happy to buy it. The tape's best song, I think, is "Laughing Babies and Sneezing Dogs," a song about living in a dreary house with too many other people in The Mission and dreaming of how, one day, we'd all live in the country together instead, in some beautiful place. Marco still lives on Capp Street. The song was recorded in 1988.

We put our own locks on the front door and slowly moved supplies in while the US moved troops slowly into the Persian Gulf. We spent weeks planning everything: who would bring the food, who would talk to police, how to maintain safety and security. By the time March 20th came, we were ready.

The two nights before the morning of the shutdown, I was out very late. One night, I went out with Bochay and wheat-pasted photocopies of the Chronicle *front page from the day after the first Gulf War started in 1991. The headline declared boldly, "Thousands Take the Bay Bridge." The next night, I went out with Ivy and Andrew, covering up billboards with big, crudely-made, hand painted signs, saying things like, "S.F. Stops Wars!" and "When the bombs fall down, we shut The City down!"*

All of our planning for the squat opening on the night of the big protests had left us without a plan for the actual day of the proposed shutdown. Many of the Punks Against War group decided to just ride our bikes around town all day. One plan was that a group of us could ride in a circle in an intersection, blocking traffic, while a couple of us used twine, or yarn to create an impassable but harmless barrier that we'd leave behind, with an anti-war banner draped over it. The rest of the time, we could join up with groups of other riders on mini-Critical Mass rides throughout town. We all agreed to do our best to not get arrested during the day so that we'd be there to run the squat opening at night.

On Wednesday, when Bush's deadline passed and the war actually started, there was a long, somewhat discouraging march through the pouring rain. Afterward, we had a long, late night meeting, during which most of the PAW group got to go inside and actually see the squat for the first time. After the meeting, Erin, who was in town, shared a bottle of wine with me at my office. Sitting there, exhausted and wet, in a fairly clean office space, just hours before the long-awaited street war, was strange. It made me think of the Hemingway war novels, the long parts where the war is actually in effect overall, but it's winter and nothing is happening—the parts when the main character's on leave, getting drunk, far from the front. So much of this year has felt that way.

On the morning of the day of the shutdown, the streets looked anything but shut down. We met up at 7th and Market at 7:00 AM. There were only five of us, all totally bleary-eyed and sleep-deprived, and traffic flowed normally all around us. My bike basket overflowed with twine, yarn, and banners. I suggested we pull these police barricades that were on the sidewalk at 6th Street across Market, but it didn't seem like there were enough of us to block the traffic pouring into town from the 6th Street freeway connection. Where was the damn shutdown we'd heard so much about?!? We had no way of knowing it at the time, but there were already people locking down at that moment all over the Financial District and at various freeway off-ramps. It would still be a couple of hours, though, before traffic this far up Market would slow to a trickle and finally stop.

SF IndyMedia reports, breaking news wire from 3/20 protests:

7:55 AM Intersections being blocked 3rd and Folsom, 5th and Mission, Mission and Van Ness, Fell and Franklin (arrests about to happen), Fell and Van Ness, Bush and Powell, Market and Sansome, recruiting station at Davis St., Bechtel HQ at Market and Beale, Harrison and Fremont freeway ramp (300 people).

8:00 AM Police violence reported outside UK consulate and outside Bechtel.

8:30 AM Lockdown on Van Ness near Market. People locked to big cement blocks. Police are sawing people out. At Pine, people are blocking street with newspaper racks. At Oak and Gough, intersection blocked by people with pink flags.

Minutes later, we were still confusedly standing at 4th and Market, with no signs of protest anywhere, trying to figure out if we could get a banner across Market Street. Suddenly, we saw these punk-looking kids walking quickly up through the crowd, on either side of the street. One across the street signaled to the two on our end, who then, in a very business-like manner, took out an enormous wrench and calmly opened the valve on the fire hydrant on the corner. The kids on the far corner got theirs open just at the same time and, suddenly, two great blasts of water shot out across Market Street, meeting in the middle of the street to form a wall of water that brought a line of cars to a screeching halt. Just as quickly, the kids had scurried off, bolting down the side streets. Fuck yeah! The shutdown was on!

8:50 AM Police say half the police force is on street. "Protests taking place all over the city." Police say 15 intersections blocked. "Worst traffic jams ever." Report that at Montgomery and Clay, police filling barricades with water to prevent cars from driving into the building. Gay Shame is holding Gough and Market—200 people.

8:55 AM Barricades at Stockton and Grant. Channel 2 says, "If you don't have to be downtown, don't go" and, "As soon as protesters are arrested, more sit down. This looks like it will go on all day." Woo-hoo!!!!! It's working!

9:50 AM 1000 people at 1st and Mission headed towards Market to meet about 1000 people that have taken over Market and Montgomery and have formed a liberated zone.

Much of the rest of the shutdown was a blur for me. I just rode my bike around all day in the sun! For a while the five of us rode the length of Brannan, bringing traffic to a crawl. Then we met up with a pretty large crew of about 30 cyclists at UN Plaza and rode around with them. We specifically chose to ride up and down from 5th to 10th Streets, weaving in and out of the South of Market freeway connector streets for a couple of hours at mid-day. This first ride set the tone for the whole day. Here we had a mid-sized, fairly diverse group of folks, ranging from gray-haired liberals to punks with black masks, riding and chanting excitedly, everyone treating each other pretty well. We chose the direction of the ride together and no one got pissed when the punks would drag dumpsters or newspaper boxes into the streets, leaving them behind us to further clog things up. The ride was fun, but vigilant and serious about making sure the streets were, in fact, shut down.

11:35 AM 1500 people heading west on Market, crowd is growing.

12:42 PM Appears to be mass arrest happening soon at 7th and Market. Police are pushing people down Market towards Civic Center. Protesters are still at Market and Kearney and Market and Montgomery. Huge police presence at Federal Building. police have pepper spray and rubber bullets loaded.

Market Street was the epicenter of everything, and in the early hours of the shutdown I saw some funny stuff there. First, there was the lone pro-war protester, who, while stuck in traffic at 8th and Market, had mounted his SUV and was holding up a homemade poster that read, "Go War!" While people half-assedly argued with him, Ivy tried to let the air out of his tires. Soon after, still in front of the Orpheum, I was leaning on this city trash can, watching some older hippie-types who were holding the intersection with linked arms and a banner, when a young Black Blocker came up to me. Through his mask he said, "Excuse me for just one second, sir," and motioned to the trash can. I stood back and watched while he, first, took the two beer bottles he was carrying and put them in the recycling receptacle on top and then, second, flipped the entire huge cement container over on its side and dragged it into the center of the intersection!

1:38 PM We are hearing reports of people trying to break into the Federal Building. There is a window broken.

It was from Market Street that you could most easily tell that the Shutdown was working. By the middle of the day, you could stand at 8th Street and look east and not see any traffic for blocks. The beauty of the decentralized, disorganized attack was that you could see results without knowing what everyone else was doing, though, on the course of our ride, we ran into some huge marches several times. At 4th and Howard, we almost got penned in with a group of hundreds of protesters that the police were trying to corral, but we rode down Minna Street, the alley, and got away, only to regroup an hour later at UN Plaza. Another time, our ride was slowed by protesters in a face-off with a line of riot cops who were guarding the SF Shopping Mall. A girl ran up to us and asked if we wanted any food. She was with Food Not Bombs, who were riding around all day with bike carts stocked with food, making sure protesters got to eat on the streets! This was the first sign that our modest group of bikers was tied in to a larger, organized event, but we still didn't know what it looked like from outside of it.

3:57 PM 4000 people are headed towards 7th and Mission to rescue some people that have been stuck there. Police seem amazed by the stamina and militancy of protesters.

6:43 Howard and Fremont Streets, crowd estimate now at 5000. Police motorcycles reportedly zooming into crowd. Traffic on the Bay Bridge backed up completely.

After riding bikes all day, around the Embarcadero, through the Broadway Tunnel, on Van Ness, and all through South of Market, PAW members split from the group to report to duty at the squat. I grabbed a six-pack and took a long awaited slug of cold, fresh Anchor Steam while standing in the middle of shut down Market Street. Just then, a man went past me pushing a shopping cart. He had a big radio in the cart that was blasting urgent local news. "...Market Street, the Financial District, and huge swaths of the city have been shut down for most of the day..." Moments later, we unfurled the banner that read, "It's not the war; it's the way we live!" over the front door of our new squat. It was a victory beer!

*From the opening of the Punks Against War zine that we handed
out for free at the squat:*

> *While the lines are being drawn and the whole world waits
> for war, we're already getting our asses kicked here at home.
> The budgets for our community's health care and education re-
> sources have been looted to finance a war that the whole world
> is against. The PATRIOT ACT has effectively suspended many
> of our civil liberties in the name of a war on terrorism that
> we are told will never end. Immigrants are being detained in-
> definitely and, here in this city, homeless people fill the streets,
> sleeping in front of vacant buildings like this one."*

At the squat, the group was putting fresh light bulbs in the hallways and toilet paper in all the bathrooms. There were buckets of
beans and rice and tons of free bread for the meal. Anandi and Zara
turned the water on. We were all moving kind of slow, because we
were so happy about how the day had gone. We shut down The
City AND we had our own building to have a party in! Meanwhile,
out in the streets, the protests were still going strong. I went out to
get a hammer from my place, a couple of blocks away, and watched
several large, unruly marches of several hundred people heading off
in different directions all at once. Passing the Orpheum, now staging
Mel Brooks's *The Producers* ("Springtime for Hitler!"), I saw it was
covered in anti-war graffiti.

8:00 PM 6000 strong at Market and Castro Streets.

*10:00 PM 500 marching down Howard. March is festive,
shows no signs of slowing down.*

11:30 PM 600 people marching through the Haight.

The scene was real sweet in the squat that night. Everybody
seemed pretty happy to get to come into an illegally occupied space
to eat a good, free meal, drink a beer, and discuss the day's events
with everyone. A year later, Erin Yanke would put out issue #7 of
her audio zine, *Life During Wartime*, which featured interviews recorded in the squat that night, with participants who talked about
the shutdown. You can hear the excitement and urgency of the day

in their voices. Listening to it over a year later, I got up and started pacing around my room, energized by the voices on the tape!

> *"Signs at protest marches proclaim 'Another world is possible,' but how? What would it look like? We don't have the means to figure it out under the system we live under. We don't have the time, we don't have money, and we don't have space, so we can't decide how we're going to live. We're not here to say, 'Let the sanctions work' or, 'Give the weapons inspectors more time.' We are here to say that we don't want to participate in a capitalist system that is dangerous to people and harmful to the world. We're here to have self-determination in our communities."*

But, in some ways, the squat event wasn't that interesting. The crowd was small, maybe only a little over a hundred people, and it was all punks. The experiment of bringing the "normal liberals" to "the next level" that Zara had envisioned never really materialized. Maybe the flyers we passed out that said "Punks Against War!" really big on them had something to do with the turnout? Looking back, this was a situation where our name worked against us. I suspect that the crowd would have grown in successive days, as we hoped, if the shutdown had continued with Thursday's energy. But Friday was to be a whole different day.

And now the war is here. The stock market is, cheerfully, rising in expectation. Bush has at last brought us to a time when brute force threatens not only reason, but MEANING. We must violate the UN's resolution in order to uphold it. We must start a war in order to have peace. It is textbook Orwellian Doublespeak, delivered with an unflagging passion and intensity that evokes the determination of Orwell's "boot stepping on a human face forever." In a few hours, our country will start to kill many thousands of innocent Iraqi civilians in an unprecedented horror show of bombing meant to "shock and awe" all opposition. This is a "liberation" that can only evoke similar "liberations" at Dresden, in Tokyo.

The Direct Action Networks' flyers leading up to the shutdown had said, basically, stay home from work and go downtown to protest the DAY AFTER the war started, and that was exactly what happened. The next day, apparently, everyone had to go back to work. Waking up in the squat, you could hear the traffic out on

Market Street and just tell that it was not going to be the same kind of day. Sure enough, without Thursday's massive numbers, Friday was one long ass-beat from one end of Market Street to the other.

On Friday, all the cops' rules went out the window. The cops had lost control of The City the day before. Now they were embarrassed and PISSED. There were riot cops everywhere, many rows thick, who weren't going to let it happen again. Anyone looking like a protester—like Ivy, Melissa, and Rachel—was to be stopped and searched. Cops were targeting bicycles, too, because the bikes had been so effective in the shutdown. They were pulling people over and threatening to confiscate bikes.

Early in the day, there were protesters locked down all over the Financial District and things were at a standstill, but there weren't enough people to sustain it. After 300 arrests by 11:00 AM, it was over. Our group rode around, watching really small protests as they were brutally attacked and watching bikes get confiscated. After a while, we decided to go home and lay low for the day until it was time to open the squat for the show and food that night.

When I reported to the squat that night to open it up, things looked bad. The cops had surrounded three separate marches and were slowly doing mass arrests, all within one block of the squat. I wasn't sure if they knew about the squat, but we were surrounded either way. "Well," I thought, "Overt IS Covert!" We went inside and began preparing for the meal and show anyway, and opened the doors as planned at 8:00. About a hundred people were eating when the cops showed up.

I was working the door. My job was to lie to them as long as possible, to keep them from getting in the door at all costs. While the three cops got out of their car, someone went inside the squat to warn everyone and prepare our evacuation plan. The cops came to the door and started asking me a lot of questions. They were loud, aggressive, but I remained calm. I said, "This is a private party. We're having dinner and music. Can I help you?" The cops wanted to know who said we could just come in and have a private dinner in someone else's building?!? I feigned shock. "I don't know what you're talking about, officer. We rented this building from John Barbagelata."

This went back and forth for several precious minutes. The cops finally produced the owner of the bar next door, who insisted that he had been entrusted by the building's real owner to watch the place. No one, to his knowledge, was to rent the place. I started to get pissed. "Look! What is this all ABOUT?!? Let's clear this up, OK? We'll CALL the landlord."

Confused by my taking the lead, the cops said, "Uh, OK..." Meanwhile, Zara was in the other room, changing his voice mail greeting so it said, "This is Barbagelata Realty. Office hours are between 9 and 5, Monday through Friday. Please leave a message."

I said, "Wait here. I'll go get the rental agreement and then we'll call the landlord." The cops waited patiently at the door while I went and checked to see how the evacuation was going. I let everyone inside know it was serious, that they were really going to come in. Then I went back to the door. Out front, there were now many more cop cars, but still only the three cops were standing there. I said, "OK, the guy is coming out with the contract. It'll just be a moment."

With this news, the cops seemed to recover their resolve. They said, "Look! We're coming in here! That's it!"

I said, "I don't think you should go in there now."

The cop looked enraged. "What do you MEAN?"

I said, "If you go in there now, you may have a situation on your hands that you can't handle," and nodded sadly. This went back and forth for a little bit, too, with the lead cop arguing with me about just what they could and could not handle, until the second cop cut the first one off and motioned for them to go inside. I saw they were going for it and tried to get the door closed and locked, but I couldn't. All three of them pushed against it, pushing me out of the way. A bunch of the other cops followed them in the door.

I am proud that our carefully planned evacuation drill worked. While I'd been delaying the cops' entrance, the back door had been opened into the alley. As the cops marched in and more and more arrived out front, they seemed to think that they were backing the crowd into the corner. But the closer they got to the crowd, the smaller the crowd got, until we had all filed calmly out the back door, thus avoiding a single arrest! With the golden dome of City Hall now in sight, I stepped into the clear on Fell Street, and ran the other way.

The two days after the war started were two of the most intense days of protest in Bay Area history. Police arrested 646 people in two days, a protest record. For weeks protests continued—sometimes spontaneous, sometimes planned—but they occurred in a city unquestionably under police control. After the protesters that shut down The City disappeared, the riot cops remained, lining the entrances of Nordstrom's or Macy's for days, as if they had always been there and you just hadn't been able to see them before.

Obviously, we had no illusions that our protest was going to stop the war from happening, but it was hard to put everything in your life on hold to plan these actions for months, and then, when it was over, have the war remain the dominant thing in your life. The "shock and awe" bombing was reducing Baghdad to rubble and the war was still happening in our own streets every day.

The day after the squat got busted, I skipped out on a legal march to go to band practice. When practice was over, I thought I'd go home and rest up for the first time in weeks, but I turned on Enemy Combatant Radio, the pirate radio station that was covering the protests, just in time to hear that the breakaway march was fighting the cops in front of my building! I showed up just in time to watch riot cops dragging a couple of my friends down the street by their hair, as the cops prepared a mass arrest.

What was hardest to take, as the war shifted into gear, was the maddening sense of suddenly living in an atmosphere of complete unreality. The local media that had been against the war and sympathetic to protesters before the war started were now saying we had to "Support the troops," and, in this most anti-Bush of cities, were now rabidly anti-protester. Clear Channel started organizing pro-war rallies across the nation and the media dutifully covered them, as if they were genuine outpourings of grassroots sentiment.

Suddenly, those of us who had shut down The City were now "The Protesters"—an alien race of simple-minded 17-year-olds who've never worked a day in their lives, numbering only in the low thousands, who had apparently descended upon The City from all across the nation simply to fuck with the good San Franciscans, who were ALREADY against the war, but just needed to get to work on time, dammit! The reality that tens of thousands of working class SF residents had stayed home from work to take part in the shutdown was being denied.

As my friends were being arrested on Market Street, I saw KRON show up. Ignoring the fact that the protesters were being hurt, the reporter ran out and, instead, started interviewing the driver of the car that was first in line on 7th, now stuck at the light.

The Protesters were now being BLAMED for the situation we were in. The cops arbitrarily declared that the shutdown had cost SF $1.8 million in police pay alone. Mayor Brown and some members of the Board of Supervisors incredibly started saying that it was because of the PROTESTS and not the war that The City's health care and education programs were going to be cut!

One night on Market Street, I saw about ten senior citizens marching on the sidewalk with signs reading things like "Grannies For Peace." Alongside trudged about 35 riot cops in full gear. This excessive force was a fairly common sight, as the cops were getting paid time-and-a-half overtime pay. At protests, I heard cops taunt, "Thanks guys! I'm finally going to get a new big screen TV out of this!"

Willie Brown made the statement to the eager press that "85% of these people protesting don't even live here!" and the news cheerfully parroted it as fact. It seemed preposterous, this claim that the protesters weren't really from San Francisco, when The City had routinely been the site for several marches of 100,000 people and over for the past eight months. I wondered what percentage of SFPD officers actually lived in The City. How many of the Financial District workers who had been blocked from getting off the freeway on their way to work actually lived in SF?

Empirical evidence would suggest that The City's residents don't really hate the protesters so much. I went to the first Critical Mass ride after the shutdown. We were cheered by the stalled drivers, many who flashed the peace sign as we cycled past. People got out of their cars to watch and wave, and some folks leaned out of a stalled #71 Haight bus to give me hi-fives as I rode by. SF gets the point: 5000 bikes in the street is NOT 5000 cars during a war for oil.

Unfortunately, Direct Action organizers started believing the bad press and publicly declared that they were switching tactics, to only directly protest the war profiteers, like Bechtel and the Carlyle Group. It does make sense, anticipating smaller numbers, to focus on more specific targets, yet there was a feeling, somehow, that the organizers were now apologizing for the very success of the shutdown. Within a week of the shutdown, the new protests had degenerated into mere civil disobedience actions, with groups linking arms, or, worse, doing yoga in front of the TransAmerica Pyramid. It seems now too easy to make fun of Yoga for Peace, a real "tactic" from the time. I will only say that history has shown how ineffectual the anti-war movement in San Francisco has been since it renounced its only successful tactics.

It took me a while to notice what was different about this morning, but then it hit me: No helicopters. I live on Market Street and

*there have been police helicopters buzzing my building for weeks,
since Bush's deadline to Iraq has passed. Is the war over and are
things back to normal? What would "normal" look like after a week
of many of The City's residents fighting the cops on the street?*

I learned a lot from the SF shutdown. I saw firsthand how much
power people have when they work together and I saw that people
have that power all the time, even in periods of history when they
may be feeling more powerless. I saw how fragile the day to day
of the system really is, how dependent it is on everyone's compli-
ance. Tactically, I learned something that folks going to ministerial
trade summits to protest could learn: that decentralized, disorganized tactics may work far better than attacking the symbolic point
of power where the most police are, like trying to "take down the
fence" at the FTAA meetings. And, of course, I had my long-term
belief reinforced that it is far better to outwit and outnumber the
cops whenever possible than it is to directly engage them in hand to
hand combat.

But most of all, I learned not to let the corporate media that we
despise decide what tactics we should be using! It doesn't make any
sense to spend half our time protesting the media as a corporate puppet of the ruling class and then try to tailor our message to please
them. When the *Chronicle* uses up that much ink denouncing the
protesters, it means they're actually threatened. Contrast the virulent press after the protest to the great congratulations the progressive community later received after Matt Gonzalez's campaign for
mayor narrowly lost. Commended for our cash-strapped enthusiasm, we were told again and again that we had actually WON!

As the war and the summer wore on, it became harder and harder
to remember just what a day in that shut down city had felt like. It
was hard, too, to listen to all the bad things that were said about us
in the media. Listening too long could warp your perspective, divide
you against your instincts about how to act out of conscience or
make you doubt your own possibility to be effective at all. We never
got a catchy name like "Battle of Seattle" to describe our historic
day. I write this to create a context to consider the success of that
day and to revive the memory of what it felt like to stand with so
many on a Market Street under the control of protesters. I want to
stand there again.

MATT GONZALEZ: THE SCAM INTERVIEW

After the passage of Care Not Cash, it was starting to seem sadly in-evitable that Newsom would carry the momentum on to win the 2003 mayor's race. No one on the Left was really challenging him and pro-gressives had spent much of 2003 organizing against the war in Iraq.

Board of Supervisors president and Green Party member Matt Gonzalez jumped in the mayor's race at the very last minute, though, and electrified progressives in The City with a feverish, month-long, low-budget campaign. The cash-strapped Gonzalez campaign rein-vigorated a war-weary SF Left, relying on a groundswell of volun-teer energy and Meet-The-Candidate house parties organized via the internet. Outspent ten to one by the Democratic Party machine's heavily favored Newsom, Gonzalez ultimately lost the runoff elec-tion, but by just a couple thousand votes.

Matt Gonzalez was possibly the fartherst-Left person to ever be elected to citywide office in SF and an unusually straightforward, honest candidate. What's more, he once asked me to sign his copy of the Turd-Filled Donut at City Hall. Make no mistake, I definitely supported him early and wanted him to win. But I had many res-ervations about the way his campaign turned out. Matt's campaign had relied on internet-organized events like "Mutts for Matt" and had bragged that Matt had "once played bass in a rock band." By emphasizing Matt's appeal to young, white artists, his campaign had alienated communities of color by not taking harder stances on is-sues like police brutality and environmental racism. I got to ask Matt his thoughts on what I called his campaign's "gentrified pro-gressivism" in this interview from summer of 2004.

Now it has been four years since the 2000 board of supervisors came in with high expectations among progressives. What would you characterize as your chief accomplishments towards a progres-sive agenda in that time?

Matt Gonzalez: The living wage initiatives, the limits on chain store regulations were big for us. We expanded health benefits for city workers to include transgender benefits. We took strong posi-tions on things like City I.D. cards for undocumented workers so they had ways to identify themselves to police officers without re-vealing their citizenship status. I think we did a lot of charter reform where we changed the balance of power so that the mayor didn't get to appoint all commissioners. We declawed Willie Brown in a lot of ways. We shared power as related to planning appointments, the police commission, the business commission. I think election reform, with Instant Runoff Voting (which should be in place by November), is big. It allows an election to be decided with one trip to the polls, where you can rank your choices First, Second, Third. It is an important reform. We're the only place in the country talking about that. Of course, in Florida, if you'd had that, folks who'd voted for Nader could have picked Gore as a second choice and he would have won. So we've done some stuff like that.

How much of a sense of "we" is there? How much of a sense is there of the supervisors elected in 2000 operating as a group?
MG: There's some camaraderie. We've certainly fallen short in some respects, I think, because we weren't as daring as we could have been, and that tends to be the simple realities, the mathematics of some of these folks staying in power. They compromise and lose some of the hardcore edge that would have accomplished more.

That leads to the next question. There's a feeling of frustration I have about how conservatives are always able to control the agenda. Part of my excitement in 2000 about this board was about the idea that the Left would now have a loud voice to say, "This is what we're going to do in this city!" and not just react to Mayor Brown all the time. Now, I wonder what happened. The Left hasn't been able to define the issues, and by early 2002, you had Newsom defining homelessness as the number one issue in town from this far-right perspective. Almost two years before the election, his platform was the standard.
MG: Well, think about it: The Mayor's got a press office. He's got all the departments working for him. For us to get something to happen, we need 8 votes out of 11 to override a veto. We have to convince his department heads that what we want to do makes sense. Otherwise, we're getting in the press with them saying, "That's a lousy idea." The public doesn't respond to that by saying, "That's just the mayor's bullshit." They say, "Wow, that sounds like a lousy idea." If you're the mayor, you can do a lot of change, rapidly. What I could do as a mayor could take me 8

or 12 years as a member of the Board of Supervisors, and that's probably doubtful.

I'm still wondering how Newsom, a supervisor, could swoop in and set the tone for the mayor's race when the new board had the same amount of time to put forth a defining agenda.

MG: I would say that the leader of the Left at that time was Tom Ammiano. Obviously, it's for the historians to decide, but I would say that Tom did not confront his likely opponent in the mayor's race. He wanted these problems to go away. I think Tom thought that if he had to avoid certain fights or tone down some of his Left rhetoric to get elected mayor, then that's what he was going to do. I don't think that was a successful strategy because I think what motivates people to go out and walk precincts and get things done is if they truly believe you're going to represent certain ideas. I got in that race late, but if you think about it, in a short amount of time, with a tenth of the resources, we clearly demonstrated that Newsom could have been defeated if he'd been confronted by opposition head on. I think there's a lesson there for progressives.

Let's talk about your campaign for mayor. There was a lot of talk about "the energy" around it and the feeling it was run in a different way than these campaigns usually are.

MG: If someone walked in (to campaign headquarters) and said they wanted to do something and started to do it, then they were doing it. There was a lot of field operation work. To counter their money, we had to walk all our campaign materials.

If there was a new base created by the campaign, what does it look like now?

MG: It's hard to answer. I think the core of much of what we were doing tended to come from centers of The City that were much younger and traditionally don't care much about politics. There were people coming from the arts community, the music community. The SF Late Night Coalition, the Bike Coalition. There were a lot of people who were looking for The City to start implementing alternative visions and to reprioritize what we were doing. The thought that there might be a mayor that someone could go speak to about saving an art space or about saving light night entertainment, about something like the hours that clubs should close, and be favorably disposed to all of this was an idea that people understood.

Do you feel that the attention from white artists or the bike lane people may have hurt you in the communities that are more traditionally part of the progressive base, like communities of color or working class communities? The five poorest neighborhoods—the neighborhoods like the Bayview that could stand to benefit most from progressive policies—all had the lowest voter turnout in a very close election.

MG: Keep in mind, I was a champion of the minimum wage proposition that passed. But, you know, the Left doesn't want to hear this, but working class neighborhoods are often the most conservative neighborhoods out there. Look at Excelsior. It's all working class people of color, but you know what? They'll support pro-death penalty initiatives, juvenile initiatives that charge juveniles as adults. They have supported some of the most reactionary things out there.

Right, but what I mean is Newsom won the Bayview but he didn't win by that much, and there weren't a lot of people who seemed to care either way. Newsom was in the Bayview a lot but he wasn't talking about getting cops to stop shooting people or about shutting down the power plant. Maybe going further to the Left or being more visible in that neighborhood would have excited people to come support you. If your ideas weren't better here, then where?

MG: We were interested in who had access to the mayor. We were looking to work on some of the economic reforms that were necessary. We were talking about tax reform, the need to restructure corporate taxation to change from a payroll to tax to a gross receipt tax to trigger an interest in hiring and not penalizing companies who were interested in hiring people. We wanted to redirect money to MUNI so that MUNI could be free. We were trying to prioritize better schools in certain areas. We were also talking about the establishment of a municipal bank so we don't have to put money with a private lender. We can take advantage of some of the huge amounts of money that sit around making money for private banks and put them to work to revitalize our neighborhoods by making loans to small businesses. We were talking about fixing some of our energy problems by using tidal energy rather than sticking to a fossil fuel reality. The police force would have been led by a progressive person who would say, you know what, we're not going to arrest peaceful marchers, even if they're in the streets, because who fucking cares? There are a lot of crimes we don't arrest people for because it costs too much and it's not in our interests. It's better to have to deal with a little inconvenience where a motorist has to wait a few minutes while a march passes by.

Do you have any regrets about the way the campaign was run?

MG: I think many of the things that caused it to fail are also the things that caused it to succeed. If that election could be repeated four or five times, we would have won a couple times. It comes down to who comes out to vote that day.

What I keep coming back to is how can the agenda be shaped by the Left? How do you think we should be more proactive?

MG: I think it's about picking an issue we want to win and going out there and fighting for it. I don't think we can only be reacting to what the establishment is putting out there. A great example of that, just like the minimum wage thing, is the example of non-citizen voting (allowing non-citizen immigrants to vote in local school board elections, a ballot measure Gonzalez is backing heavily in 2004). Both of these measures favor not just working class people but immigrant, working class people.

If you had won, what were the first couple things you would've done?

MG: I think it would have been a very progressive administration and it would have been felt in terms of who had access and who was driving the agenda. There would have been a whole mind-shift over things like economic parity. We would have been looking for business models that showed the success of being able to have that. Right now (with Newsom), we're going to have a continuation of Willie Brown being progressive on social issues and conservative on economic stuff and as long as the media promotes all the social stuff, everyone makes the mistake of thinking we have a progressive mayor, and it's simply not true.

Did you anticipate Newsom's gay marriage stance?

MG: No, but he didn't either. They thought they'd be shut down in half a day and it'd be purely symbolic. His people will tell you that they did that because they were cognizant of the fact that they had not won District 8 (The Castro) and they did that to shore up support there. They didn't expect that the judge would not shut them down, that they'd get a gay judge who didn't want to rule against them. Then the mayor just continued to issue the licenses and it became this national frenzy.

Just one last bit: Since this is for a punk rock mag, how'd you score the interview with Joe Strummer?

MG: I had a friend who was the editor of a magazine called *Vang* and they wanted someone to interview some music people. They asked me if I'd interview Tom Waits and I said no. Then they asked me if I'd interview Joe Strummer and I said yes. Strummer was certainly an icon of the period I grew up in.

In your campaign literature, you emphasized that you had "played bass in a rock band." What band?

MG: Well, that literature was intended to be kind of light to get young people to vote. We were trying to promote that I'm a tenant and don't own a car, stuff like that. But the band was here in town, called John Hartfield after the German photomontage artist. We were a trio, but we later added a second guitar. I played a total of 30 or 40 shows...

But here's the *Maximum Rock and Roll* question: What were your influences?

MG: Probably The Clash, Joy Division. Stuff like that.

That's All! Thanks!

NO JOY IN MUDVILLE

Mission Street today, like South of Market, appears trapped in some arrested state of "hip." The poorly built lofts fall apart and resemble the cheaply made public housing they have replaced. The Beauty Bar is still there, but the blue spray-painted gang graffiti won't stay hidden under the yellow paint they try to cover it with. An uneasy truce has developed between the Latino families who walk past daytime fruit stands and the nightly hipster bar crawl.

I rarely remember to notice the paint splotches on the Bayview Bank anymore, but they did catch my eye on that rainy night in December when Gonzalez lost to Newsom. I thought of election night in 1999. Tom Ammiano's insurgent campaign had been fueled by anger at the long lines of young, rich kids who came to the Mission to cram into former Latino working-class bars now turned into yuppie dives, like Doc's Clock. After Gonzalez gave his concession speech at his campaign headquarters on Duboce, he headed down Mission Street to drink a consolation beer with his supporters. In 2003, the ex-candidate now drank at Doc's Clock, too.

Much of the role of the mayor of San Francisco is symbolic, about how the mayor's personality both reflects and shapes the aspirations of our times. It was an accident of history that bought the imperious and thoroughly crooked Willie Brown back home to San Francisco just in time to preside over the thoroughly crooked dot-com times. But who else could have so embodied the era and shaped the city in his image, ruling from a golden-domed City Hall?

Gonzalez, too, was of the times, and the fact that he almost won says a lot about how much this city changed in the four years since Tom Ammiano ran his upstart write-in campaign. In 1999, Ammiano rallied all the tenants, people of color, working poor, and activists that remained after the dot-com boom. In 2003, Gonzalez instead rallied many of the young, white hipsters who remained after the dot-com BUST. The Gonzalez campaign, with its art parties and internet energy, was a gentrified progressivism, what a progressive vision looks like when it abandons traditional progressive organizing bases.

As venerable indie rocker and celebrity Gonzalez campaign volunteer Jonathan Richman played inside the bar, some friends and I drank whiskey outside in the cool rain. Even then, I'd already heard people wondering about how we could keep "the energy" alive. It seemed better to wonder how much of the energy would have been kept alive if Gonzalez had WON. Would a Gonzalez victory have ushered in a sweeping transformation of everyday life in the city with the urgency and creativity of the year's anti-war events, or would we still be standing here in the rain outside of the bar? Was this a movement or just a scene?

Staring at the old, fading paint blotches on the Bayview Bank that night, I remembered rolling down Mission Street on a flatbed truck during the anti-war parade and playing punk shows in Leed's doorway across the street. I remembered the months of dreaming of and getting away with a different way of life inside of 949 Market. I remembered Market Street shut down for a full day and the feeling of raw, unchallenged possibility in the joyful streets.

I still wished Gonzalez had won, but I only want to go to an art show in City Hall when City Hall is abandoned and taken over by squatters!

PART FOUR: UNDERGROUND

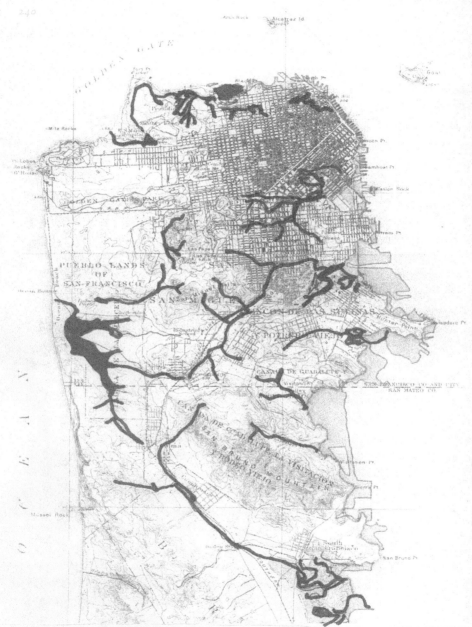

MAP OF UNDERGROUND FRESHWATER AND CREEKS
IN SAN FRANCISCO

JANUARY 2005

This was the introduction to issue #5 of SCAM from January 2005.

Wow, it's been a whole year since the FTAA protest in Miami and I've only now been able to kick my tear gas habit. I was jonesing real bad all through the protests last summer at the Republican National Convention in New York, too, but they never gave us any gas. After Miami, it was bad. I came to a week later in New Orleans on the dark end of Bourbon Street, waving around twenty-dollar bills and growling at cabbies, "There's got to be a bar somewhere in this rotten French town where a grown man with money in his pocket can get himself properly Tasered!" Back home in SF, it was worse. I started binging on mace alone in my room. And why not, eh? There's nothing like a couple quick blasts of pepper spray in the morning when coffee just won't cut it anymore. I'm not the only one. I heard that a zine symposium in Portland had to be cancelled last summer when the polyamory skillshare degenerated into a roomful of zine editors lasciviously macing each other in the dark.

Um... sorry. But that's just how these past four years have felt sometimes. This is Scam #5, a look at stuff that people have tried to do to fight back here in SF, what we've done, at least, to keep ourselves sane. It's a look at stuff that worked and stuff that didn't.

I did a lot of interviews for this issue with people who I think are doing really cool stuff. One question I asked almost everyone is, "How can we turn this around so that we're fighting for what we're for, instead of what we're against?"

It's also been a rough couple of years, but oddly rewarding ones, in a couple other ways. I've been spending a lot of time and effort trying to figure out how to deal with abuse, how to deal with having a stepfather that tried to kill me when I was a kid. And there's been a whole lot of thinking about dead friends these last few years. I had another pile of writing about as big as this one that's more about all that stuff but I'm just not quite ready to put it all out yet, honestly. I'm also not so interested in talking so much about myself these days. I'm wondering what kind of stuff we can all work on together, instead.

One last thing: after seventeen years, I quit using the name "Iggy Scam." Just so you know, I'm back to being "Erick Lyle."

The short reason is that I have actually long been sick of the name and wondered when I'd get rid of it. A kid named Toad started calling me Iggy in 1987. The longer reason involves being sick of writing from the perspective of a persona, being tired of romanticized zine writing in general, and just needing a change in my life. This year, I've been going to school, working on journalism stuff, and I quit drinking, mostly because I was just tired of doing the same old stuff and because there's a lot of stuff I want to learn. As for drinking, I can still go to the show and have fun, especially when it's The Bananas or Dead Moon!

Sometimes I wonder if he's still "Toad," though.

INTERVIEW WITH ZARA THUSTRA PT. 4

After years of graff art, now people are trying to get you involved in the art world. Your work is free on the street and cheap at shows. What's going to happen when you get in the museums?

ZARA: Yerba Buena asked me to be in the Bay Area Now, where they exhibit what they consider to be the "hot, young" artists that are "happening" now. As a "career move"—I'm learning a lot of this stuff now—what this means is if you're trying to have an art "career," you put stuff in this show and then people from all over are going to call you up and get you these shows, like in NYC, Stockholm, whatever. Like, "Come to our city so we can sell you!"

How did they hook up with you?

ZARA: I think there were told to call me by someone. They obviously don't know much about my work, but they need people to buy tickets to the gallery and I think they got word that I could bring in a lot of people. They may or may not actually like my work because they picked me for the show without seeing anything. It's like getting a video on MTV or something. Then you're guaranteed to sell a certain amount of CDs. If you're in this show, you're guaranteed to sell a certain amount of paintings.

They're investing.

ZARA: Right, and at rates of about 50 or 60%. Basically, a commercial gallery owner is like a used car salesman. They suck so bad. They're super falsely nice to you. Then they sell your painting for $1,000 and they got $500 out of it. I don't care about the money so much but the process around it is pretty slimy.

Then whoever buys it wants to sell it for $10,000.
ZARA: Yeah, it's like the big art buyers want to buy the newest toy out there. It's not the most exciting world to be in and it's devilishly false.

What are you trying to do then, by being a part of it?
ZARA: I want to be a political voice in this situation. I want to try and represent the things we've been talking about and do it in this upper class, bougie community. Plus, it's a museum, and a lot of school kids and older folks go there. On this level, anything I do is almost the most accessible it could be. A lot of different folks will go see it. I want to say something to them that I think needs to be said.

In a not-for-sale kind of way?
ZARA: They're paying me $300 to be in the show, which is pathetic. At first I thought, "I'm going to get $5000 and live off this shit all year!" I was pumped.

Basically, your presence is just making them money.
ZARA: Yeah. The "Big Time" is a total hoax and there's really nowhere to go in this society where we can do the shit that we want to do, so I'm back to square one, which is trying to speak about what I think needs to happen in this world.

What were some of the ideas you had for stuff to put in the museum show?
ZARA: The first conversation I had with them was funny. I said, 'If I'm going to be in this show, the first thing I want to do is sit down with the other thirty artists in the show and talk about what we're all thinking about right now." They were like, "Uh...THAT'S interesting...BUT, uh, it's not going to happen." I said, "This is a big deal for a lot of people and I think it's real shame that we're having this show and I'm going to be seeing all these other artists hanging their shit and we're not going to talk about the structure of the show." Another idea was to have free dinner in the museum. They said, "We don't have the budget to feed that many people."

I said, "My experience is that you can feed 150 people for $40 so let's double that and make it $80." But I guess it's not appropriate to feed people out of white buckets in Yerba Buena.

Right! "But is it ART?!?"

ZARA: So, I started thinking I'd go in and paint this huge thing that said, "This is no place to create culture." I started getting venomous. But they weren't letting me do anything. They were really editing me and letting me know that they had the power too, because if you're in the show, you've signed a contract. It's a really boring scene. It's really just another cog in the system. I was disappointed, and now, here I am, entering into this endeavor with these people and all we do is fight. It's not super fun and I'm hoping I can learn something from it.

What are you going to try to put in it?

ZARA: I'm going to paint this big landscape that has a lot of symbolic things that are happening right now, like planes and bombs crashing, I want to try to express the human emotion with animals in the painting. There's going to be dead animals, sad animals, and I'll have this hole cut out of the painting so people can walk up behind it and stick their face into the painting like at an amusement park and have their picture taken. It's supposed to look like there's all this bad shit in the world and there you are, smiling in it. It's not the end all, but hopefully it'll be good.

What ideal do you envision for art then? If you feel there's no outlet, what do you wish there was?

ZARA: It's something I talk about with a lot of people. I'm not sure. One thing I romanticize is IRA murals in Ireland. That's the real anti-colonialist shit. It's so amazing; the neighborhoods back these murals. In the Mission, we could have huge, beautiful, anti-capitalist murals that say this neighborhood is a beacon for down-ass activists, living their lives here, who don't like what capital is doing in this country or any country. I like to envision us having enough community control that we can get the property owners in this community to support pro-community messages on the sides of their buildings. I also hope the economy tanks and people have more time to be creative and work together and hang out.

What's up with your upcoming stencil tour?

ZARA: Me and SHY GIRL are going on tour to do stencils in NYC, Philly, DC. We're traveling around, doing stencils on sidewalks about giving your money away if you have it. It's just about doing public art in new places for fun. People should come to our city and do some of that!

949 MARKET REVISITED

A couple months ago, Matt Gonzalez asked me to come talk about 949 Market to his students in a class he's teaching about political art at the SF Art Institute. I asked Ivy and Zara to get together with me so we could prepare a presentation we could do together for the class.

It was an interesting situation: We had a chance to talk about anti-capitalist art events with kids about to enter the cutthroat, capitalistic art world. We would get to ask questions about who art serves and talk about how 949 Market was an example of artists working collectively to kids entering an art world that more highly values individual success. But it was also good for us to get to talk to each other again, a couple years later, about what the point of 949 had been.

It's been almost four years since 949 Market and the conditions in the city are just as bad. We've still got no community control over any aspect of our environment. We have no place to hang out as a community, no place where we can meet to talk and exchange ideas or work on projects together, and no place to make, share, and eat food. We have no not-for-profit show or practice spaces.

The situation for us is the same as it is for those kids who are now about to enter the art world. There is no option awaiting their creativity that doesn't involve fighting each other for the right to be exploited by galleries in order to possibly achieve an individual, non-collective success as some kind of brand name.

In events like 949 or the massive protests that shut down SF in 2003, or even in Gonzalez's campaign for mayor's famed energy, you can see how starved people in this city are for some sort of fulfilling collective experience.

In the end, despite some initial nervousness about speaking, we had a good talk with Matt and the kids. In closing, we broke up the students into smaller groups and asked them to try to discuss and collectively answer some questions. Questions included "What do you want your art to achieve?" and, my favorite, "Are you comfortable striving for success in a racist, sexist, homophobic society?" Hopefully, that last one may have broken a couple minds and sent a couple kids on the way to being art school dropouts, like Matt's hero, Joe Strummer.

Soon after that, we resumed regular meetings of our loose-knit affinity group, Punks Against War. We're trying to open a community space like 949 that would be, uh, more SUSTAINABLE (i.e. not a squat). We're also trying to figure out ways that we can offer up the resources of our group to other non-punks/activist communities. Is there some other way our art or writing or access to free food can be of use?

It's hard, looking for spaces. There are many vacant spaces these days, but they're still so expensive. As far as helping other groups, hotel workers were on strike and locked out at tourist hotels all throughout downtown. I approached a representative for Local 2, the union representing them, offering our help. PAW ended up, at her suggestion, feeding workers on the picket line. But the day after we went for the first time, the lockout ended. Maybe that's what happens when a bunch of vegetarians cook a meat-filled shepherd's pie: the workers say, "Okay! Enough already! We'll go back to work!" It's not always easy having regular meetings. But there's a lot of shit to work out. Right now, it feels essential to me, though; the group effort is so missing from my life. It's exciting to brainstorm ideas for what we want the space to be like. But thinking of how to pay the rent is depressing.

In the meantime, I meet landlords and go look at expensive, empty spaces. I stand in them and think, "Punk shows here, free meals over there, art making space in back, and meeting space over there."

I stand in empty spaces and wonder, "What will our world look like when we finally build it?"

50 MILLION AT 16TH/MISSION BART
5/1/04

It was a blazing hot day in May as Jimmy and I walked down Mission Street toward 16th with the generator for the show. When we passed 17th, I couldn't help it. I started looking around in the street for Matty, like I always do. When I come this way, I always wonder what it must have felt like for him to come down here every day, like a ghost haunting himself, the Mission punk guitar hero, standing around the plaza, looking.

I remembered the first show that Matty and I played together at the BART. How strange that the site of some of our biggest inspiration was also a place of so much despair. Maybe the two worlds, inspiration and desperation, are there all the time, transposed on top of each other, and we can choose which one to live in. More likely, we go back and forth between them on good days and bad. Either way, it made the BART plaza seem like a perfect place for the inspired but desperate songs of 50 Million.

When Jimmy and I showed up with the generator, there was already a bigger than usual crowd milling around for the big reunion show. There was a buzz in the air. The excitement of the first 50 Million show in a couple years mixed with the usual pre-generator show adrenalin from wondering if the cops would come and try to shut the show down and the anticipation for the first loud harsh notes of the guitar that would turn the BART plaza into an illegal, hit-and-run punk venue.

Standing in the plaza now, I could still remember the feeling of looking up from my own guitar to see a hundred or so kids filling the BART Plaza, jumping up and down and dancing, singing along, as the sun set behind the hills and the late afternoon wind came down 16th street, bending the tall palm trees across the street. The generator shows that Matty and I had helped set up years ago had always made me feel like anything would be possible in San Francisco. Cops would drive up to the shows, look at us helplessly, and just drive away.

A lot of the crowd from the first summer of generator shows was here now. It was probably the first time I'd seen all these people in one place since the memorial. It was an odd assortment including a handful of people newly clean and sober and a few people so strung out on speed that they ordinarily never left the house. Each group, ironically, was isolated in similar ways these days. Aesop was there, too, with his young kid. Matty wasn't, of course. But spread across the plaza were several packs of teenagers with patches of Matty and Aesop's old band sewn on their hoodies—they were the new kids, chain smoking and drinking cans of Sparks in the sun.

And then there were 50 Million themselves, the two brothers back from Texas, looking like they possibly hadn't slept or even drank water in the 5 years since they'd left San Francisco. With his freshly shaved head, unruly beard, and arms covered in homemade tattoos, Wade looked like a traveling punk's nightmare—like a big, scary, Texas redneck. He was standing alone by the drums, clenching and unclenching his fist, while Shell Head paced around, unshaven, bug-eyed, chattering.

Seeing them brought back a flood of memories. Just about anyone from the Mission punk scene has a great 50 Million story. There was the time that they were playing at the Tip Top and the lady who lived over the bar was trying to get them to stop playing. She poured ammonia down on them from a hole in her floor. But they didn't stop playing. Instead, Wade caught the ammonia in a cup and drank it on stage.

There was the time while I lived with 50 Million when Wade was trying to tell me a story about how he'd fought a promoter in Shreveport, Louisiana, who had ripped them off on tour. "I went to the van and got the machete," Wade growled, and then he reached behind our couch, and to my surprise, pulled out the very same machete and started to dramatize. "I told him 'You motherfucker, you better give us our money!'" he yelled as he waved it around our living room. "And then I hit him with it!"

And as he said that, Wade hit himself in his OWN arm with the machete. We both watched in wonder as blood started pumping out of the cut. Without missing a beat, Wade simply grabbed a towel off the floor and wrapped it around his arm. He turned to his wife, Tracey, and said, "C'mon baby, let's go to the hospital." They left together, just like that, holding hands, walking up Valencia, Wade holding his bleeding arm up high above his heart, wrapped in the already red towel.

Maybe the most famous 50 Million story was the one about how Wade put the "Off The Pigs" sticker on a cop right in front of Mission

Station. Wade had gone up to a cop and pretended to ask directions to Market Street. When the cop had given them, Wade thanked him and patted the cop on the back, carefully affixing the sticker at the same time. Full of neighborly good cheer, the cop didn't notice.

But his partner did. They did finally manage to get Wade cuffed and into the station, but, Wade later bragged, it took a whole lot more cops than just the two of them to finally beat his ass in the basement of Mission Station.

Some of the new kids who only knew 50 Million from the sweet, heartfelt ballads on their old records looked a little scared of these wild-eyed, sweaty, older men.

Being afraid seemed reasonable. While Matty had used Black Panthers imagery and rhetoric in Hickey's posters and album art for a cool, 60s youth movement, "Stickin' it to The Man" aesthetic, it was Wade who actually lived each day of his life as if he expected it to end in a gun battle with the police. While Matty had avidly read books about Huey P. Newton, Wade actually owned a gun that he had *named* "Huey."

Mission cops KNEW Wade. After the incident with the sticker, they picked him up and took him to the basement at Mission Station again and again. They came frequently to our old storefront on Valencia, over near the projects. They came when Shell and Wade played live shows in the storefront's display window for folks walking on Valencia, and they came the night that Wade kicked out the window. I didn't doubt Wade when he said he'd never allow a cop into our house without a warrant and was glad that the cops never came when Huey accidentally went off.

But life with 50 Million wasn't all about paranoia and violence. They could be pretty sweet guys and were genuinely enthusiastic about everything they did. One time, when I actually joined 50 Million for a couple months on drums, an amazed kid told me after a show, "You guys are like... like... a Steinbeck novel, or something." I wanted to tell him that it actually felt more like Hubert Selby, Jr. on most days, but I knew what he meant. *Tortilla Flat, Cannery Row,* that sort-of thing. And it was true: It WAS endearing, how earnestly they accepted and adapted to each new disaster in their lives. 50 Million were the only people I'd ever known who would sublet out their rooms without even going anywhere. Too broke to pay rent or to leave town, they'd find subletters and then go live with their girlfriends in other parts of the Mission.

No matter what they did, it was hard to stay mad at them anyway. One of their B-sides was a song called "Valentino," where Shell, accompanied only by a piano, addresses a lover. "I'm no Valentino," he confides, his voice solemn, cracking. "But I can love you so." Every time I hear that song, I forgive him for all the times he took all of our rent money and spent it on speed instead of giving it to the landlord. I know he just couldn't help himself.

Finally everything was set up and the band started playing. I looked around—no cops in sight! There were a lot of hits, including one of my all time favorites, "The Bud in Your Pocket," the song Shell had written about the happy day he once found drugs on the ground in the Mission. They stuck to their later, Hickey-influenced, full-rock lineup of Shell on guitar, Captain Norlon on bass, and Wade playing drums, instead of the lineup of just the two brothers playing guitars that they'd used for their first several records. I had seen 50 Million play shows with countless different lineups. Once they had booked shows 4 nights in a row before a tour and had played with 4 different lineups, Thursday through Sunday, without repeating a single song. But today, they weren't pushing it too hard. They didn't talk between songs and Wade stared vacantly at his drums, seeming alarmingly pacified by his powerful new psych meds.

Aesop was scowling, walking around telling everyone, "Reunions are stupid. This is just some fake nostalgia, greatest hits bullshit." I couldn't blame him. If I were him, I don't know if I'd want to think about the past right now either. It would be too fucking painful. But I had to disagree. It was a beautiful day and we were still actually here at the plaza, stealing the space, getting away with it. And these were only the "greatest hits" because we said so. Without that, what would we have? What else was there to separate us from an ordinary crowd of down and out people hanging around at the BART Plaza?

I looked around at the crowd. A lot of the kids who had been teenagers during the era of Hickey were here, too. Some of them were right up front, singing along. Others were lurking along the edges of the plaza, by the trashcans or BART elevator, the ones who you could usually see here anyway, trying to score.

Meanwhile, the very front of the crowd was made up of 10 or 15 teenagers who were obviously too young to have seen 50 Million before but knew every word of every song. They looked great with their hair dye and raised 40s, as they hugged each other, trying to dance and not fall over. All that was missing was a photobooth. They were all literally less than half of any member of 50 Million's age. How 50 Million's lyrics told the story of the years between them was what made the songs so beautiful and lasting to me.

Both the younger and former kids, most likely, had been brought to the Mission punk scene by Matty's songs. Hickey was undeniably the most famous band of the 90s Mission punk scene. Kids from all over the country had Hickey tattoos. Matty's songs had made places like El Farolito seem glamorous enough for kids from the suburbs and from all over the country to move to the Mission.

Now for the first time I considered the main difference between the two bands now probably best known from that era. Matty wrote lyrically clever, brilliantly catchy songs that seemed to promise young punks everywhere a life of living like rock stars in the gutter of a dying civilization. Food stamps and malt liquor! We'll stay drunk and naked! No squares at my funeral! What I appreciated now about 50 Million was that their songs never made any promises that life would be anything more than it was. Their songs about buying pills at Mission fruit stands, losing your mind again yet again, and pleading with your girlfriend to sleep over even after you got in a fight were closer to the legacy of what the new kids who moved here might actually inherit after the romance of moving to the big city wore off. Eviction threats, psych meds, the regular beatings in the basement of Mission station. It was all in the music.

And so was the BART Plaza. I noticed the crowd was all starting to move closer to the front. What does it feel like to grow up and become your favorite songs? Do you even get to choose which ones? When they finally played "Looking For You Even Though You're Gone," I couldn't help it; I found myself looking around the plaza, again—even looking up Mission Street. Oh, I don't know. Maybe we could use a little romance right about now. Or maybe we had already wanted too much, expected too much out of this old ghetto main drag. Maybe I already did know how it must have felt for Matty to come here every day. I really don't know. But 50 Million seemed to say it had all been worth it anyway. It was music that said it was worth it to just one time stand in the sun and put an "Off the Pigs" sticker on a cop's back, even if it guaranteed a lifetime of police beatings.

The wind came down 16th Street and, for a moment, looking across the crowd, I thought I could see everyone as they heard the music, not today, but as they'd once heard it, years ago, when they'd heard it for the first time. I thought I could see everyone for a second as they wished to be seen, or how they might have been, the hope still hidden close to the heart. Everyone now seemed to be singing along with the band to the same song:

We'll run away... run away...
We'll run away
To Nothing

LETTERS SECTION

I had too many good letters to choose from these past couple of years to print just a couple. So I went through the big box of mail from the last 10 years, took one line out of each letter and edited into this one big letter! This is the writing of about 50 people. Thanks for writing, and keep sending letters instead of email!

Dear sleepless, homeless, in love and insane:

I'm sitting in the morning sun by some honeysuckle outside of Woodfin. I'm trying to avoid the oppressive heat of New Orleans, and just wishing we'd get the fuck out of town and on down the road. I'm in Raleigh, hiding from the cops, drinking on plasma cash, smoking opium, trying to find a drug study to do.

Sorry I haven't written in a bit, but I'm in jail.

Kansas City is a big, dirty town with not much fun to do. Gainesville got too weird, or maybe I got too weird. Here I sit, facing the Federal Court House of Sioux Falls. I'm getting really sick of America again and really need to get the fuck out.

I'm on yet another stimulating, cross-country Greyhound trip, going from NY back to Texas. I'm sitting around, listening to DRI's first album. I'm writing this letter in the dressing room of the Sho-Bar. Ryan Fontaine was telling me to move to Minneapolis and I said, "Maybe," which is how fucked up I am right now.

I wrote this letter and then it sat in my bag through Goldsboro (NC), Asheville, Chattanooga, Athens, Tallahassee, Pensacola, New Orleans, Cleveland (MS), Birmingham, Tuscumbia (AL), and now Louisville. A condescending, self-righteous government worker told me with complete air of indignation that I was just in town for Mardi Gras and didn't deserve food stamps.

I've put so much energy into Pittsburgh, and I still believe in this city, but there's a lot of pain and heartbreak for me here now, too. I didn't know how to feel about coming back to Chicago, but it's definitely an improvement over upstate New York. Fuck, man, Texas just sucks.

I guess you've heard about the big mess I've gotten myself into.

A few of us got this big plan to home-make all the beer for the big New Year's party this year, but we already drank most of it. My new dream is to get a small apartment building, gut one of the apartments to turn into communal living space and have shows in the storefront (I forgot to mention that part). I've been collecting telephones from the Goodwill dumpster, and, if they don't work, installing them on telephone poles.

I have big plans for a garden and I'm pretty excited about it. I hope to find a barn, shack, cabin, or yurt in the next two weeks. We opened a squat—a two-story with an attic, wood frame building out at the end of Canal Street by all the decrepit cemeteries. The library here is nice—they let you sleep and don't glare at me when I smell or have bloodstains on my clothes. One fine day I'll have my solar panels and windmill and 12-volt record player, and I'll be listening to something other than the Canadian Broadcasting Corp.!

The plan, I think, is to live in Austin for "the winter" and, hopefully, sell my body to science. I wish my boyfriend could be in the prison that all my other friends are in up in Salem. Me, I'm getting out of New Orleans at some point soon.

The police are refusing us the right to march, so it seems like we may have to break the law again.

I'm going to bust ass, try to get my teeth fixed, and take a lot of painkillers and swim. I intentionally sought out demeaning employment and found it. Hey, did I tell you about the Justice For Janitors campaign I was working with? I've been really self-absorbed lately, what with my drinking and drug use and bend towards melodrama.

I've finally decided that I have to get shit done NOW instead of sitting around and waiting for it. Basically, I ride around on my bike and spray paint "Fuck gentrification!" everywhere. I'm going to help move and build the new show space down by the tracks and the river (The Pink House got sold to Christians). I'm maintaining my vision of a free school for illegal immigrants, where I teach English, history, and media literacy. We could use 50 grand or so if you have any ideas.

I'm still living in my cabin. Got a note on the front door the other day: "Hi! We are the cops! No more parties or we kick you out!" The power plant is a block away and makes this waterfall sound that makes for a good night's sleep. Isn't it awesome seeing the technologies taking a dive along with the rest of the fucking country? I spend my days drinking lots of coffee and walking through the dry riverbeds between the sheer cliff faces (man made) of Manhattan, usually ending up at ABC NO RIO. The helicopter is buzzing over again as I write this and I'm getting damn sick of it.

The rats are back, but maybe not as bad as last year. I still wake up thinking "I can't believe life exists." I want my love for this weird, fucked up, yet completely beautiful place to die, but it won't. I think its weird that everyone thinks these are the worst of times. I need to find out how to erase voice mail messages right after I leave them.

I went to NYC and looked for the punk show but when I found it, it was ANTI-FLAG. The other day, 10 cop cars came to break up the "Satanic compound" up the street where our friends live. I was riding by this sports bar and glanced in the big window on the side and saw a lot of my friends, drinking expensive beer and watching sports on a big-screen TV! I feel trapped by the whole "Getting drunk with my friends" thing. I live with four guys and its really starting to annoy me for reasons that I don't feel like going into now. Jesus! This town is going to kill me!

I am just so tired of moving, of not having a home, of not having a space for events and shows and stuff. It's raining everywhere these days. I need some inspiration and a good fuck and I'm finding nothing here but the unburied past and lots of cheap beer.

It's nice to be out of Eugene, though.

After A16 I stayed in Richmond, VA for 3 days and lived like a king in a 3-story Victorian squat, finding more dumpsters than you could ever hope to find. On the eve of Exxon Mobil's annual shareholder meeting in Dallas, Texas, we projected 100-foot tall images of floods, storms and other impacts of global warming on the building where shareholders will gather. They are trying to build luxury condos right smack in downtown so we did a skit with Mr. GorrealEstate (in a gorilla suit), marrying Ms. Government with Condozilla looming in the background.

Tom had the most brilliant sign: "WTO OWT!"

At the Inauguration, someone threw an egg at G.W. when he drove past. I just wanted to shove Timoney's bike helmet up his stupid fucking ass. Jocks came out and threatened us while saying stupid shit about how we need to go back to Iraq or with signs like "Go home treehuggers." You should have been here—not for the jail part, but for the taking over the streets! We got great press, no one got hurt or too traumatized and we actually affected the political discourse.

We just plugged our extension cord in through a lamppost and used the power strip for all the amps.

It seems as if the return of fascism has brought a return to urgency here in Gainesville as well. Apparently, during our second set, someone yelled "The cops are outside!" and me and Ella yelled "Fuck the cops!" I played too fast and fucked up constantly, busted open three knuckles, and you could see my panties but it was still badass. Jimmy hardly even sang into the mic cuz everyone knew the words and was singing along as loud as hell. At the stroke of midnight, Fred and Tootie kissed and then they played the traditional New Year's song and blew us away for about an hour and a half. It was an experiment in "How drunk can a band be and still not pass out between songs" and we, in fact, failed this test, as our drummer literally did pass out after the second to last song!

A couple guys from my prison art workshop got released and it was so amazing to hang out and drink tea like it was the most normal thing in the world. The worry's been in the back of my mind so long that it's become a part of me like a hand or a foot. It makes me wonder about what things I would take a bullet for. I kind of feel weighed down by all these people I love, since they don't really know about the hard times of the others, the responsibility is intensified and I don't want to go down with them.

I went a week without drinking without even thinking about it. I've quit drinking almost completely. Too often I feel like I'm stuck in a country song. My words sound like a Hank, jr. song when I'm in a good mood but like I'm Kitty Wells when I'm not. My co-worker today told me I was on a punk rock vision quest.

I went to Kinko's on Saturday night and I had the most fun I've ever had at a copy shop. I went shooting guns the other night with Danny the Wildman. I went swimming in Pensacola the day you left and then there was a sweet and touching, sit-down breakfast of 18 punks, with lots of food and beer and singing along to The Bananas. It wasn't like everyone was totally motivated and excited, but it seemed like everyone was doing something and not in the depths of despair.

I lied about everything but, amazingly, they still didn't arrest me.

The old St. Elmo punk house was lost to a dramatic eviction, but there's a new, bigger weirder house about to be styled. The zine library I started is now defunct because the space changed and no one cared about it but me anyway. Chad's as optimistic as one can be after losing a foot.

We're building a tank of a practice space with some shady, moldy old shit. My house is like the meeting place for all Eastern Kansas Prairie Punks. It's nice not sleeping (peeing) on other people's couches. Right now we have no phone because the whole jail is on lockdown. You're right: It IS hard to quit punk rock completely.

How come you never wrote anything with me in it, huh? Is Club Chaos still around? Sorry you got arrested on my advice. I was thinking of you, walking here, and then I saw Jorge sitting on Mission Street and I gave him a dollar, sort-of on your behalf. Last week, when I was more paranoid from lack of sleep, I would have accused you of cursing my life. What else have you been doing besides having sex and writing about it? Now that I'm not morbidly, pathetically depressed, we should hang out! You MIGHT go crazy, but maybe not.

You should have tried the dust in Montreal; its crazy shit.

I've been on a bit of a rampage lately—drinking like a fish, amassing a weekly dice crew, kissing unbelievably vapid boys. I don't think I've learned a thing about relationships in 32 and ½ years. I'm still fairly sure the breakup was the right thing to do, but, oh my, is it difficult. While she screamed insults from the safety of the house, I calmly loaded my five crates of crap, my clothes, my guitar, and my vodka into the van and drove to Little Fargo to celebrate unconsciously.

He went back to Gainesville and the only thing I'm left with is the bites from the fleas his dog left in my bed. It felt like a true "Us vs. Them" punk show.

I just want to say for the record that I am NOT always a bitter, boring, anti-social mess. Sorry if this all seems morbid. I'm not sleeping much so it's hard to be coherent. Everything's not REALLY this bad; I just haven't slept in 38 hours. It actually sounds worse on paper than it is in reality. Fuck, OK, I'm just going to send this. I've got to face it that I'm actually losing my mind and there's no way I'm going to finish a coherent letter.

Last night they negotiated with the mayor and got our lawyers in and tonight, people are locked to the front doors, demanding release for everyone. I'm just living, surviving, reflecting, learning and trying not to let my hopes up too high about anything, but also not to let go of hope completely. I can't swear to you that slogging through ten years of bitterness, resentment, hostility, and just plain drama was worth it, or that things worked out for the best.

My public defender thinks that we have a chance. Why does our struggle have to be so struggly?

Sorry about the lengthy letter; I haven't written anyone in a while and I guess all this crap was building up. Even though we'll all be dead or in jail in a few years, drop me a line!

PS. These stamps came from the Goodwill dumpster.

THE APRIL FOOL'S DAY PRO WAR PARADE

After weeks of protesting the war, we finally decided if you can't beat them, join them. Why not? Thus was born the April Fool's Day Pro-War Parade.

We all met at City Hall at 5:00 on April 1st for a pre-parade rally. Of course, all three local news networks were there, cameramen waiting on the lawn across from City Hall. The media will completely downplay the importance of WEEKS of non-stop anti-war protest, but will always bend over backwards to make a dismal, 35-person PRO-war rally seem like a significant moment in human history. As the unruly gang of punks and queers in ill-fitting suits, wigs, and weird yuppie shoes, carrying signs reading "More Blood for Oil!" and "Give War a Chance!," started showing up, though, the news crews realized they'd been had. Still, they stuck around for a bit, and the guy from KRON was totally cracking up while filming 100 of us on The City Hall steps, chanting, "We want war! France is stupid!"

Next, it was time to march. First stop was the SF Public Library, a long-time money-losing venture that has clearly been wasting taxpayers' monies for CENTURIES. Why spend all that money on BOOKS when we can use it for tanks or something? You're supposed to be quiet at the library, but fuck that! It was time to stand up and expose their unpatriotic behavior! We stood on the steps, loudly chanting, "Shut it down! Shut it down!" and demanding, "Smart bombs, not smart people!" while puzzled readers looked down at us from top floor windows. They'll see!

Next, we headed down Market Street toward Nordstrom's and the SF Shopping Mall, singing, "All we are saying, is give war a chance!" A small crew of cops had also gathered to follow us and see just what in the hell we thought we were up to. What media was left wondered if you could film cops as they attacked PRO-war marchers? The message was confusing, for sure.

People in cars honked and gave the thumbs up, obviously assuming we were one of those traitorous ANTI-war parades that everyone had been having. The crowds on the sidewalk weren't sure what was up, either. Some people got the joke, but others seemed mad and we'd have to wink and say, "April fools!" to them so they'd laugh. It was OK, though, because really the whole parade was for our own sanity anyway. After weeks of this shit we needed a good laugh.

Of course, it makes sense that no one got it; it was, after all, too obvious. With its malls, chain stores, and dying homeless people, the Market Street already, in some way, screams, "We want war!" It was implicit in our society's values, and now we were in fact at war and life was just going on. What was amazing was actually walking down this street and saying the subconscious message aloud. We yelled and chanted, "More blood for oil!" the whole way down the street until we arrived at the mall.

Anandi and I had come dressed as the Black Bloc, but, instead of spray paint and bricks, we had a spray bottle of glass cleaner and a squeegee. The Abercrombie and Fitch store at 5th Street has an enormous plate glass window that has been repeatedly broken at protest marches. When we came to it, Anandi and I broke out of the crowd, running toward the window, squeegees in hand. We quickly sprayed it with cleaner and started vigorously washing it! The crowd broke into a chant, "Bombs are dropping! Let's go shopping! Bombs are dropping! Let's go shopping!" Later, I was told that cops ran hard from the back of the crowd to grab us, only to look really, really pissed when they saw what we were actually doing.

A block away, we gathered again in front of the gleaming new Old Navy store. When we rushed the glass front door, a store employee jumped in our way, closing the door and locking it! A small line of shoppers who were about to leave the store stood helplessly now, trapped behind the glass, looking appalled and scared as Anandi and I cleaned the window just inches from their faces.

Sorry, folks. You asked for it. What we're for is what we'll get. Now you're locked in the chain store forever and it's time to clean the windows! More blood for oil!

While we carefully squeegeed the glass and the trapped shoppers scowled and pounded on the windows, the crowd of pro-war demonstraters behind us was just getting warmed up. All up and down that block of Market Street, you could here the Pledge of Allegiance being sung loud and proud, under the new Old Navy store's huge American flag.

UNDERGROUND

In late August 2005, police raided a Punks Against War planning session inside of an abandoned building South of Market. The group was meeting inside of a former Guitar Center store location to discuss plans for an enormous event to be titled "Underground" that PAW wanted to put on inside the squatted space with bands, art, and free food. One member of the group was arrested and one got away by hiding for a couple hours on a nearby rooftop. The show was eventually moved to another legal venue. This piece was salvaged from the zine Underground *that the group made for the event—the only surviving record of the last Punks Against War action.*

This show originates from many discussions that our group, Punks Against War, has had together about how increasingly isolated we are feeling in this city during the current times. Most of us feel frustrated from the current lack of politics in art and music, and the surprising lack of urgency in local activism, while also feeling personally exhausted from years of struggles here in the city. During the dot-com times, artists and activists rallied to fight displacement. But, today, while an appalling war is raging with no end in sight, health care and social services have disappeared, and Ellis Act evictions in the Mission are at a higher rate than in 2000, it seems like no one is talking about it.

That includes us. We have all, at times, felt completely overwhelmed or shut down. More than a simple protest seems to be in order, but we're not even sure where to start. And, of course, there is the curious way that living in a thoroughly anti-war city, ironically, contributes to isolation. After all, it seems pointless to talk about how awful everything is when we all already know it. We hope that tonight's show can be part of a larger process of getting people together to discuss what is going on right now and what we can do about it because the times are urgent. The excitement and power many of us felt when we came together two years ago to shut down the city at the start of the war have given way to the long silence and dead chill we've all felt since at how ultimately ineffective the protests were. Here, deep in the hidden corners of the nation's lone anti-Bush city, we're still struggling to find community, feeling more "underground" than ever.

So it's fitting that our initial idea for the "underground" show ended up being shut down before it started by the police. Most people who come to tonight's show know that it was supposed to happen directly across the street in the abandoned Guitar Center building. To make a long story shorter, the landlord for the Guitar Center space is asking an incredible $26,000 a month for it! We had no choice but to break in and try to steal the space for a show!

We have been frustrated that there are no all-ages punk spaces in this city now. There are no places where people can get together to hang out without having to spend money, no place to go at night that's not a bar. There are no places for people to come for bands to play where control of the money stays in the scene and no place where artists can actually work together collaboratively to put on collective shows, instead of just hanging their work alone next to others. Our lack of space and the kind of spaces we do art and music in contribute to our isolation.

Punks Against War has been searching for a space to rent for an event/community space for years. This is no half-assed plan. Most of us have been working together for five years and we have a lot of money saved up. Even with commercial real estate vacancies at their highest rates in years, finding an affordable space has been impossible.

There is something so lacking in our lives in the city right now that a large number of people are craving that we will gladly break into an abandoned building to try to create some vision of it. We broke into Guitar Center and excitedly found plenty of space to do whatever we could imagine. The building was empty except some wall-sized posters of Carlos Santana and Jimi Hendrix that had been left behind. We decided to paint drag clothes on all the male guitar gods and have the bands play in front of them. Another huge room, separate from the rock room, could be filled with furniture and be a quiet room where we could serve free food. Two huge rooms were designated to be the art rooms—whole rooms where artists were going to build tunnels and caves, full of art they came up with related to the theme of "underground." Ironically, after weeks of planning meetings where we discussed things like how to safely and calmly evacuate 500 people from an illegal show if the cops came, there were only seven people in the squat when the cops shut it down. Just a couple nights before this show, the artists were discussing their plans inside the Guitar Center when fifteen cops with guns drawn (and a fire truck!) showed up to kick them out. The landlord was notified and the space was sealed up. Most likely, Guitar Center will remain vacant, like so many properties in the Mid-Market and SOMA redevelopment areas, and the landlord will one day receive redevelopment money to tear down this "blighted" property and build condos. Meanwhile, we'll keep looking for a space of our own.

Which brings us back to our theme, "underground." In the generator and squat shows, in graffiti, in street protests, we all seek out this place, a place of refuge and comfort with glimpses of the world we want to live in—unregulated spaces in an appallingly regulated world. There is much strength, beauty, and creativity in this, the "SF underground." But there is the powerlessness of isolation, too. When the FBI convenes grand juries and the rest of the country outlaws gay marriage, the underground is a dangerous place. Seen in this way, it is not just a haven, but also an awful place, a psychologically debilitating place we've been thrust into. Tonight is about celebrating what we have and can make together and about asking questions. How can our ideas leave this ghetto to go out and change the larger world? And, if we have all found ourselves in the underground due to our politics, ideas, or sexuality, how do we make this a safe place and take care of each other now that we're here?

OUR HEARTS ARE OUR SHIELDS

On my way to City Hall to the show, I saw that half the storefronts on Market Street were still abandoned. But one thing was different lately: the doorways of the empty buildings that used to be full of homeless people were now blocked off with police barricades so no one could sleep there. So much for Care Not Cash. I headed through UN Plaza and on to Civic Center Plaza in my thrift store suit, carrying my guitar case, looking myself much like a drifter just washed up on these shores, a ghost from the old 7th and Market Greyhound station. Looking around, I wondered, "How had everything turned out so horrible?" I thought about the war. I thought about the bitter breakup and dissolution of our group, Punks Against War. How had things gone so wrong?

I blamed everyone else. I blamed myself. I blamed everything, really. But maybe I blamed myself mostly. And like everyone else, in the absence of group activity, I suffered alone. On some days, I really thought that even the war could be my fault—that I just wasn't doing enough to stop it. In the barren Civic Center Plaza, the rows of trees stood limbless, leafless, their trunks barbarically trimmed back, looking like rows of returned war veterans, amputees. I assumed that The City deliberately trimmed them that way to keep lines of sight into the park clear for the police, to keep foliage from growing that could potentially provide shelter to a homeless person in the rain. I considered the maimed trees in front of resplendent City Hall —the broad steps, the classic façade, the golden dome. It looked like a landscape from one of Zara's paintings. This was supposed to be the symbolic heart of the city and somehow, ironically, these stunted trees in this desolate place had really captured the spirit of the new San Francisco. Despite myself, I felt a little better. I'd spent so much time critiquing our own political actions and ideas these past few years. But if these were the values of the city we lived in, how could any of it really be our fault?

As the sheriffs inside the door of City Hall checked my guitar case, though, I looked up at the long marble staircase and got excited. It was funny that I'd always said that I didn't even want to go to an art show at City Hall and now here I was playing a show at one. How had this happened? When Matt Gonzalez had been the President of the Board of Supervisors, he held monthly art openings in his office in City Hall. Now that Matt had quit politics and gone back to law practice, his Green Party successor in District 5, Ross Mirkarimi, had continued the tradition. Not knowing what he was getting into, Ross had asked Zara Thustra to do this month's show. Zara's plan was to throw a big, 949 Market-style party in City Hall featuring his art, his friends' art, free zines and posters, a huge, free meal, and Ivy and I playing an acoustic show on the staircase under the rotunda. The full-color postcard invitations for the event announced the show's title, "Free Dinner at City Hall." Zara had been handing them out everywhere in town for weeks.

Upstairs, Mirkarimi's people were still freaking out. Zara had wanted to serve the dinner under the rotunda. The people in Mirkarimi's office didn't want there to be food at all. So, he offered to feed in the long hallways in front of all the supervisors' offices. They weren't into that either. Zara told them the cards were already printed. They said, why did you do that? So Zara just went ahead and brought in the food. Finally, they opened up a conference room down the hall from Mirkarimi's office and said the food had to stay there.

When I got upstairs, the party was still kind of dead. Some of the usual gallery crowd was in Mirkarimi's office, milling around, drinking wine. I found the punks down the hall in the conference room in hiding together around the long table that was piled high with various vegan entrees and snacks. Some others were self-consciously dressed up like me, looking like they were expecting to get thrown out of the building at any minute.

But it was OUR show. I grabbed a plate of food and went to check out the art. Mirkarimi's office looked like a crime scene. Zara had used a lot of bright, fluorescent colors—dripping oranges and hot pinks that seemed almost to have been stabbed or slashed on with a knife. The paintings were jarring, urgent—you could almost still smell fresh spray paint in the orderly office—and full of pain and caring. It was the closest I'd seen Zara come to the sincerity and vulnerability of his Yerba Buena Bay Area Now piece in the three years since. Rows of text were scrawled across the pieces and I was struck by one painting with the top to bottom handwritten epigraph, "Our hearts are our shields. Our love is our loss. Our poison is our policy." Somewhere in there, Zara's art had come close to describing my true feelings about playing a show in this building: the art was full of the excitement of making a positive statement with hundreds of our friends in this shitty place combined with the vague sadness that what I really want is for this place's power to simply go away.

Soon the event started to really go off, as more and more of us showed up. The halls and offices filled with punks, activists, artists, and freaks, all eating the food and drinking, checking out the art, reading the zines. Everyone was dressed up, too. Ivy showed up, looking great in a homemade, gold-sequined gown provided by Annie Danger. People were out on Supervisor Mirkarimi's balcony, smoking weed and looking out across The City. City Hall was ours!

Of course, some folks were there, too, giving us shit just for having a show in City Hall at all, calling Zara a sell-out for even doing it. I could understand the objections to having an art show in the very seat of the government that we spent so much time protesting against. I even felt weird about dressing up—as if I was showing deference to the power the building represented. But, the truth is that we would do this kind of event anywhere in town where we could get away with it. The people who were doing this event at City Hall had found perfection one time together at 949 Market and now we carried around the pieces of that vision with us like exiles, looking for any place where we could recreate that dream together.

When there were maybe 200 of us at the show, Zara went around quietly giving the order for everyone to go sit on the marble stairs in the rotunda so the music could start. This was another part of the "art show" that Mirkarimi's people hadn't exactly known about, so we were under pressure to all get in there and sit down before they knew what was up. While everyone assembled on the stairs, Ivy and I went down to the bottom of the stairs to sing up at them, because singing from the top of the government's stairs seemed somehow too fascist. Concerned for the time and the sheriffs, I grabbed the guitar, put my head down and started playing, "No Joy in Mudville."

It was Friday night, after 5:30, and the building seemed oddly cleared out except for us. The sound of Ivy's voice echoed mightily in the rotunda, filling City Hall with the sound of music. I looked up a couple times at the stone angels circling the ceiling. It was quite gorgeous, really—especially the hundreds of punks draped all across every surface. I thought people were sitting because they were too self-conscious to dance in City Hall, but I was told later that people were sitting out of reverence for the scene of all of us there together, partying in City Hall. We went on to play "Fuck

You, Motherfucker!" which Ivy dedicated to Mayor Newsom. The shouts of 200 people yelling, "Fuck you, Gavin!" directly at the mayor's office in unison filled the building. But if he heard us, there was no sign, and we kept on playing.

Next up, Tracey from the Deep Throats took over my guitar to play some songs. Tracey looked beautiful—five o'clock shadow and heels, the self-inflicted knife wound on her throat from last year now healed nicely just over the neckline of her dress. Her operatic voice resounded throughout the hall as she sang the fitting hit, "Telling the Truth Will Get You Nowhere." I looked at the punks on the stairs and thought of the black and white photos hung in the North Light Court, the photos celebrating the student activists that had been hosed down the front steps of City Hall—the photos that seemed to be about the dream of what a city might be. Here, I thought, we finally had our group photo in City Hall, and it would only be taken by surveillance cameras. Next, Tracey sang a song that ended with the repeated chorus, "When I died for 15 minutes, I didn't see a light," and the sheriffs were standing by her side the whole time, telling her to quit playing.

But when the song ended, I grabbed the guitar and headed directly into the center of the crowd at the top of the stairs. I yelled, "Hey! They want to shut this down, but let's all stand up and dance and keep this going!" People gathered around Ivy and me, effectively protecting us from the cops, and we continued on, playing "The City That Never Sleeps," "I'm Not Ashamed," and the song we named after Zara's painting, "If This Is What We're For, This is What We'll Get." As the crowd started to dance around us, I saw Zara at the edge of the crowd, arguing with the sheriffs, holding them off until we finished the last song for the dancing crowd.

And then, just like that, it was over and we were all filing outside. An aide from Mirkarimi's office came up to Zara and said, "Wow, you guys just, like, took over City Hall, man!" But it was Friday night and everyone was already going their separate ways, looking for the next event. Now that we'd finally taken over City Hall after all these years, power seemed to actually be somewhere else.

I thought of all the events like this one that I'd wished had somehow been able to last longer. It was another page in our secret history—a history that also pointed to an alternate future, like blueprints for buildings that had never been made or a map of a republic that had never been born, but that we were all somehow still exiled from. People were getting on their bikes and riding away.

The mayor had left the building and even the sheriffs were going home. But, somewhere, the surveillance camera footage of our show was playing and the hundreds of punks were still dancing under The City Hall rotunda. I thought of the years that had passed since I'd moved back to The City, young and excited. I tried to hold the image of our group photo in my head for a bit longer. From the top of The City Hall steps, all I could see were the rows of trees in the plaza, cut back and maimed, warped into their weird shapes, and the Truth Mural looking down over everything, waiting. But in the group photo—the photo they'd never hang in the North Light Court —the punks on the stairs were still dancing, their faces open and expectant, as if looking off at something just off camera.

As if still waiting for it all to begin.

ABOUT THE AUTHOR

Still proudly unemployed, Erick Lyle has been setting up punk shows and protests, touring the country in his various bands, and editing his zine, SCAM, since 1991. His writing has appeared on NPR's *This American Life,* in *Raritan* and the *San Francisco Bay Guardian,* and various book anthologies. He is currently playing music in Black Rainbow and Onion Flavored Rings. He lives in downtown San Francisco.

Printed in the United States
by Baker & Taylor Publisher Services